THE JERSEY GAME

The History of Modern Baseball from Its Birth to the Big Leagues in the Garden State

RUTGERS UNIVERSITY PRESS New Brunswick, New Jersey

THE JERSEY GAME

James M. DiClerico and Barry J. Pavelec

Library of Congress Cataloging-in-Publication Data
DiClerico, James M., 1939–
    The Jersey game : the history of modern baseball from its birth to
the big leagues in the Garden State / by James M. DiClerico and
Barry J. Pavelec.
        p.   cm.
    Includes bibliographical references and index.
    ISBN 0-8135-1652-8
    1. Baseball—New Jersey—History.   I. Pavelec, Barry J.
II. Title.
GV863.N5D53   1991
796.357′09749—dc20   90-44860
                                                            CIP

To
Mike DiClerico and Bill Pavelec,
two New Jersey catchers
whose names and baseball exploits
appear in no record books
but who paid for the balls, bats, and gloves,
bought the tickets and hot dogs
at Ebbets Field and the Polo Grounds,
got up and got out for endless catches,
and told the stories of Ruth, Hubbell, and Walker,
which fueled the dream for another generation

CONTENTS

LIST OF ILLUSTRATIONS

PREFACE

Baseball books abound. Some are novels, but nonfiction works predominate. Many of these are narrowly focused—dealing with a single player, one team, a league, an era, or even a race of men who played the game. Others treat the subject broadly, sometimes encyclopedically, often statistically (for it is the most statistical of games).

But when talk of professional baseball returning to New Jersey grew loud in 1988, the authors of this volume, lifelong residents of New Jersey and friends for more than thirty years, wondered what the state had contributed to the game. When we began looking for answers, there was no source that gave a complete look at New Jersey's history in baseball. To our delight, though, the piecemeal evidence suggested that New Jersey may well have had a pivotal relationship to the national pastime. We ultimately became convinced that the state really was—and to some extent continues to be—the crossroads of baseball.

As this realization grew, so did the conviction that the story deserved to be recorded in a book of its own. New Jerseyans, currently without a team in professional baseball, should have the means to explore their heritage in the game. We decided to write the story of New Jersey baseball.

As the book progressed, the old controversy about baseball's origins emerged again—and sent us digging deeper for answers. Like most people who follow baseball closely, we had long since discounted Abner Doubleday as the founder of the national game. The notion that he "invented baseball" in 1839 in his hometown of Cooperstown, New York, is no longer accepted by the sport's scholars. Historians of the game agree that baseball's bosses created the myth in 1905 to "prove" that the sport was purely American. In 1939 the baseball powers attempted to institutionalize the fable by establishing the Baseball Hall of Fame in Cooperstown.

What was being calculated by Doubleday in the summer of 1839 was the trajectory of cannonballs, not baseballs. Doubleday was attending the U.S. Military Academy, from which he would graduate in 1842 and go on to a distinguished career in the army. Doubleday did, however, start something—the Civil War. It was he who ordered the first shot fired in defense of Fort Sumter. Later he held brief command of the Union forces at Gettysburg on the first day of the battle there. The only New Jersey connection with this mythical inventor of baseball was that Doubleday died in Mendham, New Jersey, in 1893.

Early in our research we made a pilgrimage to the Hoboken site of what we and most baseball authorities accepted as the first recorded match game played by the rules of Alexander Cartwright, the man who owns the strongest claim to the title "Father of Baseball." We photographed that 1846 game's commemorative plaque, now behind the fence of a coffee factory, and wandered a few blocks away to another monument celebrating the event's centennial, more conveniently located in downtown Hoboken.

But even as we retraced this baseball "first," came a counterclaim: a newspaper article on the perennial "birthplace of baseball" battle between New York and New Jersey quoted a recently published book suggesting that the first truly "recorded" game (recorded, that is, in a newspaper) had been played in Brooklyn in 1845. But Hoboken may rest easy (even if the city has to move up its newly announced sesquicentennial). The claim for Brooklyn is demonstrably mistaken, as the reader will discover in the pages that follow.

We came across many other baseball controversies in our research. Although many truly are matters of opinion ("Was the great black shortstop John Henry Lloyd as good as Honus Wagner?"), others stem from contradictions in the records and reportage of the game. Especially in the early days, newspaper accounts of baseball games made up in color what they lacked in accuracy. It was not that sports journalists of earlier times were necessarily less fastidious than today's. But they had to contend with constantly changing rules (a walk was counted as an error this year, a hit next); with players performing under assumed names; with teams and leagues coming, going, and changing names faster than some players changed undershirts. Add to this the phenomenon of "factoids"—pieces of misinformation first recorded by careless or misled writers, and then repeated time and again until generally accepted as fact.

This book could not have told a story nearly as rich or accurate without the groundwork laid by a dedicated, persistent, hardworking, and undoubtedly eye-weary group called the Society for American Baseball Research (SABR). Among other things, SABR members have for years been poring over early newspapers, scorebooks, and other artifacts, trying to reconstruct a faithful record of the early days of the game. One of their objectives has been to wipe out the factoids—and in our opinion they have had excellent but not total success. We hope we have helped their cause along by not repeating questionable information without trying to verify it first, and by digging hard for new material.

We have, unabashedly but with tremendous gratitude, used the work of SABR, because it contributes to the foundation literature of baseball. This gratitude extends, of course, to the authors and editors of such works and their own contributions. Among our key general sources were *Total Base-*

ball, edited by John Thorn and Pete Palmer with David Reuther; *The Historical Baseball Abstract* by Bill James; and *The Baseball Encyclopedia,* edited by Joseph L. Reichler.

Individual chapters owe much to some of more narrowly focused works. Our central sources for the story of the Negro Leagues, for example, were *Only the Ball Was White* by Robert W. Peterson, *Blackball Stars* by John B. Holway, and *Sol White's Baseball Guide* by Sol White. The minor league chapter owes much to Randolph Linthurst and three of his books: *Journal of Leo Smith: Story of a Nineteenth Century Shortstop, The 1947 Trenton Giants,* and *Newark Bears.* For information on the early days of New Jersey baseball we turned, as do most writers on the subject, to the best and most complete stories on the subject: *Baseball: The Early Years* by Harold Seymour; *Baseball (1845–1881) from the Newspaper Accounts* by Preston D. Orem; *The Man Who Invented Baseball* by Harold Peterson; the understandably biased *Base Ball* by Albert G. Spalding; that treasure trove of early team facts including the only known account of Camden town ball play, *The Book of American Pastimes* by Charles A. Peverelly; and the newer, more scientific work by George B. Kirsch, *The Creation of American Team Sports.*

For some chapters, books either were not available or told less than we wanted to know about New Jersey's involvement. So like the members of SABR, we pored over newspaper microfilm for hours. The papers we used most extensively were the *Newark Evening News, Jersey Journal, Paterson Evening News, Trenton Times, New York Times,* and *Philadelphia Inquirer.*

We consulted official league records and spoke to people in the research departments of such organizations as the Hall of Fame in Cooperstown and the National Association of Professional Baseball Leagues (the governing body of minor league baseball). One of us visited the Hall of Fame during this writing and the other checked out the sites of some long-gone ball parks and one that is still there.

We did not choose to interview ballplayers or other participants in the game extensively, first, because this would have been impossible for the chapters on the early years. Equally important, our focus was less on "how it felt to be there"—which clearly requires first-person accounts— and more on "how it came to be." For readers interested in the former, we can recommend many of the sources listed in our bibliography.

Our work is not totally bereft of firsthand discussion with experts, though. In particular we acknowledge the help Lawrence Hogan of Union County College gave us with the Negro League chapter and the fortunate, if inadvertent, contribution of Jane G. Hartye, associate curator of the

Stevens Institute of Technology. Working in the library that sits exactly on the site of Elysian Fields, Hartye included in some material sent to us the first reference to the October 21, 1845, *New York Herald* announcement that led to the 1989 findings described in this volume.

These pages recount numerous national baseball milestones with strong New Jersey ties as well as the high points of the state's own internal experience with the game. (A guide to these key moments appears as Appendix B.) As far as was practical, we structured the book chronologically but chose to cover specific topics (the minor leagues, black baseball, amateur ball) from their beginnings in the last century to today in their own chapters. The chapter on New Jersey's short-lived major league experience, covering but a brief moment, thus became something of a still frame in a motion picture. Its position between the minor league and Negro League chapters is imperfect, but reflects its place in the midst of the developing story of these better-known New Jersey aspects of the game.

Finally, it should be obvious that this work—almost certainly like all works on baseball—is a work of love. We never played major league or even minor league ball. In fact, one of us opted for track and the other for tennis after one year of high school ball. Both went on to play lacrosse in college and for ten years more, created a magazine on the sport, and even refereed it occasionally.

But as kids on the sandlots of Milltown and New Brunswick, Elizabeth and Cranford, we could never get enough of baseball. Like so many of our generation, we played it by day, listened late into the night to radio broadcasts of games from the "West" (Chicago and St. Louis then), and died for the rare chance to see our "home" teams play, at the Polo Grounds (the N.Y. Giants) for one of us, Ebbets Field (the Brooklyn Dodgers) for the other. (We couldn't have coauthored a postcard in the emotional aftermath of October 3, 1951, when Bobby Thomson hit a home run in the last of the ninth to win the pennant for the Giants over the Dodgers.)

We hope that our love of the game, coupled with our pride in our state, makes this a book that other New Jerseyans will consider a touchstone as the story of New Jersey and baseball moves on to its next chapter.

James M. DiClerico
Barry J. Pavelec
May 1990

THE JERSEY GAME

INTRODUCTION

Newark, Oct. 12—Echoes of New York's "Subway Series" of the 1940s and 1950s reverberated here today as the Newark Peps, champions of the Federal League, and the Camden Canners, winners of the American League pennant, met in game 1 of what sportswriters have already dubbed the "Turnpike Series."

Although Camden helped found the American League in 1901 and Newark has been in the Federal League since its second season (1915), the teams have never before met in the World Series. The closest they came was three years ago, when both finished atop their leagues but Newark lost to St. Louis, the National League standard-bearer, in the preseries playoffs. This year, in a Federal vs. National playoff, Newark thumped the senior-circuit champion Hoboken Knickerbockers four games to one. The Knicks, oldest of New Jersey's major league teams, helped inaugurate the National League in 1876 and this year won their seventeenth pennant.

Fantasy? Well, yes. But had a couple of balls bounced a little differently, it might have been fact. A team called the Knickerbockers actually did play in Hoboken in the infancy of baseball. It contributed centrally to the game's early development and was invited to help form the National League in 1876. But the Knickerbockers demurred, preferring to stick with the "gentlemen's" (amateur) game.

The Newark Peps were real, too. What's more, this team played in a league—the Federal—that had talents to match its major league aspirations. Unfortunately, the league could not survive the triple whammy of World War I, a dearth of fans, and the opportunism of some of its owners.

As for Camden, there never was a team called the Canners. But there was, in the 1880s, the Merritt—a good enough team to form the early nucleus of what generations later would become the Los Angeles Dodgers. More on point, there was the 1927 threat of Philadelphia Athletics owner Benjamin Shibe that he would move his team to Camden, where games could be played on Sunday. Shibe, who built the first concrete-and-steel stadium (Shibe Park) and invented the cork-center baseball, clearly considered Camden a major league city. So let us suppose that the City of Brotherly Love refused to give Shibe his way (as Brooklyn and New York refused O'Malley and Stoneham three decades later). Then we might today be reading not about the American League's Oakland (via Kansas

City) Athletics, but rather about the Camden Athletics (or "Canners," in honor of a well-known enterprise that just announced its intention to stop canning in Camden).

Though such major league dreams have not and may never come true (a referendum for a new stadium in the Meadowlands was defeated in 1987), New Jersey may well see a second heyday of the minor league version of the game. The state certainly saw some glory the first time around—in Newark, in Trenton, in Jersey City, in Paterson, and from time to time in at least a dozen other cities around the state. And if major league dreams have not become reality for the state and its cities, they decidedly have for many New Jersey natives. Over three hundred have put their names into major league record books.

New Jersey has also played a central and colorful role in the amateur version of baseball. The state has had its Little League and Babe Ruth champs, its collegiate powerhouses, its representatives on Olympic squads. Trenton serves, in fact, as the seat of government for all of U.S. amateur baseball.

The past may not be prologue for New Jersey and baseball. But it is a proud and important past, one that New Jersey baseball fans should enjoy reliving as they read here about the men, the teams, and the events that make the state truly "the crossroads of baseball."

CHAPTER 1

A Game Is Born in Jersey

The Beginnings of Modern Baseball

The Commodore, John Cox Stevens, scion of the family that made Hoboken's Elysian Fields the recreation mecca of its day. (S. C. Williams Library, Stevens Institute of Technology, Hoboken)

A t midafternoon on October 21, 1845, John Cox Stevens reined his horse, stopping his carriage to allow a throng of people to pass as they walked from the Hoboken ferry dock to the heights above. For a Tuesday afternoon the size of the crowd and its obvious destination pleased him. The pleasure seekers had used the Stevens ferries to reach Hoboken from lower Manhattan and were obviously en route to the playgrounds on the cliffs above, which his late father had named "Elysian Fields" and whose attractions had helped keep him and his family wealthy. Stevens was on his way to the docks below, where his yacht *Gimcrack* was anchored. On her decks a year before he had helped form the New York Yacht Club and had received the title "commodore" in return for the Elysian Fields clubhouse he donated to the new organization.

"Hello, Commodore," shouted a young man from the crowd. He was Billy Tucker, son of tobacconist Abraham Tucker, whose New York shop on lower Broadway was not far from the sumptuous home maintained there by Stevens and known by the locals as "the Stevens Palace."

"Billy!" Stevens replied in recognition, and seeing the bat on the young man's shoulder asked, "Another town ball game? I thought you boys had enough of that last Friday."

"Oh, we weren't playing town ball last Friday," Tucker called back brightly. "That old-fashioned game belongs to my father and his cronies. We've got new rules and a new club called the Knickerbockers that plays nothing but the new game. We put the rules in our charter. I'll show you a copy the next time you come to the shop."

"A new game?" Stevens retorted. "Come on, I've been watching base ball since I was a boy. And as for 'chartered' base ball clubs, I remember the Olympics playing near our railroad terminal in Camden a dozen years ago. They put *their* rules in *their* charter. And, by the way, no one in New York City played base ball better than your father!"

Tucker smiled. "I know he was good," he replied. "But after watching the game we Knicks played among ourselves on Friday, even he prefers our new rules. We all had a roaring good time! Commodore, why don't you come up and watch the game today? My old club, New York, is going to give the new rules a try against the Brooklyn team. It will be the first time two different clubs play each other under the new rules."

With that Tucker waved good-bye with his bat and continued up the hill. Stevens went down to the waterfront to turn his attention to his first love, yachting. In just five short years he would make his most enduring mark on American sports by winning the first America's Cup on a yacht representing his New York Yacht Club. Whether he saw the New York Base

Ball Club (Tucker's "old club") beat the Brooklyn club that afternoon is unknown. What is now known is that at 2:00 P.M. on Tuesday, October 21, 1845, the first match game of modern baseball began on Elysian Fields in Hoboken, New Jersey, fully eight months before the game between New York and the Knickerbockers that has until today erroneously borne that monumental designation.

THE COMMODORE'S AWARENESS of the baseball of the mid-1840s was probably greater than most. He was of that class of sportsmen who were regularly organizing clubs, in the fashion of the day, to participate in their favorite diversions. His own New York Yacht Club was not dissimilar from the many horse racing, shooting, rowing, cricket and other sporting clubs forming at the time. Thanks to the ferry service his family provided between Manhattan and Hoboken in the north and Philadelphia and Camden in the south, access to the playgrounds of New Jersey was easy for all manner of sportsman and athlete from the neighboring states.

When the Stevens family brought the Camden & Amboy Railroad (the nation's first) to Camden in 1832, its right-of-way passed near the Market Street playing fields of the two groups of baseball players who, in May 1833, merged and formally organized as the Olympic Ball Club of Philadelphia.

But the game Stevens might have seen in Camden or the one Abraham Tucker or thousands of other American men played in New York City and throughout the East from before the Revolution was not the game Billy Tucker played that afternoon of October 21, 1845.

The game of the commodore's acquaintance, usually called "base ball" or "town ball," was a direct descendant of the English game of rounders. Its rules required that every member of a team bat before the other team came up, and it featured "soaking" a runner (that is, hitting him with the ball after a fairly struck hit) and an unlimited number of players on a team.

By the time Billy Tucker had grown to early manhood, his father was among the acknowledged "best of the best" in New York City at the soon-to-be-outmoded game, along with Colonel James Lee, Dr. Franklin Ransom, James Fisher, and William Vail. Billy Tucker was not a bad ballplayer either, joining other young men for regular evening and weekend contests on the rapidly disappearing open spaces of Manhattan.

As the summer of 1845 neared an end Tucker was approached by another player, Alexander Cartwright, a clerk at the Union Bank, who told Tucker of some new ideas about the old game. These ideas would change the game forever and eventually earn for Cartwright the title "Father of Baseball." Cartwright loved the camaraderie of ball playing and the chance to get out in the still clear air of New York City from late spring until late fall, but it was the game itself that most interested him. He knew that in its present state it could be boring for both players and spectators. He knew that standing in the field waiting to bat while an entire opposing team batted was no way to pass what was supposed to be an "active" afternoon. He knew that being hit with the ball while running the bases was not a pleasant or efficient way to be put out. He knew that stationing mobs of players in the outfield and two catchers behind the batter (as was then allowed) was unwieldy. Most of all he knew that with the application of some simple logic he could turn this old-fashioned game into an exciting athletic event.

In approaching Billy Tucker, Cartwright had been discriminating. By 1845 Billy was already an active member of the New York Base Ball Club, which had been organized in 1843. His roommate, William Wheaton, was both a ballplayer and a lawyer—not a bad combination to assist in the organization of a new sporting club. The two shared membership in the New York Base Ball Club and an apartment above Tucker's lower Broadway tobacco shop.

Cartwright and his ball playing friends had been gathering since the spring of 1842 in mid-Manhattan, first at a field near Madison Square, then at a site on the edge of a delightful body of fresh water called Sunfish Pond, and finally on grounds near the north slope of Murray Hill near Third Avenue. He probably spoke with Tucker and Wheaton after a Murray Hill game of town ball in early September and explained his new ideas for improving the sport. Tucker and Wheaton were excited by his suggested changes, and although they were not about to leave the New York team, they agreed to Cartwright's suggestions that they help form a new organization to promulgate, promote, and play under his new base ball rules.

With two other young New York area ballplayers, Duncan Curry and Ebenezer Dupignac, they began recruiting for a club to be called the New York Knickerbockers, taking the name of the volunteer fire fighting organization to which Cartwright had belonged. Lawyer Wheaton volunteered his legal skills to draw up a constitution for the club and, along with roommate Tucker, to formalize and fine-tune the distinctive new rules. By the end of September they had found enough members to support the new club and had completed the by-laws.

But recruiting and rulemaking seemed to be the least of the problems facing them and all New York City base ball players. Active Manhattanites had to face the reality of the rapid urbanization of Manhattan and the loss of their traditional playing fields. The fields and pathways surrounding Sunfish Pond (situated between modern Thirty-second and Thirty-first streets at Park Avenue) had been an important playground for New Yorkers for years, but by the mid-1840s the effluent coming from Peter Cooper's glue factory at Thirty-third Street had so polluted the water that the city fathers decided to fill it in. Without the pond the site became not so much a playground as an opportunity for development—a chance not wasted by the real estate barons of the day. The newer site near Third Avenue was soon to be closed to accommodate a new railroad right-of-way. Urban progress was rapidly driving base ball out of Manhattan.

Fortunately there were alternative recreational sites for New Yorkers. Thanks to the extensive ferry service available to the east and west of Manhattan Island, the playgrounds of Brooklyn and New Jersey were just minutes away. For the new Knickerbockers, Hoboken was the obvious choice. Years of intense and effective effort by the Stevens family to build their ferry business and sell off their vast land holdings on the heights above the Hudson had made the beautiful and expansive Elysian Fields a mecca for fun and games for New York's active young men. Playing fields, hotels with more than ample bars and dining facilities, beautiful vistas overlooking the Hudson and such diversions as Barnum's staged "buffalo hunts" and the "Ioway" Indian encampment (really just an extended stopover for Chief White Cloud's entourage on their return journey from England) taking place that very summer made Hoboken the Disneyland of its day—and all just fifteen minutes from Manhattan.

On September 23, 1845, a group of nearly thirty young men met at McCarty's Hotel not far from what is now Hudson and Twelfth streets in modern Hoboken. There Tucker and Wheaton, the two-man Committee on By-laws, presented their suggested charter to the new team and were rewarded both with its adoption and with election to the offices of secretary-treasurer and vice-president, respectively. The only other officer elected that day was fellow organizer Duncan Curry, who became the first president. Alexander Cartwright had to wait another year before being elected secretary.

Cartwright's suggested playing rules, as codified by lawyer Wheaton with suggestions by Billy Tucker, were included in the charter. They read:

Bird's-eye view of New York City and environs by John Bachman shows the location of Hoboken (foreground) and its appealing rustic setting. A baseball game is in progress at the lower left in this 1866 drawing. (I. N. Phelps Stokes Collection, Miriam & Ira D. Wallach Division of Art, Prints and Photographs, The New York Public Library, Astor, Lenox and Tilden Foundations)

1st. Members must strictly observe the time agreed upon for exercise, and be punctual in their attendance.

2nd. When assembled for exercise, the President, or in his absence, the Vice-President, shall appoint an Umpire, who shall keep the game in a book provided for that purpose, and note all violations of the By-Laws and Rules during the time of exercise.

3rd. The presiding officer shall designate two members as Captains, who shall retire and make the match to be played, observing at the same time that the players opposite to each other should be as nearly equal as possible, the choice of sides to be then tossed for, and the first in hand [first up] to be decided in a like manner.

4th. The bases shall be from "home" to second base, forty-two paces; from first to third base, forty-two paces, equidistant.

5th. No stump match [pick-up game] shall be played on a regular day of practice.

6th. If there should not be a sufficient number of members of the Club present at the time agreed upon to commence exercise, gentlemen not members may be chosen in to make up the match, which shall not be broken up to take in members that may afterwards appear; but in all cases, members shall have the preference, when present, at the making of a match.

7th. If members appear after the game is commenced, they may be chosen in if mutually agreed upon.

8th. The game to consist of twenty-one counts, or aces [runs scored first by one team]; but at the conclusion an equal number of hands [outs] must be played.

9th. The ball must be pitched, not thrown, for the bat.

10th. A ball knocked out of the field, or outside the range of the first or third base, is foul.

11th. Three balls being struck at and missed and the last one caught, is a hand out; if not caught is considered fair, and the striker bound to run.

12th. If a ball be struck, or tipped, and caught, either flying or on the first bound, is a hand out.

13th. A player running the bases shall be out, if the ball is in the hands of an adversary on the base, or the runner is touched with it before he makes his base; it being understood, however, that in no instance is a ball to be thrown at him.

14th. A player running who shall prevent an adversary from catching or getting the ball before making his base, is a hand out.

15th. Three hands out, all out.

16th. Players must take their strike in regular turn.

17th. All disputes and differences relative to the game, to be decided by the Umpire, from which there is no appeal.

18th. No ace or base can be made on a foul strike.

19th. A runner cannot be put out in making one base, when a balk is made by the pitcher.

20th. But one base allowed when a ball bounds out of the field when struck.

Modern baseball in a form clearly recognizable even a century and a half later had been born—at least on paper.

Within a few days the new club played its first informal intrasquad game under the new rules. The record book whose purchase had been authorized by the charter had not yet arrived, so no documentation exists (although forty-two runs were scored according to later recollection). It was the first game of modern baseball and was played in late September or early October 1845 in Hoboken.

By October 6, the scorebook had arrived. On that Monday evening a small band of brokers, doctors, lawyers, postal clerks, and merchants took the Stevens Barclay Street ferry across the Hudson after work and climbed the hill to Elysian Fields for the first recorded game of modern baseball. William Wheaton, the only true expert in the new rules and in the art of arbitration, became the game's first umpire. His strict adherence to the rules resulted in one of the club's newest members, Wall Street broker Archie Gourlie, becoming the first player to be fined when he prolonged a discussion over a call just a little too long.

In this Knicks versus Knicks contest Billy Tucker's side gave its all, and he drove in three runs. Teammate Alexander Cartwright contributed a single run in an 11–8 losing effort. Retiring to McCarty's for beer and cigars

KNICKERBOCKER BALL CLUB.

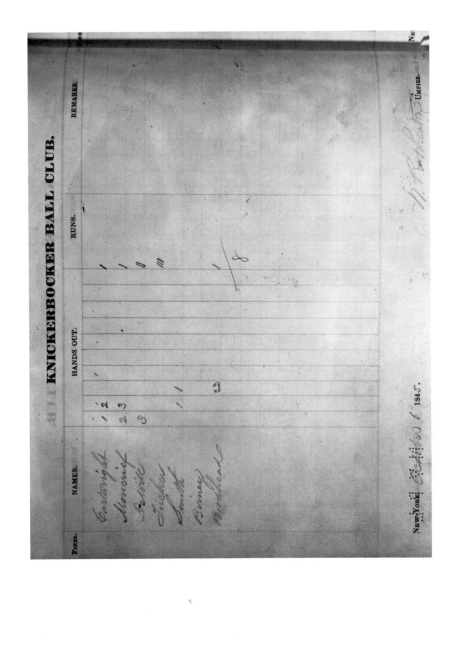

PAGES.	NAMES.	HANDS OUT.		RUNS.		REMARKS.
	Cartright	1	'	I		
	Howard	2		I		
	Davis	3		II		
	Tucker			III		
	Smith		/			
	Birney			I		
	Bertharad		23	8		

New-York ‹...› 6 1845.

‹signature› Umpire.

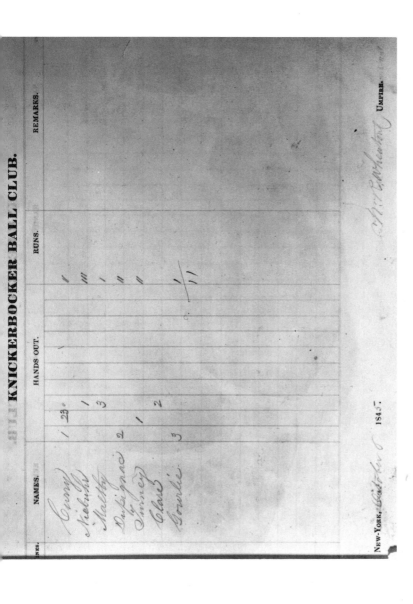

New York Knickerbockers' scorebook, now in The New York Public Library, provides first documentation of a game of modern baseball, October 6, 1845. (Spalding Collection, Rare Books and Manuscripts Division, The New York Public Library, Astor, Lenox and Tilden Foundations)

after the game, passing the scorebook around from table to table, all must have agreed they were on to something. By the seventeenth of the month they had played four contests. That Friday evening Wheaton and Curry were teammates in a lively 25–23 winning effort.

It was undoubtedly, as Tucker told Commodore Stevens the following Tuesday, "a roaring good time": a Friday evening's relaxation after the week's work was done, two fines issued for overexuberance, beer and cigars at McCarty's, a pleasant sail home across the beautiful Hudson filled with returning sailboats and singing rowers.

When Tucker and Wheaton returned to their Broadway apartment that night, probably in the company of Abraham Tucker and Ed Cone, another who had played that night and who also had dual membership in the Knick and New York clubs, someone probably suggested that they try to convert the older team to the new rules. Perhaps, they thought, it would be a good idea to have New York challenge another town ball club to a match of the new game.

Although much of early sports competition in the United States involved members of the same club, games between two distinct organizations ("match play") was not unusual by 1845. Separate cricket teams had engaged each other for years. Match play in town ball was common in Camden and Boston, and probably even in New York, though there are no records to prove this. But there had never been a match game under the new Knickerbocker base ball rules.

Wheaton and Tucker, by now convinced that the new rules were the wave of the future, were anxious to play the new game as much as possible. After the exciting Friday, October 17, contest, they may have used a cricket match in Brooklyn as the occasion to issue a challenge on behalf of their New York Base Ball Club to the Brooklyn Base Ball Club, made up primarily of cricketeers from the Union Star Cricket Club of Brooklyn. Elysian Fields, Hoboken, was designated as the meeting place. The appointed time was 2:00 P.M. on Tuesday, October 21, 1845.

The Union Star Club had already discovered the power of the press in building awareness of their activities and encouraging spectators. So a player probably suggested contacting the *New York Herald*, circulation forty thousand, to announce the scheduled contest. Unfortunately the announcement failed to appear in Monday afternoon's editions. So on Monday night, October 20, the only people who knew the first match game in the history of modern baseball was to take place the next afternoon were the players and their friends.

On the afternoon of Tuesday, October 21, 1845, as the participants in the scheduled event wrapped up their work in the banks, brokerage houses, shops, and offices of Manhattan and Brooklyn, the *Herald* hit the streets with this day-late but historically significant announcement:

> The New York Base Ball Club will play a match of baseball against the Brooklyn Club tomorrow afternoon at 2 o'clock, at the Elysian Field, Hoboken.

That afternoon young gentlemen carried base ball bats as they headed west, meeting in small clusters and mingling with the New Jersey commuters. Reaching the dock at the foot of Barclay Street, the players boarded the steam ferries shuttling commuters from the Manhattan to Hoboken and Jersey City. It took only a few minutes to cross to the New Jersey side, followed by a short walk from the commuter terminal to the ball field.

William Wheaton, the recognized expert in the new rules, likely was called upon to umpire just as he had been a few weeks earlier at the first Knick intrasquad game. The Knickerbocker game was new to most of the players, and Wheaton and Tucker must have had to explain a few things from time to time. Although its similarity to town ball made the game easy to play, its unique features gave the contest a new pace and excitement. Most distinctive was the rule that the teams at bat and in the field were to exchange places after just three outs, not after an entire team had batted. This was a mercy to players in the field when all hell was breaking loose at bat. On the base paths, too, things were different. Tagging the runner survived in the Cartwright variation, but hitting the runner with a thrown ball did not. This doubtless sped up the contest, since poorly thrown or effectively dodged balls probably resulted in many extra bases or runs under the old rules.

On Wednesday afternoon, October 22, the participants eagerly read the following item in the *Herald*: "Base Ball Match—A very closely contested match at this well known and old fashioned game took place yesterday at Hoboken between nine Brooklyn men and nine New Yorkers. We were informed last evening that the Brooklynites were the victors." But the *Herald* had gotten the story wrong! The inexperienced Brooklyn team had in fact lost. So the error was pointed out to the paper and, on Thursday, for the third consecutive day, the seminal event in modern baseball got exposure in the *Herald*: "Base Ball Play—We were misinformed in relation to the result of the Base Ball Match reported yesterday. It appears that the New York men beat their Brooklyn opponents with great ease but the latter earnestly promise to return the compliment with compound interest,

a. THE NEW YORK BASE BALL CLUB will play a match of base ball against the Brooklyn Club, to-morrow afternoon, at 2 o'clock, at the Elysian Fields, Hoboken.

b. BASE BALL MATCH.—A very closely contested match at this well known and old fashioned game took place yesterday at Hoboken, between nine Brooklyn men and nine New Yorkers. We were informed last evening that the Brooklynites were the victors.

c. BASE BALL PLAY.—The subjoined is the result of the return match between the New York Base Ball Club and the Brooklyn players, which came off on the ground of the Brooklyn Star Cricket Club yesterday. Messrs. Johnson, Wheaton and Van Nostrand were the umpires.

NEW YORK BALL CLUB.			BROOKLYN CLUB.		
	Hands out.	*Runs.*		*Hands out.*	*Runs.*
Davis,.....	2	4	Hunt......	1	3
Murphy ...	0	6	Hines........	2	2
Vail.......	2	4	Gilmore....	3	2
Kline......	1	4	Hardy......	2	2
Miller.....	2	5	Sharp.......	2	2
Case......	2	4	Meyers.....	0	3
Tucker....	2	4	Whaley.....	2	2
Winslow...	1	6	Forman.....	1	3
	12	37		12	19

d. BASE BALL PLAY.—We were misinformed in relation to the result of the Base Ball Match reported yesterday. It appears that the New York men beat their Brooklyn opponents with great ease, but the latter earnestly promise to return the compliment, with compound interest, on a repetition of the play which is to be made to-morrow on Brooklyn, on the ground belonging to the Union Star Cricket Club.

a.—*The New York Herald*, October 21, 1845
b.—*The New York Herald*, October 22, 1845
c.—*The New York Herald*, October 23, 1845
d.—*The New York Herald*, October 25, 1845

on a repetition of the play which is to be made tomorrow on the ground belonging to the Union Star Cricket Club."

On Friday the same group of ballplayers took the ferry, this time to Brooklyn, and played the return contest. That game got reported by the *Herald* as well, this time with a box score, a device already familiar to newspaper readers who routinely saw cricket contests so described.

Base Ball Play—The subjoined is the result of the return match between the New York Base Ball Club and the Brooklyn players, which came off on the ground of the Brooklyn Star Cricket Club yesterday. Messrs. Johnson, Wheaton and Van Nostrand were the Umpires.

NEW YORK BALL CLUB

Name	Hands Out	Runs
Davis	2	4
Murphy	0	6
Vail	2	4
Kline	1	4
Miller	2	5
Case	2	4
Tucker	2	4
Winslow	1	6
TOTALS:	12	37

BROOKLYN CLUB

Name	Hands Out	Runs
Hunt	1	3
Hines	2	2
Gilmore	2	2
Hardy	2	2
Sharp	2	2
Meyers	0	3
Whaley	2	2
Forman	1	3
TOTALS:	12	19

The Knickerbocker rules seem to have been applied. In the first game the teams were matched nine to a side. In the second, four-inning contest the New York team scored the required twenty-one aces (and sixteen for good measure) with twelve hands out, then home-standing Brooklyn fell short at just nineteen with an equal number of hands out.

By November 1845 there were two senior clubs and at least one junior club playing and partying at Hoboken's Elysian Fields. The new Knicker-bockers had been joined by the New York team, the latter now firmly converted to the new rules. The *Herald* reported New York's celebration ending its second year:

New York Base Ball Club—The second anniversary of this Club came off yesterday, on the ground in the Elysian fields. The game was as follows

	Runs		Runs
Murphy	4	Winslow	4
Johnson	4	Case	4
Lyon	3	Granger	1
Wheaton	4	Lalor	3
Sweet	3	Cone	1
Seaman	1	Sweet	4
Venn	2	Harold	3
Gilmore	1	Clair	1
Tucker	3	Wilson	1
TOTALS	24		23

J. M. Marsh, Esq. Umpire and Scorer.

After the match, the parties took dinner at Mr. McCarty's Hoboken, as a wind up for the season. The Club were honored by the presence of representatives from the Union Star Cricket Club, The Knickerbocker Clubs, senior and junior, and other gentlemen of note.

It is not hard to imagine that at this celebration and for the next six months, the new version of base ball was the subject of much lively conversation. On May 5, 1846, the Knicks held their first meeting of the new year. Curry was reelected president, Dan Adams replaced Wheaton as vice-president, Cartwright became secretary, and Tucker retained his treasurer's post. A month later, on June 6, the Knicks named their first honorary members, Colonel James Lee and Abraham Tucker, and they appointed a committee consisting of Curry, Adams, and Billy Tucker to arrange a match game with the New York Club.

Long thought to be the first match game, this contest, played on June 19, 1846, was actually eight months later than the Hoboken contest and the Brooklyn return match between New York and Brooklyn. This time Billy Tucker aligned himself with the Knicks and ended up on the losing side. Cartwright umpired. The final score was 23–1 in favor of New York.

In almost every baseball history including the first, *The Book of American Pastimes* written by Charles Peverelly in 1866, the New York Base Ball Club, though given recognition for its participation in this contest, has been called an "unorganized squad of ball players" or "a shadowy group," or has been otherwise dismissed as unimportant.

Clearly, though, the New York team was no will-o'-the-wisp. It was a club that saw to it that its games would be announced to the forty thousand readers of the *New York Herald*, with accurate box scores included whenever possible, and a club that publicly celebrated its second anniversary with an impressive banquet.

The New York Base Ball Club was not the first to play modern baseball, but it was, along with the Brooklyn Baseball Club, the first to play in a match game. It did not have staying power, however, and the Knickerbockers seemed to have momentum going for it. Before long, members of the New York team began showing up more and more in the lineup for the Knick's intrasquad games, the only kind it played, with the exception of the June 19, 1846, contest, until 1851.

Cartwright headed west in March 1849, while Billy Tucker stuck with the team until April 6, 1850, when he "regretfully" tendered his resignation. He could not stay away, however, and was back on the field on June 3, 1851, when the team journeyed to the Red House Grounds in Harlem for its first away game with Washington (history's fourth recorded match contest). The Knicks won 21–11. In 1853 Tucker was again appointed to the rules committee and in 1857 and 1858 was voted a director of the club.

IN 1939, the Abner Doubleday myth was receiving great play by the baseball powers—to legitimize the Cooperstown, New York, location of the soon-to-be-opened Baseball Hall of Fame and also to justify a centennial

Across the street from Hoboken's Elysian Park, last vestige of the Elysian Fields, stands a plaque commemorating the Knickerbockers' first match game, which followed by eight months a New York versus Brooklyn contest on the same site. (Authors' Collection)

celebration of the "birth" of the game. Robert W. Henderson, in "Baseball and Rounders," a thoroughly researched article on the origins of the sport for the *Bulletin of the New York Public Library*, scientifically debunked the legend for all time and honored the real pioneers of the game, writing, "To Alexander J. Cartwright, D. F. Curry, E. R. Dupignac, Jr., W. H. Tucker and W. R. Wheaton, and the other men who organized the Knickerbocker Club of New York in the year 1845, should go much greater credit than any being directed towards Doubleday, and we suggest that an American centennial celebration should commemorate this Knickerbocker group as the originators of the modern American game, rather than Abner Doubleday, whose contribution to baseball is so slight and so uncertain."

Henderson might have added that Hoboken, New Jersey—not Cooperstown, New York; Brooklyn, New York; New York, New York; or anyplace else, New York—should be given credit for being the real birthplace of modern baseball. And today, Hoboken, New Jersey, and the rest of the baseball world should be setting its sights on October 21, 1995, as the date to celebrate the 150th anniversary of the first match game.

CHAPTER 2

They Came to Play

New Jersey Nurtures Competitive Baseball

Currier & Ives print, published in 1865, shows an Elysian Fields game of base ball thought by some historians to have been played a decade earlier by the New York Knickerbockers. (Newark Public Library)

By the early 1850s Hoboken, long known to New Yorkers as the "stronghold of lager beer," had also established itself as the stronghold of the New York game of base ball. New clubs immediately gravitated to Elysian Fields for competition and instruction. In 1852 the Gotham Base Ball Club was created when a group of new players joined and renamed the Washington Club. The Eagle Club was created in the fall of 1853 and its members immediately asked the Knickerbockers to help in organizing a committee to establish formal rules.

In 1854—the first season when there were more than two teams—the Knicks, Eagles, and Gotham held a multiclub, postseason party on December 15 at Fijux's, 11 Barclay Street, New York. Absent was a fourth new squad that called Elysian Fields home: the Empire Club, formed on October 23. The party was described a decade later: "An equal delegation was present, and an excellent bill of fare presented. The utmost hilarity prevailed, and everything passed off in a happy manner. A song, composed for the occasion by James Whyte Davis of the Knickerbocker Club, was so well received that the Eagle Club had it printed. It was entitled 'Ball Days' and abounded in witty allusions to the principal players of the three clubs."

In these early days teams often formed when a group of sports-minded fans were impressed by what they had witnessed at Elysian Fields. Writing in 1866, Van Brunt Wycoff, told of the formation of the Excelsiors, one of the most influential teams of the era: "While witnessing a game played November 10 or 17, 1854, between the Knickerbockers and Eagles, it occurred to John H. Suydam and several others to 'get up' a Base Ball Club, and accordingly on Thanksgiving Day in November of that year they met for practice, but under no especial organization. They styled themselves the 'J.Y.B.B.C.' (Jolly Young Bachelors Base Ball Club)." At their December 8 meeting, at New York's Florence Hotel, this new team took the name Excelsior Baseball Club. They were the first team based in Brooklyn to play regularly under the New York rules.

The next year, in May, New Jersey's first team was formed in Newark, followed shortly by the Pioneer Club of Jersey City, founded in June. Two other New Jersey teams, Hoboken and Star, were based at Elysian Fields. The Putnam Club, with grounds in the Williamsburg section of Brooklyn, also came into being in 1855, as did the Union Club of Morrisania of Westchester County.

By 1856 the press was already calling baseball the "national game." Perhaps the first such claim appeared in the fall of that year in *Porter's Spirit of the Times*: "With the fall of the leaf and diminution of the daylight, many of the out-of-door sports and pastimes come to a close for the season. The manly and exhilarating pastimes of Base Ball, Cricket, Foot Ball, and Racket are not playable. . . . We feel a degree of old Knickerbocker pride at the continued prevalence of Base Ball as the National game in the region of the Manhattanese."

In the December 6 issue, in answer to numerous requests, *Porter's* printed the rules of the game and gave a boost to the new sport. New clubs soon converted from town ball to the New York game. Until this time all teams were "gentlemen's" clubs, but in 1856 the elitist dam broke, and the common man came in. The Atlantics of Jamaica and Henry Eckford's team of Greenpoint were composed of shipwrights and mechanics working for him in the "island" section of Brooklyn. Others followed: Long Island working men formed the Pastime Club, policemen from New York City proper the Manhattans, saloonkeepers the Phantoms, schoolteachers the Metropolitans, and dairymen the Pocahontas Club.

The "class" teams did eventually play the upstarts, but not without a sneer. The Eckfords and the Atlantics thrust again and again into the realm of the lofty at Hoboken. Soon games were played, but the gentlemen tried to avoid them. Prior to one contest, the Eckfords were told of a standing rule among the elite clubs to play only against others who used the Hoboken fields. Not mentioned was the fact that the rule was created only to avoid the match.

Teams were springing up everywhere. The Liberty Club of New Brunswick was founded on March 1, 1857, with the Star emerging in the same city later that year. The year also saw Amity of Rahway forming along with Hamilton in Jersey City and Nassau in Princeton.

On October 6, 1857, the Wayne Base Ball Club disbanded, with some members moving to Excelsior. This put several New Jersey players on what was to become one of the top teams of the 1860s.

Many clubs formed junior or "muffin" teams, which fed members into the senior teams. Among them were the Harmony Club, Enterprise, and Star clubs of Brooklyn. (Star would have an impact on New Jersey in the fall of 1858, when three of its members matriculated at Princeton University, bringing along their baseball paraphernalia and converting the college's ball team to the New York game.)

The growth in new ball clubs had reduced the influence of the Knickerbockers, but they were still honored for their "gentlemanly" style. The Putnams gave homage to the founding Knickerbockers and suggested the growing lapses of demeanor by other teams with one of their songs:

> And should any club by their cunning and trick
> Dishonor the game that it plays
> Let them take my advice and go to "Old Knick"
> And there learn to better their ways.

The Knicks, while still recognized and respected for their pioneering efforts, were finding it increasingly uncomfortable to play among the "greasy mechanics" who increasingly were finding their way to bat. They avoided match games with the more common teams and remained content to practice among themselves and continue their tradition of sumptuous dining.

The growth in the number and geographical spread of teams, coupled with the pride in performance each felt, brought a growing desire for more match play throughout the New York metropolitan area. Finally the Knicks, in their role as founders and keepers of the flame, came under pressure to call a convention, ostensibly to consolidate the rules. Bowing to the other teams, which were anxious to expand match play and put some structure into the sport, they agreed to place an ad in *Porter's Spirit of the Times*: "Pursuant to the above resolution the various Base Ball Clubs of this city and vicinity are requested each to select three representatives to meet at 462 Broome Street, in the city of New York, on Thursday, the 22nd day of January next, at half-past seven o'clock P.M."

At a subsequent meeting (May 1857) it was decided to call a larger convention of all regular organized baseball clubs. This second event took place in New York City on March 10, 1858. Liberty of New Brunswick sent two members, and although casual historians say the other twenty-five teams came from New York and Brooklyn, Amity and Nassau are listed in attendance. Because names were commonly shared in those early times, these were not necessarily the Rahway and Princeton teams, but may have been.

At the gathering, the newer clubs voted to create a formal association. The resulting National Association of Base Ball Players, the first formal baseball organization in the country, effectively cut the Knicks out of any position of power, ending their primacy in the game.

About fifty teams were competing in the New York metropolitan area by the 1858 season, with another sixty muffin teams. Brooklyn, Harlem, and Long Island saw increasing play by New York and Brooklyn teams. Hoboken's Elysian Fields was easily the most popular playing venue for the entire area, with Englewood another New Jersey favorite.

The scene at Hoboken during the height of the baseball season in the sport's first "golden age" can only be imagined. Writing in 1902, William A. Shephard, a third baseman who had played at Elysian Fields against the famous stars of the day before he headed west in 1861, recalled the scene he witnessed at the end of the 1850s:

> Almost half a century ago my brother and I, boys of fifteen or sixteen, claimed every available holiday and hurried across the Hoboken Ferry to Elysian Fields, the rendezvous of New York base ball players.
>
> The beauty of those fields still linger [sic] with me although I have not seen them for nearly a lifetime. A walk of about a mile and a half from the ferry, up the Jersey shore of the Hudson River, along a road that skirted the river bank on one side and was hugged by trees and thicket on the other, brought one suddenly to an opening in the "forest primeval." This open spot was a level, grass-covered plain, some two hundred yards across, and as deep, surrounded upon three sides by the typical eastern undergrowth and woods and on the east by the Hudson River. It was a perfect greensward. Nature must have foreseen the needs of base ball, and designed the place especially for that purpose.

Shephard, who had competed against the greats of the East—George and Harry Wright, John Oliver, and Jim Creighton—played for the San Francisco Pacifics in 1869 when the Cincinnati Red Stockings, the United States' first all-professional team, came to town.

In 1858 the growing popularity of baseball inspired its first direct commercial exploitation and touched off a new fanaticism for the sport, which carried it into the Civil War era. In July, August, and September, "picked nines" (players selected at random) from New York and Brooklyn clubs met in a best two-out-of-three competition at the Fashion Race Course, a major horse racing facility in Newtown, Long Island (now Queens).

These all-star squads played for the Championship of New York. On July 20 the series got under way with the first game ever at which admission was charged. Fifteen hundred spectators, most of whom had to come by the Fulton Ferry from Hunters Point, saw New York defeat Brooklyn. The second match took place on August 19, with Brooklyn winning 29–8. The final and deciding contest was scheduled for September 10.

Both the previous games had involved teams composed of players from all the major teams in the two cities. In the final game, Brooklyn used six from the Atlantics and three from the Eckfords. New York used players from all of its four teams. The final score was 29–18 in favor of New York before what the press called "the largest crowd ever to see a baseball contest."

THE SPREAD OF THE NEW GAME

In 1859 more New Jersey teams joined the party: Live Oak of Orange, Union of Elizabeth, Lone Star of Jersey City, and Independent of Somerville, to name a few.

Meanwhile enthusiasm for Alexander Cartwright's game was spreading beyond the New York metropolitan area. In 1857 the Tri-Mountain Club of Boston adopted the New York game, which had been introduced by E. G. Saltzman, who had played second base for the Gotham Club. (Saltzman later introduced the game to North Carolina.) Tri-Mountain was followed by several other New England squads in 1858 and 1859.

But the Massachusetts game (old town ball) was making a strong final stand. The first organized team in Massachusetts had been the Olympic Club of Boston, followed by the Elm Tree Club of the same city. The two played their first match game in the summer of 1855. More clubs followed until, in 1857, the Olympics established a set of distinct town ball–type rules, which were soon adopted by several other clubs.

On May 13, 1858, the Massachusetts Association of Base Ball Players was formed at Dedham. The rules adopted by the convention included variations from the New York game:

Rule 4. The bases shall be wooden stakes, projecting four feet from the ground.

Rule 8. The ball must be thrown—not pitched or tossed—to the Bat, on the side preferred by the Striker, and within reach of his Bat.

Rule 14. If a player, while running the bases, be hit with the ball thrown by one of the opposite side, before he has touched the home bound, while off a Base, he shall be considered out.

Rule 17. In playing all match games, one hundred tallies shall constitute the game, the making of which by either Club, that Club shall be judged the winner.

Rule 18. Not less than ten nor more than fourteen players from each Club, shall constitute a match in all games.

In the summer of 1859 Massachusetts rules prevailed in the first intercollegiate game of baseball, played between Williams College and Amherst. But town ball was boring and thus doomed. In one of the last games under the Massachusetts rules, two clubs played from 11:00 A.M. to 5:00 P.M. one day in October 1859 and from 10:00 A.M. to 3:30 P.M. the next day, for a total of eighty innings. Said *Porter's Spirit of the Times* in an editorial: "This thing cannot last, and the Massachusetts game will surely die a natural death when the New England clubs come to realize the superiority of baseball, 'the New York game,' as played under the rules adopted by the National Association of Baseball Players."

The Tri-Mountain Club defeated the Portland (Maine) Club on the Boston Common in 1858 in the first-ever play of the New York game in New England. At least seven other clubs were formed later that year to play by the New York rules.

THE YEAR 1860 saw a general blossoming of the New York game. The top teams were taking advantage of the growing railroad networks to spread the game and their fame throughout the East. Team tours brought attention to the sport and launched heated intertown rivalries, which had never existed before.

Brooklyn's Excelsior Club was the first to have an impact on the game beyond the confines of its metropolitan New York home, thanks to major tours to upstate New York, Philadelphia, and Baltimore in 1860 and to New England in 1862. Top teams had already been playing away games at the end of steamer lines and along railroads. Liberty of New Brunswick, for example, had welcomed (and lost to) Brooklyn's Atlantics in 1859 through the convenience of the steam ferry, and were beaten on their home ground by the Philadelphia Athletics that same year courtesy of the railroad. But the multigame Excelsior tours were a new baseball phenomenon.

Even as the Civil War became imminent, baseball continued to grow in popularity. After the start of hostilities, fans in the North showed as much interest in news of the baseball field as in dispatches from the battlefield.

Not every contest was worthy of reporting, however. On September 21,

1861, at Hoboken, a match was held with nine picked players on one side and eighteen on the other. Half of the latter were cricketeers, the rest top baseball players from leading clubs, including the Mutuals. The eighteen-man team was allowed six outs to an inning, but still lost 45–16. Superstar Jim Creighton pitched for the winners.

A few years later things took a turn for the truly silly. In 1864 and 1865 winter games were played on ice at Sylvan Pond in Hoboken. A February 1864 game had to be halted because of a thaw. Bases were powdered charcoal circles; the ball was soft and inelastic, the runner could "overskate" a base by five feet, then had to try for the next.

The following winter the Atlantics and Gothams played an ice baseball series for a silver ball. The Atlantics won 32–5 on January 12, 1865, at Capitoline Skating Pond in Brooklyn. Gotham took the second game at Sylvan Pond in Hoboken 39–19. Atlantic won the rubber match 50–30 on Washington Skating Pond in Brooklyn.

Winter ball was not that unusual. In 1865 the Philadelphia Athletics, as enthusiastic a group as has ever played the game, scheduled a double-header against Burlington and Mount Holly on December 9. The first game in Burlington went off smoothly, but the Mount Holly game had to be stopped in the seventh inning because of a snow storm. The teams called it a season and left the field for a "fine banquet" at the Mount Holly Hotel.

Other competition made more sense. On October 21, 1861, fifteen thousand fans gathered at Elysian Fields for an all-star game between New York and Brooklyn for a silver ball trophy presented by Frank Queen of the *New York Clipper.* Brooklyn, headed by a strong Atlantic contingent, won 18–6 with a strong performance by pitcher Jim Creighton. Al Reach, later a sporting goods magnate, played for Brooklyn. Harry Wright of the Knickerbockers, who seven years later would found the first professional ball club, played for New York.

THE IMPACT OF THE CIVIL WAR

The Civil War eventually monopolized the nation's attention. Young men were, after all, going off to war in faraway places and some were coming home dead or maimed. For most of the soldiers, the war nevertheless started as an adventure, something to look forward to, a time of excitement. With that attitude, many ballplayers packed up their bats and balls along with their canteens and carbines.

The impact of the war on baseball has long been debated. Some say it spread the sport to the South and West. But emigrating New Yorkers and New Jerseyans with baseball experience had taken it to those regions long before the hostilities began. Teams in the Carolinas and New Orleans were in full competition before the first shot was fired at Fort Sumter. It is likely, though, that the game played in camps (including prison camps) caught the attention of local citizens. The enthusiasm and ability of many of the best players might well have made such an impression that the locals took up the sport when the fighting stopped. Finally, the massive migration of ex-soldiers after the war brought more and more experienced players south and west, and the game flourished.

Formal competition did not die off during the war. Spirited and significant contests went on throughout the years of conflict. An important innovation introduced during the war was the concept of state and regional championships. Along with New York and Pennsylvania, New Jersey was a leader in developing such competition.

In the fall of 1862 the Princeton Nassaus became the champions of New Jersey by twice defeating the 1861 champions, the Stars of New Brunswick. The first game was played on September 24, 1862, at Princeton and was won 22–16 by the Nassaus. The return game was played on October 11 at New Brunswick.

In 1865 the first "Grand Match for the Championship of the United States" attracted a crowd of fifteen to twenty thousand to Elysian Fields on August 3. By 11:00 A.M. crowds started to arrive. By 1:00 P.M. all "platform seats" were occupied. From 1:00 to 3:00 P.M. Hoboken ferries were loaded down to the water's edge. Arriving railroad cars were packed, and since wagons and carts were at a premium, many had to walk to the fields. The game was scheduled to begin at 3:00 P.M. but it took forty-five minutes to clear a space to play. The Atlantics led the Mutuals 13–12 with the Mutuals at bat in the sixth when a thunderstorm broke and the game was called. Later that month the U.S. champion Atlantics defeated Newark's Eureka, champions of New Jersey, before seven thousand on August 18, 21, and 20.

ALTHOUGH MOST TEAMS now made "road trips" and several undertook extended tours via the new modes of transportation, Hoboken's Elysian Fields remained the center of baseball. A local newspaper reviewed improvements made to the grounds: "For several years past the ball grounds

Brooklyn's Atlantics and Mutuals meet at Hoboken for the 1865 Championship of the United States. Caption beneath the woodcut from *Frank Leslie's Illustrated Newspaper* **of August 26 reads: "CATCHING OUT THE ATLANTICS ON A 'FOUL BALL.'" (S. C. Williams Library, Stevens Institute of Technology, Hoboken)**

in the northern end of Elysian Fields had been the scene of matches between the Mutuals, Gothams, Actives and other clubs. Now, with the permission of Edwin Stevens, these three clubs were enlarging and improving the grounds, cutting down several trees, removing rocks, leveling and turfing, as well as erecting several rows of seats for spectators. The work was done under the supervision of Coroner John Wildey, president of the Mutuals." More than one thousand were present at the grand opening of the improved Elysian Fields on May 25, 1865, and saw the Mutuals beat a "picked nine" 25–13.

By 1866 the improved fields at Hoboken were teeming with sportsmen and their ladies. To get an idea of the kind of entourage that surrounded a game, one need only look at the size of the membership of the important clubs of the era and consider how many friends and family tagged along. The major Hoboken-based clubs, besides the Knickerbockers and Gothams, included the Eagles with 85 members, Empire (74), Active (150), Jefferson (50), Social (70), and Eclectic (76). Excelsior, based in Brooklyn, had 370 members, including 5 who were still with the team from the Wayne Base Ball Club when they joined with Excelsior in 1857. Atlantic had 220, Eckford 150. Liberty of New Brunswick had 75. Most Hoboken-based clubs had their own clubhouses at the Elysian Fields. The Eagles had clubrooms large enough to permit indoor practice in bad weather.

On September 13 the first game for the 1866 U.S. Championship was staged at Hoboken between the Mutuals and the Atlantics. According to a New York newspaper report, fifteen thousand spectators filled "every fence, shed and other prominence on which a human being could be poised within view of Elysian Fields." The Mutuals led 14–8 at end of the seventh, but in the eighth the "misjudgment of the umpire seemed to demoralize the Mutuals." The Atlantics scored nine runs to make the final score Atlantics 17, Mutuals 15.

The series continued in Philadelphia with an advance sale of eight thousand tickets at twenty-five cents each. Scalpers were getting five dollars for elevated seats on a chair or bench. Nearly twenty thousand finally came to the ball park, some placing bets of up to one thousand dollars on Brooklyn. But by the third inning there were no takers for bets against Brooklyn. The Athletics, who had won thirty games that year and lost only to Irvington, were too much for Brooklyn. With seven runs in the tenth inning, they won 12–6.

In 1867 the Stevens family banned championship games at the Elysian Fields because of crowd disorders, gambling, and suspicion of fixed games. Consequently, the Mutuals moved to Brooklyn's Union Grounds that year.

In 1869 the lower portion of Elysian Fields, where the Knickerbockers still played, was cut up to accommodate sewers and streets for the expansion of Hoboken. The city had grown from 2,668 in 1850 to over 20,000. The Empire Club, which used the upper part of the grounds, invited the "old-timers" to use their grounds. Still active in 1870, the Knickerbockers built a new clubhouse on the reduced Elysian Fields.

HOBOKEN was not the only pleasure spot in Jersey. Another was Irvington, or "Camptown," as it was known until the original Christy Minstrels made Stephen Foster's "Camptown Races" a popular hit of the early 1850s, much to the embarrassment of the residents.

Camptown's elite—including many professional and business people who worked in Newark, Jersey City, and New York—had already become upset with the reputation of their town, described by a clergyman as "the rendezvous of the fast and wicked young men of Newark and Orange, the goal of strawrides and the Gretna Green of dance, frolic and fun. The road to Newark [is] bad and dangerous. Robbers lurk in the thick woods." So the town changed its name to Irvington, honoring a popular writer of the day, Washington Irving.

Shortly after the end of the Civil War a group of young men, employees of the Belcher Rule Company in Irvington, formed a ball club. It became one of the best in the country and a source of some players who eventually went on to the major leagues. The Irvington Base Ball Club was, according to the *Newark Daily Advertiser*, "second to but one or two clubs, and fearlessly and, for the most part, successfully contest[ing] with the crack nines of the country."

The Irvington club was a great draw. On May 16, 1867, five thousand traveled to the Eureka grounds (four miles from Newark) to see Irvington beat the Newark team. Then they came home to their Ferry and Adams Street grounds and beat the Actives 25–16. They had enclosed their grounds that year with a high board fence, erected seats, and made other improvements.

On June 4, Irvington played Morrisania's Unions before seven thousand at home. Newspapers reported that "despite intense heat and

The Mutuals of Brooklyn, backed by New York City's notorious "Boss" Tweed, were the first powerhouse in baseball. In this photo from about 1871, Rynie Wolters, who pitched for the 1873 Elizabeth Resolutes, is seated second from right. Another future Resolute, Marty Swandell, is standing at Wolters's right shoulder. (Spalding Collection, Miriam & Ira D. Wallach Division of Art, Prints and Photographs, The New York Public Library, Astor, Lenox and Tilden Foundations)

transportation difficulties, including the efforts of the Jersey Horse Railroad Company, running from Newark to Irvington, to cram the greatest number of people into the smallest possible space . . . the crowd of overgrown boys with men's hats and loud neckties, loud voices and little sense, who annoyed everyone near them by their blackguardism, by degrees cooled down."

Describing Morrisania's play, the report went on: "Pabor pitched more wildly than usual; Birdsall, although as neat as ever, was not so sure on the catch; Goldie made a most horrid and, for him, extraordinary muff; Ketcham, although still quick, was slippery in the fingers; Smith, though lively and earnest as always, could not play short; and Austin, who judged flies very nicely and got them in his hands, could not keep them there." Irvington won easily.

On June 28 the infamous pickpocket game occurred. Long before game time the road from Newark to Irvington (Springfield Boulevard) was lined with vehicles of every sort. Filled with food and drink, people flocked to see the Irvingtons face off against the Mutuals.

The Mutuals had stayed at the St. Nicholas Hotel in Newark, arriving at the ball park in grand style via two hotel coaches. Just before 3:00 P.M., as the game was about to begin, a downpour occurred making the field one huge New Jersey–style swamp. When play finally did get under way it was, according to press reports, "marked by several disgraceful fights, the first started by some pickpockets from New York as a distraction to ply their trade. A detective Dunn of New York City's 6th Precinct saw what was going on and collared one practitioner whereupon his colleagues started an even greater row. Members of both ball clubs under the guidance of Coroner Wildey joined in to stop the altercation but not without Hugh Campbell of the Irvington team being hit in the face with an umbrella. Finally the game was played with Mutuals winning by just one run, 17 to 16."

Irvington beat the Eckfords and the Stars late in July, then drew a crowd of four thousand on August 5 for a game with the Atlantics. The out-of-towners had taken the ferry from New York to Jersey City, then the New Jersey Railroad to Newark. From there they boarded any and all wheeled vehicles they could find and traveled out Springfield Boulevard to the Irvington grounds. Irvington beat them 34–32.

Irvington was, in 1867–1868, one of the best teams in the country, drawing good crowds wherever they went. For a game with Union at Union's grounds in Melrose (just north of Harlem and Mott Haven) the Harlem Railroad system set up a thirteen-car special train.

The 1867 season was the zenith for the amateur team. Shortly thereafter players began to be lured away by other clubs with offers of cash or, in the case of the Mutual team then controlled by the Tweed ring, even New York City jobs. Irvington, stocked with great players, was an obvious target for such raiding. The once dominant team lost most of its best men and closed the 1868 season with three straight losses, including a final 16–13 heartbreaker against the college men of the Seton Hall Alerts.

IN 1867 AND 1868 baseball had mixed reviews in the newspapers. The *Paterson Press* said in 1867 that baseball "frenzy" was destroying "all regular business habits," and predicted, with accuracy, that the time would come when "every member of the first class nines of the country will be a paid professional player, and hundreds of our young men will aim at such a position as one of the most shining pinnacles that fame can boast."

The following year the *Newark Advertiser* said, "People have baseball on the brain to an extent hitherto unequaled." Young men were slighting everything "to worship at the shrine of baseball vanity—not for exercise, but for the plaudits of the crowd." The game was "a curse." It created "strong, muscular, lazy boys, whose sole ambition is to be good ball players, to forsake their work."

In spite of the growing public enthusiasm for the national game, or because of it, a new and enduring force was making itself felt in baseball, and its name was "money."

Betting, to this day a serious problem in baseball, was already a fixture at major games. Henry Chadwick, first among significant baseball writers, recalled:

Two Brooklyn cranks [fans] had a wager of $100 a side on John Holden's making a home run. One was an Atlantic rooter, the other an Excelsior fan. In this game I noticed that when Holden went to bat he was very particular in selecting his bat. It appears that the man who had bet on him went to him and told him that he would give him $25 of his bet if he made the hit; so Jack was very anxious. Matt O'Brien was pitching, and Jack, after waiting for a good ball, got one to suit him, and sent it flying over Harry Wright's head at right center, and made the round of the bases before the ball was returned, thus winning the $25.

Shortly after the end of the Civil War, in spite of its baseball tradition and beauty, Elysian Fields became the scene of the first great scandal in the game. On September 28, 1865, the Mutuals played the Eckfords. The pregame odds opened at five to three in favor of the Mutuals, then fell to five to four, dropped to even, and finally favored the Eckfords at game time. Before three thousand fans, the Mutuals fielded well and led 5–4 after four innings. Then in the fifth, catcher Wansley started giving up numerous passed balls, and some of the infielders booted easy grounders. The Eckfords scored eleven runs and went on to win the game 23–11. They made five double plays, almost unheard of in that day.

Catcher Wansley and third baseman Duffy were accused of throwing the game and offering shortstop Devyr money to assist. (Devyr had indeed made some peculiar plays.) Wansley and Duffy were expelled. Devyr was out for the 1866 season but apparently reinstated for the next. Wansley was reinstated in December 1870 but was never again wanted by first-class clubs.

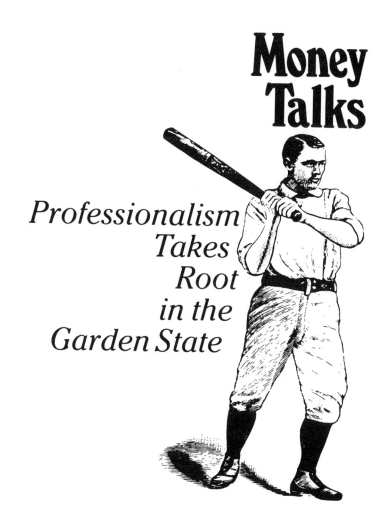

CHAPTER 3

Money
Talks

*Professionalism
Takes
Root
in the
Garden State*

The 1869 Cincinnati Red Stocking Base Ball Club, first all-professional team, featured three Jersey stalwarts: catcher Doug Allison (standing, center), left fielder Andy Leonard (standing, far right), and second baseman Charlie Sweasy (seated, far left). (Spalding Collection, Miriam & Ira D. Wallach Division of Art, Prints and Photographs, The New York Public Library, Astor, Lenox and Tilden Foundations)

As baseball became more popular, it became more important to win. Winning meant prestige. Winning meant respect. And often, winning meant money for team supporters, whose betting frenzy went unabated through the 1850s and 1860s.

The best assurance of winning was to have the best players. Very early that translated to "the best players that money could buy." A look at the dealings of amateur baseball in its infancy will show that paying amateur athletes under the table is not a phenomenon of our era alone.

As early as 1859 the National Association of Base Ball Players had a rule against professionalism, but "recruiting" players to change teams was common. Offers of cash and other inducements to switch teams occurred often enough to have a clear impact on the game.

A common but subtle insult was to refer to a team as an "eclectic nine." An eclectic team had a liberal sprinkling of players recruited from other teams, usually of greater talent than the resident members. The famous pitcher James P. Creighton and outfielder George H. Flanley were scouted while playing for the Niagara Club of Buffalo against Brooklyn's Star Club in July 1859. By September they were regulars on Star. The Excelsiors, one of the wealthiest teams of the time, were able to "induce" both players to jump to their team over the winter of 1859–1860.

During the turmoil of the Civil War, baseball continued on its path toward professionalism. It was a time, after all, when cash payments could still buy a man outright, if he was black and lived in the South, or could provide a man with a substitute to serve in the Union Army in the conflict that would end that first obscenity.

By the end of the war, conflicting attitudes about money and baseball created contradictory approaches to the problem. The popular Philadelphia Athletics, whose 1866 tour delighted and enriched other squads in the East, paid at least four of their players outright. But another top team, the Washington Nationals, forcefully refused reimbursement for expenses while touring that summer and playing several New Jersey teams, including Liberty in New Brunswick. They cited the unwritten rule that "gentlemen should cover their own costs."

In 1868 the National Association of Base Ball Players made a fateful and, as it turned out, fatal decision to divide players into professionals and amateurs. New Jersey's nationally recognized Irvington team had nine members designated as professionals:

Mike Campbell, first base

Eaton, second base

Buckley, third base

Mills, shortstop

Lines, left field

Bailey, center field

Lewis, right field

Sattles, catcher

Hugh Campbell, pitcher

The team had already suffered when cash payments induced one of its best players, Stockman, to join New York's rich and increasingly professional Mutuals. Shortstop Mills also left for the "Mutes," but for some reason returned to Irvington that same year.

Prior to the opening of the 1869 season leading baseball writer Henry Chadwick wrote that several "commercialized" teams were ready for action: the Troy Haymakers; the Atlantics and the Mutuals of Brooklyn; the Athletics of Philadelphia; the Unions of Lansingburgh, New York; the Buckeyes and the Red Stocking Club of Cincinnati; and the Marylands of Baltimore. The Red Stockings were the first all-paid, all-contracted team of professionals. An amateur team since 1866, they had been reorganized as a professional team by Harry Wright, a mainstay of eastern baseball since Knickerbocker days, when he had been a regular on the Elysian Fields. The former cricket player and successful jeweler was also a shrewd businessman who could predict the trends in baseball. His creation of the first pro team was really just an above-the-table manifestation of what had been the practice for years.

Wright selected a few Cincinnati area semipro players and then turned his attention east to stock his team. When he got to New Jersey, he chose three players who would go on to distinguished careers in the game. From a Jersey City team he took twenty-two-year-old catcher Doug Allison, a marble cutter born in Philadelphia and a well-known ballplayer. From Newark came two hatters, twenty-three-year-old Andrew J. Leonard, born in Ireland, who was assigned left field, and twenty-two-year-old Newark-born Charles James Sweasy, placed at second. Both Leonard and Sweasy had played infield for the Irvington team in 1866. The New Jersey trio were paid eight hundred dollars per man for the season. (Player-manager Wright paid himself twelve hundred dollars and his brother George, another top player from the East, fourteen hundred.)

The New Jersey boys eventually moved from Cincinnati to the new professional leagues as they were created. Doug Allison was on the 1873 Elizabeth Resolutes, the New Jersey entry in the first professional baseball league, and in 1876 he joined one of the first National League teams, Hartford. Sweasy played in the National Association of Base Ball Players and was on the first National League team from Cincinnati. Leonard was perhaps the best player of the group. His career in the National Association, first with the Washington Olympics (1871) and continuing with the Boston team (1872–1875), placed him on the all-time, all-star team for the short-lived league (selected in the 1988 volume of *The Bill James Historical Baseball Abstract*). From 1871 to 1875 (the life of the league) Leonard appeared in the outfield in 266 games with 1,334 at bats, 424 hits, and 350 runs. His overall batting average was .318. On James's National Association All-Star Team he was joined by such players as Deacon White, Cap Anson, George Wright, Albert Spalding, and Candy Cummings.

When the National League was formed in 1876, Leonard was picked for the first Boston entry. He and Wright amazed and entertained fans before games by flipping the ball high into the air and catching it with one hand (a difficult achievement in those preglove days). They would bounce the ball off their biceps and catch it, or throw it from behind the back over head or shoulder, snatching it before it hit the ground. Though nothing special today, in the 1860s this was an amazing demonstration.

The Cincinnati Red Stockings shocked the baseball world, not because they were all professionals (the public was less than sensitive to the nuances of play-for-pay), but because they were so damn good! In their second season, 1869, Wright took them on a tour of the established baseball world. The Red Stockings went from coast to coast, traveling nearly twelve thousand miles and appearing before over two hundred thousand fans. They had gate receipts of $29,726.26 and expenses of $29,724.87, for a profit of $1.39. The team beat every opponent in the Midwest and California. Their final record was 56 and 1. They scored 2,395 runs against only 574 allowed.

During the eastern swing, on their way from defeating the Mutuals (before thirty-five hundred), the Atlantics (ten thousand at the Capitoline grounds), and the Eckfords (eight thousand at Union grounds) in New York, they stopped off en route to Philadelphia to show the country folks of Irvington their former players, Leonard and Sweasy. The game was mercifully called at the end of the seventh, with the visitors leading 20–4, to allow the Cincinnati team to catch their train. During the game, catcher Allison used the rules of the day to make a double play. With runners on first and second, he intentionally dropped the third strike on the batter, who under the prevailing rules was required to run to first, forcing men on base to advance. He then threw to George Wright at second to force out the runner from first. Wright then threw to first to get the batter for the second out.

In 1870 the National Association of Base Ball Players, in an attempt to confront the growing trend of professional domination, changed its organization so that only elected representatives from state associations could be voting members. No longer would representatives directly from teams control the organization. But the strong clubs easily circumvented these efforts by controlling who the state associations sent to the annual convention.

Soon "professional" teams once again dominated proceedings. Henry Chadwick said, "The meetings [were] controlled almost entirely by an unscrupulous clique of men hailing from the professional clubs assisted by tools selected from some of the amateur organizations." Thus the fall meeting of the association found amateurs staging a walkout. Not satisfied with the ambiguous nature of the National Association, ten representatives of professional teams met at Colliers' in Manhattan on March 17, 1871, to create the National Association of Professional Base Ball Players. Under its rules, a team that wanted to be a member had simply to petition the permanent committee before May 1, 1871, and pay a $10 entry fee, an amount equivalent to about $150 today. The rules stipulated that each team play every other at least five times before season's end on November 1. The pennant would go to the team with the most wins.

In 1872 the National Association of Professional Base Ball Players had eleven clubs, including five "cooperative" nines, which were not expected to perform well or even finish the season. Their job was just to make sure enough games were played. A portion of the gate receipts made up their salaries. They included the Eckfords, the Atlantics, the Olympics, the Nationals, and the Mansfields. The better players among these clubs were shifted during the season to the stronger nines, foreshadowing the practice of bringing minor leaguers up to the majors today.

The idea of a league of professional teams caught on—with the clubs and with the public at large. By 1873 the professional brand of baseball had become the focus of the game. In New Jersey the Resolutes of Elizabeth paid their ten-dollar annual fee to join the league and became New Jersey's first major league team. (The debate as to whether the National Association of Professional Base Ball Players was a major league goes on.

The fact is, in 1873 it was simply the only professional league, and the organizers in Elizabeth certainly thought they were joining the big time.) It was, indeed, big-time. Fifteen to twenty thousand people could be counted on to watch the Mutuals play the Atlantics in Hoboken. The *New York Times* said, in comparing it with the amateur glory days of the sport, it "seemed like old times."

The Resolutes' lineup was familiar, featuring Doug Allison from Cincinnati's by then defunct professional team and several former stars from the Irvington nine. The full team from opening day was: Favel Wordsworth, Rynie Wolters, Marty Swandell, Ben Laughlin, John Farrow, Fred Crane, Jim Clinton, Mike Campbell, Hugh Campbell, Eddie Booth, Henry Auston, Frank Fleet, Art Allison, Doug Allison, and the manager, John Benjamin.

Under Benjamin, born in Elizabeth in 1837, the team played its home games at Waverly Fairgrounds, a field with a wooden grandstand, bordered by Frelinghuysen Avenue, Haynes Avenue, and Lower Road, now on the border of Newark and Elizabeth. (The site is the current location of B'nai Jeshuron Cemetery and Weequahic City Park.) Of the five new teams that year, the Resolutes and the Marylands of Baltimore were described as hopelessly weak and not expected to last beyond July 4.

Elizabeth got off to a roaring stop by losing to its weak sister, Baltimore, 7–3. In its road debut it faced off against Brooklyn in a steady rain before five hundred fans. The game was scheduled to start at 4:00 P.M., but the teams agreed to begin an hour earlier to get in enough innings to keep the gate money. To the horror of Brooklyn, the Resolutes built the score to 8–0 in its favor in three innings. In those days, that was enough play to keep the gate receipts, so the home team called the game, declaring it "no contest."

The Resolutes then recorded an exhibition win against the strong Atlantics 12–9, were beaten by Princeton University 6–2, then shocked the league and the fans by beating Boston 6–4 on Memorial Day in Boston. But the miracle season was not to be. By mid-June the Resolutes were fading fast and had abandoned Waverly, playing home games in Brooklyn along with the Mutuals and the Atlantics. So poor had the team's reputation become that bettors were wagering on the number of innings competing teams would need to beat them. On June 16 the odds favored the Atlantics to have enough runs to win by the second inning, a bet rewarded when the Brooklyn team trounced the Resolutes 10–0. In one game against the Mutuals the five hundred fans seemed to be paying more attention to the out-of-town scores coming by way of runners from the local

The Irvington Base Ball Club reunion in 1897 brought together some of New Jersey's professional standouts of the 1870s, including (front row, from left) Rynie Wolters, Stockman, Charlie Sweasy, and (standing) John Farrow (far left) and Mike Campbell (far right). (Irvington Public Library)

telegraph office and posted on a scoreboard by innings on the grounds. Meanwhile, pitcher Wolters, formerly of Irvington and one of the game's best, was throwing so hard that he injured two catchers. The team dispensed with his services and he left baseball to pursue a career of peddling in Newark.

On June 30 the Resolutes' league record stood at 1 and 13. The team planned to disband but agreed to play three games in Boston before announcing that intention so the games could count for the championship. Boston had had difficulty for two years in a row in obtaining an opponent for the Fourth of July and had scheduled the Resolutes as a last resort. Under league rules, the Resolutes' announcement of their intention to disband would have meant that games played with them would not count in the final standings.

A large crowd came to the Elizabeth-Boston doubleheader on the Fourth, and in the morning the Resolutes could do no wrong, beating Boston 11–2. In the afternoon Boston scored twenty-one runs in the ninth inning to win 32–3. At Elizabeth's next game, only three hundred saw the Resolutes get beaten by the Atlantics, but they did see a first. During the 23–1 game not a single error was committed (at the time errors included walks, wild pitches, and mishandled pitches by the catcher).

By end of July the Resolutes had disbanded after winning two and losing twenty-one. Thus ended New Jersey's first entry in the majors. It would be forty-two years until another New Jersey team, the Newark Peps, could stand with the big boys of organized baseball. But the big boys kept coming to the state in the meantime for other reasons. One of the most important could be stated in a word, and the word was *Sunday.*

SUNDAY GAMES

When the New York area was dominated by the Dutch, Sundays were deadly serious times for its residents. The Knickerbocker sabbath, as described in *The World of Washington Irving,* was "a long solemn Sunday. . . . Then only the tolling of church-bells broke the silence, and heavy chains were drawn across the streets to keep any traffic away from the windows of the churches."

The coming of the tradition-bound English with their legacy of keeping the Lord's Day holy had not made things much more liberal by the time baseball became popular. Section 265 of the New York City Penal Code, for example, prohibited "racing, gaming and other public sports on the first day of the week." Not all clergy were against the sport, though. Soon after the Civil War a Brooklyn pastor of the Puritan Congregational church had some kind words for it:

> [Baseball is a game] whose regulations are calculated to prevent the ill feelings engendered by other games; and one, moreover, which serves to attract our young men from places of bad repute, and to supply the right kind of exercise and amusement. This opinion has been practically endorsed by several clergymen of Philadelphia who last year formed themselves into a base ball club for the purpose of healthful and moral recreation, in imitation of the hundreds of English parsons who take such delight in playing cricket on commons of these villages. . . . Their sermons are stronger and more attractive, their physical ability greater, and their intellects clearer and brighter for the relaxation from their arduous cares and trying duties.

While most northeastern cities and towns took their otherworldly responsibilities seriously and tried to ban all ball play on the sabbath, a more relaxed attitude prevailed in the U.S. hinterlands, where continental Europeans had settled and influenced the social patterns of the area. Sundays were a time to escape from the seriousness of the week and, if the opportunity presented itself, to have a good time. Thus in most areas of New Jersey ball play was considered an acceptable activity. Not so, however, in New York, New England, and Pennsylvania.

In the early days of the National League, teams from areas where Sunday ball was banned sought other venues to earn some weekend cash. Many players simply went to neighboring states and played in pickup games. But league contests were held as well. New Jersey became the site for games played by New York and Philadelphia teams and for exhibitions by visiting squads when in those cities for league contests.

In the fall of 1877, for example, St. Louis used a Sunday off to play the by then amateur Elizabeth Resolutes, who managed to beat the league team 5–2. On September 17, 1877, Hartford of the National League went to Orange, New Jersey, to play the local amateurs. Hartford was leading 8–3 in the sixth when a heavy rain started, and the leaguers sought shelter in the somewhat shabby dressing room. A major league New Jersey rain storm flooded the dressing room and all the streets in the area, so when the Hartford boys made for the train station, they had to walk half a mile with water over their shoe tops.

At the winter meeting of the league that year, a rule was passed to prevent any member team from playing any games on Sunday. Individual players were prohibited from playing in nonleague games as well. There was an ulterior motive behind the rule, however. The league saw the Sunday ban as a way to punish certain teams that had run afoul of the league powers. In 1880 it used the rule to expel Cincinnati from the league, punishment for leasing its field to a nonleague club and making four thousand dollars selling beer during games on Sunday.

It was not until April 17, 1892, that the National League had an official game on Sunday. Still, teams in cities that banned Sunday ball were prevented from playing such contests. Not that clubs did not try to bend the rules to arrange contests in their own parks. A favorite ploy was to schedule a concert of sacred songs for which an admission was charged and then stage a "free" baseball game for those attending. The key was to avoid playing ball for pay, technically the prohibited activity.

The club owners counterattacked other business operators who earned money on Sunday. They demanded, for example, that theater owners be banned from operating on Sunday. In Columbus, Ohio, they succeeded in getting trolley operation banned, ironically cutting into church attendance. Still, the easiest way for teams to avoid the problem was to journey across state or municipal borders to more lively venues. For the New York, Brooklyn, Philadelphia, and even Boston teams, New Jersey was an attractive site.

Late in the 1898 season the Giants and the Dodgers, both down in the standings at the time, met for the first time in a Sunday game. They played on September 18 at the West New York Field Club grounds, also known as the Weehawken Cricket Grounds, in Weehawken. (It was a field where important ball games had been played for many years; in 1887 the National Association's Mets had played their Sunday games on the site.) Over four thousand saw the Giants win 7–3. In October the Dodgers played Washington on the Weehawken field. In 1899 the Giants played Louisville there on June 4 and August 13.

At the turn of the century only five major league clubs—in Chicago, St. Louis, and Cincinnati—could play on Sunday. Before the end of World War I, Detroit, Cleveland, and Washington, D.C., would join the group, and fifteen years after the war, New York, Boston, Philadelphia, and Pittsburgh would be on the list. This left plenty of time for New Jersey to continue hosting Sunday major league contests.

Trenton's Mike Tiernan, shown in an 1890 preseason
Harper's Weekly "action" pose, was a key member of
the first of the great New York Giant teams. As if to justify this pose, Tiernan went from thirty-three stolen
bases in 1889 to fifty-six in 1890. Hall-of-Famer King
Kelly of "Slide, Kelly, slide" fame had only fifty-one
that year.

The New York Highlanders (later the Yankees) first played Sunday ball in New Jersey on July 17, 1904, in a game against Detroit at Wiedenmayer's Park in Newark. But even in New Jersey, playing Sunday ball involved sacrifices. At an exhibition game in Jersey City on Sunday, April 18, 1909, the Highlanders, having had several runins with the law over Sunday ball, saw fit to distribute cards asking patrons to avoid all cheering and rooting to keep the noise down. The thousand or more fans generally complied, and the Highlanders won 6–3 in what might have been one of the quietest contests ever held.

Things changed only slowly. In 1913 four Brooklyn boys were locked up for twenty-four hours for throwing a ball around Prospect Park. On August 19, 1916, the New York Giants played in the New York Polo Grounds for the first time in history on a Sunday. The owners were called into court, but because the fans had allegedly paid to hear a sacred concert before the game, the case was dismissed. Not until 1918 could teams play in New York on Sunday with impunity. That year Catholic Al Smith ran for governor of New York on a platform that promised Sunday baseball. Flamboyant Mayor James J. Walker masterminded passage of a bill permitting Sunday games.

In the last year of New York's Sunday prohibition, the Dodgers, Giants, and Yankees all used Harrison Field across the Passaic River from Newark for Sunday contests. (This was the field built a few years earlier for the Newark Peps of the Federal League.) When the ban was lifted in New York, so great was the rush to schedule games in town on Sundays that the New York Giants evicted the Yankees from the Polo Grounds, a move that would result in the building of Yankee Stadium.

Things still were not so liberal in Pennsylvania, however. There the conflict continued well into the late 1920s. At the end of that decade, Philadelphia's baseball powers, including Connie Mack and Benjamin Shibe, threatened to move their team, the Athletics, lock, stock, and bat-boy to Camden, where it was believed they could play Sunday ball. They announced that they would build a major facility there for Sunday games and return baseball to the New Jersey town where organized Philadelphia play was born. But after a test game played by the Athletics in 1926, a Camden court declared the activity "worldly employment," in violation of its Sunday blue law.

The following year Shibe got assurances from "liberal leaders across the river" that they would change the law and arrange for his club to play permanently in Camden, including on Sundays. The Pennsylvania powers were not swayed, the state's supreme court voting seven to two against

Sunday ball. Shibe formed a syndicate to purchase land, build a multimillion-dollar stadium, and shift his franchise across the river. A month later the Pennsylvania House of Representatives finally passed an amendment to the blue law that would allow a local option. Still, it was not until 1934 that local law allowed the Athletics and the Phillies, as well as the Pittsburgh Pirates to play on Sunday. And well into the 1950s Sunday games had to conclude by a "decent" hour in the Keystone State.

With the final acceptance of Sunday ball in New York and Philadelphia, New Jersey saw American and National League players during the season only when their teams played occasional exhibitions with minor league clubs or college nines, or when one or more came across the Hudson or Delaware to play in the dozens of weekend or nighttime pickup games that took place all over the state. In 1938, for instance, Hank Greenberg, Ducky Medwick, and Billy Urbanski could be seen playing against a black team led by Satchel Paige in a night game in Bound Brook. Illumination was provided by lights mounted atop running pickup trucks.

The off-season was another matter, however. In the spring, especially, New Jerseyans had a special opportunity to see the big leaguers. For well before the turn of the century, New Jersey's resort towns had become spring training sites for top teams.

In 1888 Harry Wright took his Chicago White Sox to Cape May rather than to Savannah, Georgia, as had been the tradition. The regimen called for his players to rise at 6:00 A.M., douse one another with buckets of sea-water, and hike the Cape May beach for an hour before breakfast, which Wright said "made them look pretty sick." The balance of the day was spent on long workouts with Indian clubs and dumbbells, and more hiking. After supper the team could relax until 10:30 lights out.

In 1897 the New York Giants abandoned Jacksonville, Florida, for Lakewood, then an aristocratic resort patronized by the Vanderbilts and the Belmonts. The *New York World* claimed that Lakewood had only three classes of people: wealthy New Yorkers, invalids staying for their health, and ballplayers.

The next year the Brooklyn Dodgers and New York Giants, by now great rivals, spent spring training within twelve miles of each other. The Giants went to Lakewood, while the Dodgers worked out at Allaire, a small country town with a few houses, a country store, and a tendency toward swampiness. The Giants' owner, Andrew Freedman, who lived in Red Bank, was a realtor-politician and a member of Tammany Hall. In 1896 he had paid fifty thousand dollars to acquire the team, which was reeling from baseball's first experience at unionization and the resulting labor

Continuing a long tradition, the 1934 Philadelphia Athletics visited Lakewood, New Jersey, to play the local team. Jersey boys Frankie Hayes and Doc Cramer (standing, third and fourth from right) were among the Philadelphia players managed by Lena Blackburne. (Richard Steele)

strife called the Brotherhood War. The Giants were so weak that other National League teams had to subsidize them.

Lakewood offered Freedman a site close to his home and, more important, close to New York, where he could easily attend meetings of the Tammany machine. He and his team could enjoy the luxury of the resort atmosphere. But one rainy night, Freedman, dressed in his finest evening clothes, went to a Lakewood hotel dining room hoping to rub shoulders with the aristocracy. Instead, one of the Vanderbilts mistook him for a waiter and called him over to tend to a table. Freedman's reaction was not recorded.

Freedman advocated running baseball like a business, ridding the league of weak franchises, having a strong leader at the helm. To the surprise of the powers of baseball, he followed his beliefs. In 1899, aware of declining public support for the game and a variety of shady deals within the National League structure that clouded its future, he proposed a baseball trust composed of the "most powerful and wealthy" franchises. They should be in the most profitable cities, staffed by the best players even if that meant annual redistribution of talent. He was calling for a baseball "syndicate."

In August 1901, at a secret meeting at Freedman's Red Bank home, the trust was, in fact, created. It went on to raid existing teams of talent and to set up the first stages of absolute control over professional ball to the financial benefit of its owners. The reaction of the entrenched National League powers against the trust, coupled with the creation of the new American League, established organized professional baseball as we know it today. Once again, events in New Jersey, secret and nefarious as these might have been, were critical in shaping the national game.

Florida eventually took over as spring training site of choice for most teams, but in 1943, adhering to Commissioner Kenesaw Mountain Landis's directive not to travel great distances on trains needed for the war effort, the Giants returned to Lakewood. As they had fifty years before, the team traveled by ferry from Manhattan to New Jersey, then by train to Lakewood, and finally by horse and wagon to the Brannick Arms (which had previously seen duty as Shilkraut's Vegetarian Hotel).

The following year the New York Yankees were in Asbury Park, where Manager McCarthy and venerable general manager Ed Barrow were trying to plug gaps made by the departure of stars Joe DiMaggio, Phil Rizzuto, and Red Ruffing for wartime service. In 1945 they moved to Atlantic City, where they were close to the Red Sox, working out in nearby Pleasantville.

Lakewood's Brannick Arms hotel, named for New York Giants secretary Eddie Brannick, was spring training home to the team during World War II. Practice took place at Ott Field in nearby Ocean County Park, former estate of John D. Rockefeller. (Bettman Archives)

THE DODGERS' AND GIANTS' NEW JERSEY ROOTS

In 1956 and 1957 New Jersey had its last chance to see major league teams compete in league play. In those years the Dodgers made a final gesture to demonstrate how serious they were about moving from cramped Ebbets Field in congested downtown Brooklyn by playing seven games in Jersey City's Roosevelt Stadium. In one such game, won by Willie Mays's home run, both teams—the Dodgers and the New York Giants—had been favorites with New Jersey fans for decades. Unmentioned (and probably little known) at the time was that both teams had New Jersey roots.

The Giants' story begins in 1880. John B. Day, a prosperous young tobacco merchant from New York City who wanted to play baseball, created a team in Orange called the Metropolitans (the second to use that name) and appointed himself pitcher. Since it was his team, no one objected. When he took his team across the harbor to Brooklyn to play one of the more established nines, he did not last the game and ended up in the stands watching his team go down to defeat. Sitting next to him in the stands was James Mutrie, an aspiring sportsman and promoter. Mutrie, who had just ridden a bicycle from Boston to New York, asked Day how he would like to create a baseball team that would not only whip the team that had just vanquished the Orange Metropolitans but would become the top team in all of baseball.

Mutrie, who had failed in a recent attempt to get August Belmont to create a ball club, had more success with Day. A few weeks later they jointly formed the Metropolitan Exhibition Company and created the third New York area team to be called the Mets. The team opened in 1880 as an independent club playing some home games in New Jersey but most in Brooklyn. The team used the Union and the Capitoline grounds in Brooklyn, venues that had once been among the finest ball yards in the East but that by the 1880s had become rough and ragged and far from the heart of the city. Attendance was poor in both Brooklyn and New Jersey.

Day and Mutrie looked around for a better site and came upon the new Polo Grounds at 110th Street, owned by *New York Herald* publisher James Gordon Bennett, Jr. They struck a deal with Bennett, and the new team at the new field was an instant success. During the winter Day and Mutrie went about scheduling games with other independents and local college nines, including Seton Hall, all anxious to play in New York City. In 1881 the Mets played college teams and independents as well as five dozen

At a mid-1950s Jersey City rally, Brooklyn Dodger catcher Roy Campanella caps Governor Robert Meyner, flanked by Parks Commissioner Joshua Ringle (left) and Mayor Bernard Berry. Owner Walter O'Malley (standing, right) had hinted at moving the Dodgers to Jersey City, where they actually played fifteen "home" games at Roosevelt Stadium in 1956 and 1957. (New Jersey Room, Jersey City Public Library)

games against National League teams. The next season they helped form a two-team league with a Philadelphia squad. In 1883 they joined the American Association, although many thought they would enter the National League. Day and Mutrie did get into the National League, but with an entirely new team recruited mainly from the Troy (New York) Haymakers, which had folded. Mutrie managed the American Association Mets, and John Clapp was brought in to handle the New York Nationals. Day simultaneously accommodated his two New York teams in the Polo Grounds by stringing a canvas fence between two diamonds. The Nationals went on to become the New York Giants, and the Mets went out of business in 1885.

In 1889 the New York Giants had to open their season in Jersey City because the original Polo Grounds field had been closed to allow for the extension of 111th Street. They played Boston on April 24 and 25, 1889, at Oakland Park, located at Oakland Avenue, Hoboken Avenue, Concord Street, and Fleet Street near Newark Avenue. Their new Polo Grounds at 155th Street and Eighth Avenue was opened on July 8, allowing them to return to New York.

In 1890 the Player's League, organized by a group of ballplayers in competition with organized baseball, put a team into the park immediately adjacent to the Giants' field. On May 12, 1890, the Giant rookie "Silent Mike" Tiernan, a native of Trenton, actually hit a home run from one park into the other while a Player's League game was going on. Fans at both games cheered. When the Player's League collapsed, the Giants moved into its horseshoe-shaped park, bringing the name Polo Grounds along, and used it until they moved to San Francisco in 1958. The current New York Mets used it for two years (1962 and 1963) until Shea Stadium was built.

And what of the Dodgers? As the reader will discover in the next chapter, the team that now plays in Los Angeles was born of a squad that once called Camden home.

NEW JERSEY has had more than its share of both amateur and professional baseball, and despite never having been the permanent home of a National or American League team, the state has enjoyed considerable success in the professional arena. The history of professional baseball in

New Jersey starts with the boys who were paid to play for Irvington. It goes on to the Elizabeth Resolutes, the state's entry into the first professional league. But its greatest and most glorious chapter focuses on New Jersey's long and distinguished minor league record, recounted in the following chapter.

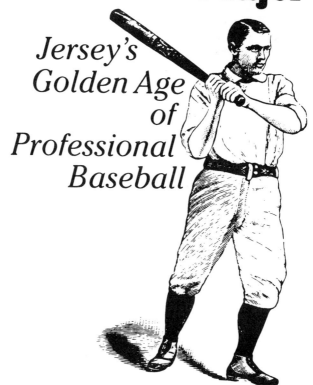

CHAPTER 4

When the Minors Were Major

Jersey's Golden Age of Professional Baseball

The Domestics, Newark's first professional team, played in the Eastern League in 1884–1885. (Courtesy of Newark Public Library)

Charlie Johnson, twenty-three, played in six games for the Philadelphia Phillies in 1908. In sixteen at-bats he collected four hits for a .250 average. He had one triple, two RBIs, and two runs scored. He walked once, stole no bases. This was the sum of Charlie's career in the major leagues. It earned him a single, undistinguished line in their official annals.

Why, then, does Charlie Johnson rate any mention at all in this book? Charlie, as it happens, had a significantly better time of it in the minor leagues, becoming the *only* player for a New Jersey team to lead the minor leagues in season batting or pitching in the modern era (post-1900). In 1912, playing for Trenton in the Tri-State League, Charlie topped all forty-seven minor leagues teams, with a .403 batting average. In 109 games and 400 at-bats, he stroked 161 hits and scored 86 runs. He also stole 22 bases. Records for that year fail to mention how many four-baggers he slugged, shedding little light on the validity of his nickname: "Home Run."

Charlie Johnson is one of an intriguing group of ballplayers who simply tore up the minor leagues but somehow never made it big in the majors. And that, in essence, echoes the story of New Jersey in organized baseball. Except for a brief fling with the Federal League in 1915 and cameo appearances by teams from New York, the state has never made it in big-time baseball. But, oh, what a glorious record in the minors! One New Jersey team—the 1937 Newark Bears—appears on virtually every expert's list of the top minor league teams of all time. And then there were the 1883 Camden Merritt, the 1932 Newark Bears, the 1947 Trenton Giants, the 1950 Jersey City Little Giants, and others.

The story ends—for the time being, at least—with the Jersey City team of 1960–1961. It began nearly ninety years earlier.

THE EARLY HISTORY OF THE MINORS

There were no minor or major leagues before 1876—just loose-knit groups of teams with no set schedules, no pay scales, no contracts worth anything, no league-appointed umpires to guarantee impartiality. The National League brought all these innovations to baseball that year, defining "major league" in the process.

But still there were no official minor leagues. The other leagues of the era claimed to rival the National League as majors, and one—the American Association—made it stick for sixteen years. (Today's American

Association is one of two "Triple A" leagues, the highest of the minors.) Another so-called major league was the International Association, which included a Jersey City entry (1879–1880). But this was neither a league nor major by the standards of the National League and American Association.

It was not until 1883 that the true minor leagues came along. These pioneers were the Northwestern League and the Interstate Association, with Camden and Trenton fielding teams in the latter. These leagues mirrored the National League and American Association but had lower pay scales and accepted subordinate status. What followed, until well into this century, was a period of more or less constant but tense cooperation—or cooperative tension—between the majors and the minors. The early minors generally were not the farm teams of major league clubs, as so many are today. Though some were reserve or B teams of major league teams or had working arrangements with them, the majority were independents, struggling to survive in a system akin to sleeping with a five-hundred-pound bear: he'll keep you warm if you can manage not to get crushed.

As Table 1 shows, New Jersey teams played a major role in the development of the minor leagues for the next ninety years.

Especially in the early years, minor league teams often had no name other than that of the city they called home. This was true, for example, of the Trenton, Harrisburg, and Brooklyn teams in the Interstate Association of 1883. But there were some teams with nicknames—the Quicksteps (Wilmington), the Active (Reading), the Anthracite (Pottsville), the Merritt (Camden)—names you do not hear much anymore.

FROM THE CAMDEN MERRITT TO THE L.A. DODGERS

Dodger manager Tommy Lasorda probably does not know this, but the team he managed to glory in the 1988 World Series can trace its roots to Camden more than a century earlier.

When the Interstate Association helped originate minor league baseball in 1883, the Camden club—named for state senator Albert Merritt, Republican of Camden—proved an artistic success from the outset. By the end of May they boasted a record of 10–1, having thrashed their Trenton rivals in three games by a combined score of 41–12. The Camden lineup featured:

Robert Emslie	pitcher
Samuel Kimber	pitcher
Rooney Sweeney	catcher
Charlie Householder	first base
William Greenwood	second base
Frank Fennelly	shortstop
Fred Warner	third base
Bertleback	outfield
Kenzel	outfield
Frank Gardner	outfield
Jack Corcoran	outfield

But even as the Merritts were tearing up the Interstate Association, their owners were going broke. Rumors of the team's demise began circulating as early as May 28, and on July 20 Senator Merritt confirmed that the end was near. A report in the *Trenton Times* quoted Merritt blaming "poor support received from Camden people." The article went on to say that Merritt, "his purse heavily drained in trying to keep the nine on its feet, thinks proximity to Philadelphia makes Camden an undesirable place to locate a club."

On the evening of July 20, with the team's record standing at a spectacular twenty-seven wins against only six losses, the directors met and voted to disband.

Meanwhile in Brooklyn, Charles H. Byrne and his partner, George T. Taylor, were facing something of the opposite situation. Fans seemed willing to patronize the club's new ball yard, Washington Park. But the team, in sports vernacular, stunk up the place. Byrne and Taylor had put it together earlier that year by running newspaper ads asking, according to a report in the *New York Clipper*, for "men of intelligence and not corner-lot tough guys who may happen to possess some ability as players. Players whose habits and way unfit them for thorough teamwork need not trouble themselves to apply for positions on the new Brooklyn club's team." Forty men of character applied and the partners signed up sixteen of them.

By July, with the Brooklyns stuck at the bottom of the heap, Byrne and Taylor probably were wondering if a few corner-lot toughs would have been so bad after all. They were spared that distasteful solution when the

TABLE 1
New Jersey's Minor League Baseball Teams Over the Years

Location	Years Active	Name	League
Asbury Park	1914		Atlantic League
Atlantic City	1885		Eastern League
	1912–1913		Tri-State League
Bloomfield	1914		Atlantic League
Bloomingdale	1946–1948		North Atlantic League
Camden	1883	Merritt	Interstate Association
	1904		Tri-State League
Elizabeth*	1873	Resolutes	National Association
	1892		Central New Jersey League
	1907		Atlantic League
	1908		Union League
	1909		Atlantic League
Hoboken*	1886		Interstate League
Jersey City	1879–1880		International Association
	1886		Eastern League
	1887		International League
	1888		Central League
	1889–1890		Atlantic Association
	1900		Atlantic League
	1902–1915	Skeeters	International League
	1918–1933	Skeeters	International League
	1937–1950	Little Giants	International League
	1960–1961	Jerseys	International League
Long Branch	1913		New York–New Jersey League
	1914		Atlantic League
Newark	1884–1885	Domestics	Eastern League
	1886	Little Giants	Eastern League
	1887	Little Giants	International League

(continued)

TABLE 1 (*Continued*)

Location	Years Active	Name	League
	1888		Central League
	1889–1890		Atlantic Association
	1896		Atlantic League
	1899–1900		Atlantic League
	1900		Eastern League
	1902–1915	Indians	International League
	1907		Atlantic League
	1916–1949	Bears	International League
New Brunswick	1948		Colonial League
Paterson	1886		Interstate League
	1896–1899		Atlantic League
	1904–1906		Hudson River League
	1908		Union League
	1913		New York–New Jersey League
	1914		Atlantic League
Perth Amboy	1914		Atlantic League
Plainfield*	1892		Central New Jersey League
Trenton	1883		Interstate Association
	1884–1885		Eastern League
	1907–1914		Tri-State League
	1936–1937		New York–Penn League
	1938		Eastern League
	1939–1950	Giants	Interstate League
Washington†			

SOURCES: William Vanles, Research Department, Baseball Hall of Fame; R. J. Sparks, National Association of Professional Baseball Leagues.

*Elizabeth, Hoboken and Plainfield appear in the minor league records of the Baseball Hall of Fame, but not on the lists of the National Association of Professional Baseball Leagues (NAPBL), the governing body of minor league baseball.

†Washington appears on the NAPBL list, but not in the Hall of Fame records; the NAPBL list gives no date or league for a Washington team, nor is it explicit about which of New Jersey's several Washingtons the team may have called home.

The Camden Baseball Club of 1885 was the semi-pro successor to the 1883 Camden Merritt, which disbanded at mid-season and sold most of its players to the fledgling forerunner of the Brooklyn Dodgers. Fourth from right is Camden-born William "Kid" Gleason, who went on to manage the ill-fated Chicago Black Sox of 1919. (Courtesy of Camden County Cultural & Heritage Commission)

quality roster of the Merritt went on the block. The July 23, 1883, edition of the *Trenton Times* described the scene: "The disbandment of the Merritt club, of Camden, attracted to Philadelphia on Saturday the managers of various clubs, including those of Trenton, Harrisburg, Brooklyn, Baltimore and Easton, each eager to get hold of some of the Merritt's crack players." (The Merritt's team batting average at that point was .274, nearly twenty points higher than that of their closest rival.) The *Times* went on to report that Taylor of Brooklyn had arrived a day earlier and offered to transfer the entire team, promising to pay increased salaries to all hands whether they played every game or not. Called in by the board of directors, several players said Taylor's offer was acceptable in theory but that they might individually go for more money being dangled by other teams.

In aggregate, the monthly payroll of the Merritt then stood at $1,315: $150 each for Emslie and Gardner; $125 for Sweeney, Corcoran, Fennelly, Householder, and Greenwood; $100 for Warner, Bertleback, and Kimber; and $90 for Kenzel. (The differences were said to relate not to ability but rather to when the players joined the club.) So hot was the demand for some of the players that salaries of $300 and $400 a month were being offered.

"This rather staggered Taylor," the *Trenton Times* article continued, "but he set about securing as many of the players as his purse could reach. Greenwood, the second baseman, was his first choice, and satisfactory terms were made with him at once. Corcoran, Kimber, Householder and Kenzel also were gathered in." (Fennelly and Warner joined the migration to Brooklyn, too.)

Adding the erstwhile Merritt players had a salubrious effect on Brooklyn, commencing immediately and lasting through the long and ultimately successful drive to overtake Harrisburg for the first Interstate pennant. (The Merritt club, its record forever frozen at twenty-seven wins and eight losses as of the disbandment date of July 23, 1883, still owned by far the best record in the league. But by folding it had lost its claim to the prize.) Trenton, meanwhile, fared better against its former tormentors from Camden when they switched into Brooklyn uniforms, beating them 12–4 in an August game and 9–3 in a late September contest. Raising its record above .500, the Trentons finished third in the league.

Byrne and Taylor subsequently moved their Brooklyn team to the American Association (then a major league) and later to the National League. It was officially known for several decades thereafter as the Superbas, with "Trolley Dodgers" a nickname stemming from the many trolley lines that crisscrossed Brooklyn. "Dodgers" eventually stuck, the

Ebbets took over, the Boys of Summer won hearts and broke them—and Los Angeles finally lured the team away. But it all began in Camden.

Just how good was the Camden squad of 1883? Much is made—and properly so—of the fact that all the starters of the great Newark Bears of 1937 went on to play in the majors. The Merritt all but matched that feat, sending two pitchers and every other starter except one outfielder on to the big leagues.

The Camden Merritt had been laid low by a gate too small, at sixty-seven hundred dollars, to cover about five thousand dollars of salaries and twenty-five hundred dollars of field improvements through the date of its demise. The Trenton team of 1893 determined not to follow suit, especially not by letting the freeloader problem go unchallenged. The *Trenton Times* of August 28, 1883, caustically described the financially debilitating circumstances:

> The successful business men who own wagons but who have not a quarter to pay for admittance to the ball grounds are growing numerous again. The field outside the fence is thick with these generous citizens every afternoon. So many people were on one of the wagons yesterday that a spectator mistook it for a new grand stand which he supposed had been lately erected. One man, who has money enough to be in two businesses, drives out regularly. He has the reputation of never missing a game and never paying to see one. Then in the evening he leads the discussion in his grocery on the merits of the players and is always the "maddest" man in town when the Trentons fail to play well.

A few weeks later, the *Times* reported the team's reaction to these non-paying fans: "The stockholders of the Trenton club address THE TIMES as follows: 'By request of many of the paying patrons of the Trenton Base Ball Club the management of the club have secured the name or number of wagons belonging to some of our most prominent business men that continually stand outside the fence during all games, and by publishing them you will confer a favor on not only the management but also on those that pay.' We hold the names for future publication."

If this did not eliminate the problem, it is likely that at least some amelioration resulted. For Trenton not only completed the 1883 season—beating Philadelphia's major league team and losing narrowly to Detroit in the process—but was on hand to help organize the first Eastern League for 1884.

TRENTON AND THE EASTERN LEAGUES

With Camden out of the picture in 1884, Newark joined Trenton in the Eastern League to carry on New Jersey's fledgling tradition in the minors. The Trenton team not only fared far better than their Newark brethren but also had their exploits colorfully chronicled in the *Journal of Leo Smith: Story of a Nineteenth Century Shortstop*, by Randolph Linthurst, who constructed the work from newspaper accounts of the day. The *Journal* is a fascinating look at both the early days of minor league baseball and the Garden State's first professional baseball champions.

Backbiting and *backing in* are two terms that concisely sum up the 1884 Trentons. It was not a happy team by Leo Smith's account. Smith himself misses no occasion to criticize third baseman Bill Schenck, who later played three seasons in the majors to Smith's one. A pitcher named Con (Cornelius) Murphy evidently irritated his teammates to the point that some of them refused to take the field when he was on the mound (or "in the holes," as they called it). In one game, after bickering with his catcher on the field, Murphy fired a ball to the plate when the catcher was not looking and nearly decapitated him. In another game, pitcher-outfielder John Fox threw his bat at teammate John Shetzline after striking out. When Trenton returned to the field, Fox went and sat on the fence, refusing to play.

Despite all that, Trenton did win the first championship of the Eastern League—by backing in. All season long they trailed the league-leading Wilmington Quicksteps by a wide margin while battling the Virginia Club of Richmond and the Reading Actives for second place. But Reading disbanded on August 2. Richmond went over to the American Association on August 5. And Wilmington defected to the Union Association (a short-lived major league) on August 19. The final standings on September 30 of the five surviving Eastern League teams saw Trenton in first with a win-loss record of 50–40 and no other club over .500. The Newark Domestics finished third at 38–46.

The ninety games making up Trenton's league record for the year did not make the season. Those were just the "championship" games—contests against other members of the league. In the typical fashion of the day, Trenton played some fifty additional games against college and other amateur clubs as well as against major league nines. Near the end of April, according to Leo Smith's journal, the Trentons "won impressively" over Princeton University (11–4), "massacred" Lafayette College (21–5), and "battered" Rutgers (14–4). Earlier in the month, though, they had dropped one, 7–1, to the National League's Providence Grays and their star pitcher, Charley Radbourn. Providence went on to win the National League pennant that year by ten and a half games. Radbourn recorded sixty victories while losing only twelve, earning himself the number-one spot on the all-time major league "wins in a season" list. (Though the records are supposedly made to be broken, Radbourn's seems untouchable, even if the majors start playing year round.)

Trenton had better luck with some other major league clubs in 1884. On June 6 they lost a 9–8 squeaker to Brooklyn (still made up partly of former Camden Merritt) thanks, says Smith, to bad umpiring. In July the New York Giants came to town and had "no picnic" downing Trenton by 7–5. In August Trenton led Brooklyn, 3–0, before the game was cancelled in the third inning due to poor weather. And later that month the Trenton nine defeated Cleveland of the National League 6–5, before a crowd of a thousand at the new ball yard in Chambersburg.

Playing college and other amateur teams as well as major league pros made for some interesting juxtapositions in Trenton's 1884 season. For instance, two days before beating the major leaguers from Cleveland, Trenton had dropped a 3–2 decision to an amateur squad from Millville.

In addition to Smith and Schenck, several other members of the 1884 Trentons went on to the major leagues. Catcher Tom Daly, who was nineteen that year, broke in with Chicago of the National League in 1887 and finished up with Cincinnati in 1903. He had a respectable .278 lifetime batting average, once leading the National League in season doubles. He caught a no-hitter and helped win a pennant.

Pitcher Joseph ("Cyclone") Miller spent two seasons in the big time, winning thirteen and losing eleven. Con Murphy won seven, lost twenty-two for three different teams in two seasons six years apart. Catcher Marshall Quinton, left fielder Washington Williams, and pitcher John Fox appeared in a combined grand total of nine major league games.

But the greatest impact on baseball by a member of the 1884 Trenton team undoubtedly was made by its manager, Patrick Thomas Powers. Native Trentonian Powers went on to manage Rochester of the American Association in 1890, finishing fifth, and the 1892 New York Giants, eighth in the National League. He became president of the International League in 1893, holding that post until 1911, with a sabbatical in 1906. According to the official history of the league, "under Powers the International League became an institution"—an accomplishment recognized by his election to the league's Hall of Fame in 1961. In 1915 he joined with oilman Harry

Sinclair to bring the Federal League Peps to Newark and give the Garden State its brief moment in the major leagues.

ATLANTIC CITY joined the Eastern League briefly in 1885, while in mid-season of that year the league's Trenton franchise moved to Jersey City. The following season found Jersey City and Newark still in the Eastern League and Hoboken and Paterson in the newly formed Interstate League (not to be confused with the earlier Interstate Association, which had become the Eastern League). Then, in 1887, the Eastern League, reduced to Jersey City and Newark clubs only, merged into the International League, which had been formed the previous year by the amalgamation of the New York State and Ontario leagues. Paterson began a decade-long hiatus from organized baseball in 1887, while Hoboken disappeared for good.

On this latter point there may be some confusion. For fifteen years later, on June 16, 1902, the *New York Times* reported that a Hoboken team had the day before beaten Boston 7–4, to the delight of a crowd of four thousand at the St. George Cricket Grounds in Hoboken. It was, the *Times* said, Hoboken's second win over the National League's Boston franchise that year. The winning pitcher for Hoboken was "Deegan"—probably W. John ("Dummy") Deegan, who had won none and lost one for the New York Giants in 1901, his only season in the majors. He was amply supported by the three hits of third baseman "Cusick"—arguably Andrew Daniel ("Tony") Cusick, who had concluded a four-year major league stint with the Philadelphia Phillies fifteen years earlier. It is likely that the team described by the *Times* as being from Hoboken was actually Jersey City's new International League franchise. The presence of Dummy Deegan on the team supports this idea. If the New York Giants wanted to stash Deegan somewhere in 1902 in case they needed to recall him later, Jersey City would have been a logical place (the Giants and the Jersey City franchise were closely related). The reader is left to ponder whether the *Times* might have confused Hoboken and Jersey City, perhaps because the Jersey City club may have been using the St. George Cricket Grounds in Hoboken that year.

A rift between the International League's "northern" and "southern" teams (Newark and Jersey City were considered southern) caused its demise in 1888. The northern teams reorganized as the International Asso-

The oxymoronic Little Giants of 1886, first of several New Jersey teams to carry that name, succeeded the Domestics as Newark's entry in the Eastern League. (Courtesy of Newark Public Library)

ciation, and Newark and Jersey City helped form the new Central League, which metamorphosed into the Atlantic Association and then the Atlantic League. Jersey City and Newark alone represented the state from 1888 to 1890, and for the next five seasons New Jersey had no league teams at all. But those were poor years in general for the national pastime. The depression of 1892–93 caused a sharp dropoff in the number of minor leagues (from seventeen starting and ten finishing the 1890 season to only seven starting and three finishing in 1893).

Newark came back with a vengeance in the new Atlantic League of 1896, bringing the state its first professional baseball championship since the Trenton nine of a dozen years earlier. But it was the rival Paterson Atlantics who, in retrospect, really made baseball history that year.

The leader of the Paterson bunch in 1896 was Edward Barrow, baseball executive extraordinaire, elected to the Hall of Fame in 1953. Barrow's later accomplishments involved the Yankees:

- switching Babe Ruth from the mound to the outfield
- developing the New York Yankees farm system
- creating the Yankee dynasty (a club that had never topped its league before Barrow's arrival went on to win fourteen pennants and ten World Series during his twenty-four years as general manager and president)
- originating the practice of painting distances on outfield fences (at Yankee Stadium)
- first putting large numbers on players' uniforms

In 1896, Ed Barrow and the city of Paterson accelerated the career of the best shortstop and possibly the greatest player of all time, Honus Wagner. He was the second inductee into the Hall of Fame, behind Cobb and ahead of Ruth.

A year earlier, in 1895, a kid known as John Peter Wagner played a total of 129 games at shortstop for three different teams—Adrian in the Michigan State League, Steubenville (Ohio) in the Tri-State League, and Warren (Pennsylvania) of the Iron-Oil League. He batted .377.

Getting wind of this rising star, Barrow traveled to one of his games and signed him on the spot for the 1896 season at a salary of three hundred dollars. On opening day in Paterson, "Big Hannis" (so-called by the Paterson newspaper in apparent reference to his German heritage) manned first base rather than shortstop. In fact, he never played short at all that

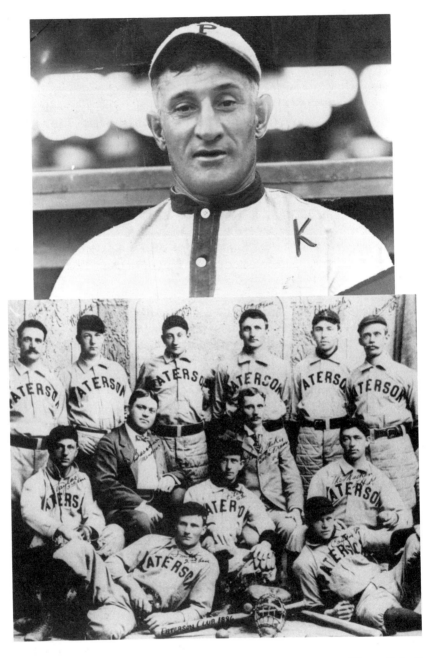

Hall-of-Fame shortstop Honus Wagner, standing third from left, played right field and all base positions for the 1896–1897 Paterson Atlantics before advancing to the major leagues. He had been brought to New Jersey by Edward Barrow, seated in street clothes, who later built the first New York Yankee dynasty. (Old Timers A.A. of Greater Paterson)

year, moving sometimes to third and occasionally patrolling the outfield. Barrow's great eye for talent seemed to have a blind spot when it came to Wagner's skills at shortstop.

Wagner's magnificent career might have ended for good on July 11, 1896, when he collided with his team's catcher and severely injured his knee. Reporting the accident, the *Evening News* expressed what many Paterson fans must have been thinking: "Let us hope Hannis Wagner's absence will not be long. This means no insult to Killacky, but first base is not Jack's position." It was no longer Wagner's either. When he returned to action on July 17, he was stationed at second.

The 1897 season saw Wagner settle into third for the Paterson club. He continued blasting enemy pitching (batting .379 in the first one hundred games), but he gave back a lot of runs with the worst fielding he would do in his twenty-two-year professional career. He erred forty-one times for a .898 fielding average (in contrast to his lifetime .949). The *Evening News* described one of his miscues—throwing over the head of his first baseman—as "*a brilliant exhibition of stupidity.*"

But the Paterson media would not have "Big Hannis" to kick around much longer. On July 17, two days after his "brilliant exhibition of stupidity," Barrow sold Wagner's contract to Louisville of the National League for eight hundred dollars. Commenting on Wagner's sale to Louisville, the *Evening News* neatly made a sow's ear out of a silk purse: "Popular as Wagner has been in this city, it was apparent of late that he had not been playing his game and had become a source of weakness to the team. If he played good ball Paterson would have kept him." But this was hardly a fit of Steinbrennerian pique on Barrow's part. To the contrary, he thought a great deal of Wagner and wanted him to get a chance in the big leagues. Louisville eventually merged with the Pittsburgh Pirates when the National League cut back from twelve to eight teams, and Wagner stayed with the team until his retirement in 1917.

In truth, it took Wagner another three seasons to really hit his stride. At Louisville in 1897–1899, he averaged .321 at bat. Not too shabby, but hardly up to his next ten seasons, when his lowest average was .330, his highest soared to .381, and he led the National League seven times. Similarly, he stole an average of thirty-two bases in two full seasons at Louisville—but in the next ten years never had fewer than thirty-five, pilfered a high of sixty-one, and led the league five times. (While Wagner was pacing the National League with sixty-one steals in 1907, Cobb was topping the American League with forty-nine.)

MAJOR LEAGUE WARS

Despite losing Wagner, Paterson carried on in minor league baseball in New Jersey in 1898. Newark returned to the Atlantic League in 1899, to be joined by Jersey City in 1900 as Paterson faded once again. The next year saw the Garden State without a professional team for the only time in the first half of the twentieth century. Then Newark and Jersey City both regained teams in the International League in 1902, replacing Syracuse and Hartford—and both remained more or less continuously in organized baseball through 1950. From time to time they were joined by teams from Asbury Park, Atlantic City, Bloomfield, Bloomingdale, Camden, Elizabeth, Long Branch, New Brunswick, Paterson, Perth Amboy, Trenton, and (possibly) Washington. The high-water mark came in 1914 when nine New Jersey cities had minor league baseball teams spread across three different circuits. But for the first twelve years of the century, the state had little to brag about in professional baseball as Newark and Jersey City were perennial also-rans in the International League. Better times were soon to come.

The new principal owner of the International League Newark franchise in 1912 was none other than Charles H. Ebbets, Sr. Ebbets had risen from ticket seller to take majority control of the National League Brooklyn Superbas a decade earlier. The team was about to change its name to the Dodgers and occupy brand-new Ebbets Field (in 1913) and emerge from the league's second division under new manager "Uncle" Wilbert Robinson (in 1914). But the Newark club—called the Indians—stole a march on its parent, nailing the International League flag in 1913 to give Newark and New Jersey their first baseball championship in seventeen years.

Despite unsettling early-season rumors that Charley Ebbets was already looking to unload his newly acquired team, the Indians got off to a fast start and kept extending their lead throughout August. Also known as Redskins, Warriors, and Braves, they built a late-August lead of twelve games over the runnerup Rochester Hustlers, also known as "the Flower City Crew." The rest of the International League of 1913 included, in rough order of performance, the Baltimore Orioles, the Buffalo Bisons, the Montreal Royals, the Toronto Maple Leafs, the Providence Grays, and the Jersey City Skeeters (also called the "Pests" and the "Insects").

One reason for the Indians' success was the strong left arm of "swarthy" Wyatt Arnold ("Watty") Lee. A former major leaguer (three seasons with the Washington Senators and one with the Pittsburgh Pirates), Lee fared especially well against the defending champion Maple Leafs. He started nine games against them and won seven, including four shutouts. Lee's supporting cast (in batting order and with major league experience in parentheses) included:

Jack Dalton, right field (Brooklyn Dodgers, 1910, 1914; Buffalo Buf-Feds, 1915; Detroit Tigers 1916)

Bert Tooley, shortstop (Brooklyn Dodgers, 1911–1912)

Hi Meyers, center field (Brooklyn Dodgers, 1909, 1911, 1914–1922; St. Louis Cardinals, 1923–1925)

Harry Swacina, first base (Pittsburgh Pirates, 1907–1908; Baltimore Terrapins, 1914–1915)

Bill Zimmerman, left field (Brooklyn Dodgers, 1915)

Eddie Zimmerman, third base (St. Louis Cardinals, 1906; Brooklyn Dodgers, 1911)

Gus Getz, second base (Boston Braves, 1909–1910; Brooklyn Dodgers, 1914–1916; Cincinnati Reds, 1917; Cleveland Indians, 1918)

Bob Higgins, catcher (Cleveland Indians, 1909; Brooklyn Dodgers, 1911–1912)

Player-manager Harry Smith (formerly a ten-season major leaguer with the Philadelphia Athletics, Pittsburgh Pirates, and Boston Braves) spelled Higgins behind the plate.

In a collapse that nearly foreshadowed the Dodger debacle of 1951, when Brooklyn's thirteen and a half game lead in early August disappeared by season's end, the Indians watched their lead of August dwindle to just three and a half games by September 12. Five days later, despite a 5–1 whipping of Providence, the lead over onrushing Rochester had dropped to just one and a half games. In a paroxysm of nerves, the *Newark Evening News* of Thursday, September 18, demanded that one game of the season-ending doubleheader scheduled for the following Sunday at Jersey City be moved up to Friday. The thinking was that rain on Sunday could wash out two nearly certain Indian wins over the hapless Skeeters and let the Hustlers back into the pennant.

Jersey City club president Thomas Fogarty finally agreed to let one of the Sunday games be added to one scheduled for Saturday at Newark's Weidenmayer's Park. A record crowd turned out for that newly cobbled doubleheader and was rewarded with Newark's pennant-clinching 2–1 win in the first game as Rochester was losing to Toronto. Fogarty, however, paid dearly for his act of generosity when only one thousand fans came to Roosevelt Stadium for the meaningless season finale the following day. A league record was set, though, as the Braves beat the Insects 5–4 in a game lasting only fifty-eight minutes.

With a closing spurt of five straight wins, Newark had finished with a 95–57 mark, four games ahead of Rochester. Jersey City brought up the International League rear with 101 losses against only 53 wins.

Newark Mayor Jacob Haussling, out of town at a conference when the Indians clinched, sent club president George Solomon a telegram that said simply, "My sincere congratulations to you and club. Newark Knows How."

This might have been the start of a minor league dynasty like that of the Newark Bears of the 1930s or the Baltimore Orioles before they went big-league. But 1914 was a horrible year for the Indians and 1915 rang down the curtain as the Federal League muscled the Indians off to Harrisburg.

The 1914 Indians, with Charles H. Ebbets, Jr., as general manager, got left at the starting gate and owned a bleak 56–83 record by mid-September. They finished strong, beating Babe Ruth and his Baltimore Orioles on September 21 and almost spoiling the Providence Grays' rush to nip Rochester (rechristened the "Red Wings") for the pennant. They also made sure that the rival Skeeters of Jersey City stayed in the International League basement. But the year-end books showed a loss of eighty thousand dollars.

The coming of the Federal League Peps in 1915 was akin to tossing a concrete block to a drowning man. A few loyalists continued trekking to Weidenmayer's Park to cheer the Indians, but most baseball buffs of Newark and environs flocked to Federal Park in Harrison to watch the major leaguers. The Ebbetses, no dummies, sold their interest in the Indians on April 15 to George Solomon, a native of Newark and their erstwhile partner. Solomon brought in two new partners—C. H. and H. W. Medicus—and a new manager, Jimmy Callahan, who had skippered the Chicago White Sox for four seasons and would later manage the Pittsburgh Pirates for two.

None of these moves made the slightest difference. By Memorial Day, the Indians stood dead last in the International League with a 9–16 record. And although they almost reached .500 by July 1, that day they played their last game in Newark for 1915 and then decamped for Harrisburg. Their troubles in Newark probably had been at their worst a few days earlier when, as the *New York Times* reported on June 26, they were sued for $1,750 in back rent by the owners of their ball park, the Reliable Improvement Co. of Newark.

Newark was not the only International League franchise to be hurt by the Federal League. The Baltimore Orioles also gave up, moving to Richmond. Only Buffalo, of the three International League towns invaded by the Federal League, hung on to its International League franchise. In the course of this invasion, the International League came to be known as "the Belgium of Baseball," after that country's long history of being overrun by invading armies.

When the "major league wars" ended in the winter of 1915–1916 with the demise of the Federal League, Solomon and the International League brought the Indians back to Newark. But with the Jersey City Skeeters gone to Baltimore, the cellar was available and the Indians grabbed it, finishing 53–87. It would take sixteen years, a change of name, and several changes of ownership before the Newark entry in the International League would amount to much again. Then it would not only match but exceed the glory of the 1913 Indians.

NEWARK'S GLORY

From 1915 on, the story of minor league baseball in New Jersey focuses on just three cities—Newark, Trenton, and Jersey City (forgetting New Brunswick's brief flirtation with the ill-fated Colonial League in 1948). The story begins in Newark.

After returning to the International League in 1916, the Newark franchise stumbled through a decade of professionally mediocre and financially debilitating seasons. A "Newark-Providence-Newark shuffle in 1925–26," as the official league history calls it, did not solve the problems. Neither did a name change from Indians to Bears. Nor the rain-delayed opening on May 15, 1926, of brand-new Davids Stadium (named for team owner Charles L. Davids and later renamed Ruppert Stadium). Though the new ball yard got the "Grizzlies" out of Newark Schools Stadium, where they had opened the 1926 season, and Bloomfield's Sprague Field, which seemed to jinx their play, the team finished third in the league, ten games behind first-place Toronto.

Newark's Ruppert Stadium, opened in 1926 and origi-
nally called Davids Stadium, was home to the Newark
Bears, seen here on opening day in 1936. (Courtesy of
Newark Public Library)

The following year saw little improvement in terms of either finances or play—though the Bears did have a heartening spring training in Pensacola, Florida, and capped the season by splitting an exhibition doubleheader with the highly rated Cuban Stars of the Negro Leagues. Nonetheless, the year ended in bankruptcy.

Paul Block, publisher of the *Toledo Blade* and *Pittsburgh Post-Gazette*, bought the team at a receiver's sale after the 1927 season for an outlay of just over half a million dollars. Though his commitment was strong (he invested heavily to acquire better players), his timing was awful. The stock market crash of October 1929 and the ensuing Great Depression knocked the stuffing out of baseball, along with nearly everything else. Minor league teams suffered especially; whereas twenty-six leagues started the 1929 season, only twenty-three were around for opening day in 1930, dropping to fourteen by 1933—the low for the century after 1918. Making things even bleaker for Newark, the International League's Rochester club—now part of Branch Rickey's Cardinal farm system—seemed to have a lock on first place, reeling off four straight championships during the years Block owned the Bears (1928–1931).

Block undoubtedly was happy to see Colonel Jacob Ruppert come along at the close of the 1931 season. The millionaire brewer and owner of the New York Yankees, vowing to return the Yanks to American League primacy, felt that a farm system on Rickey's model was the only way to go. Despite the opposition of organized baseball's first commissioner, Judge Kenesaw Mountain Landis, Ruppert set his sights on Newark as the centerpiece of his minor league system.

The acquisition took place in November 1931, with about six hundred thousand dollars reportedly changing hands (six times what Ruppert had paid for Babe Ruth a few years earlier). In the depths of a depression that would take several more years to run its course, and despite heavy unemployment in Newark, 345,001 fans would spin the turnstiles of Ruppert Stadium the following season, setting a new International League record. Colonel Ruppert's promise to build a contender for the city clearly struck a responsive chord in people with more hope in their hearts than money in their pockets.

Ruppert wasted little time making good on his promise. The 1932 Bears, loaded with major leaguers either starting or finishing their careers, ran away with the pennant. They won 109 games while losing only 59, finishing fifteen and a half games ahead of the second-place Baltimore Orioles. They had the league's top pitcher in Don Brennan (twenty-five wins) and its second-best hitter in Dixie Walker (behind George Puccinelli, who led all minor leagues that year and had departed Rochester for the parent St. Louis Cardinals by season's end). They beat the Minneapolis Millers four games to two in the Little World Series. The batting star of the series was thirty-six-year-old Charlie Hargreaves (born in Trenton, died in Neptune), who slammed three home runs and averaged .471.

Although the 1937 Bears earn high praise whenever the discussion turns to the great minor league teams of all-time, you could argue for the 1932 Grizzlies and have plenty of ammunition. The fame of the 1937 team rests on three achievements—finishing twenty-five and a half games in front (on 109 wins and 43 losses), winning the Little World Series, and sending every regular on the team to the majors. The 1932 club did not overwhelm the league quite as boldly, but won just as many games; they matched the Little World Series achievement (giving the opposition one less win in the bargain); and they counted fourteen past or future major leaguers among their regulars. (Table 2 shows the Bears of 1932 and their major league records.)

Whether the 1932 Bears were as good as the 1937 Bears or not, enough of their players moved on to the majors in 1933 to force the team into a multiyear rebuilding program. The result was the 1937 wonder team, which included:

Charlie Keller, who would play thirteen seasons in the outfield for the Yankees and Tigers, leading the league twice in walks and once in "production" (a combination of on-base percentage and slugging average). In 1937 "King Kong"—who stood only five foot ten but hit a lot of home runs—led the International League in batting average, hits, and runs scored.

Joe Gordon, future Yankee and Cleveland Indian second baseman for eleven summers, part of outstanding double-play combinations with Frank Crosetti and Phil Rizzuto.

Babe Dahlgren, best known for replacing Lou Gehrig at first base for the Yankees in 1939 after launching a twelve-season major league career with the Boston Red Sox in 1935; played third base for the 1937 Bears.

George McQuinn, who returned to the majors after starring at first base for the Bears; compiled a twelve-year big league career, mostly with the St. Louis Browns, where he hit .324 and .316 in his two best years.

The 1937 Newark Bears, one of the greatest minor league teams of all time, lost the first three games of the Little World Series, then stormed back with four straight wins to take the title. Every regular on the team went on to a major league career. (Randolph Linthurst)

TABLE 2
The 1932 Newark Bears and Their Major League Records

Player/Position*	Major League Seasons	Major League Accomplishments*
Johnny Neun, first base	6 (1935–1931) Detroit (A), Boston (N)[†]	Lifetime .289 average
Red Rolfe, shortstop	10 (1931, 1934–1942) New York (A)	Led American League in runs, hits, doubles (1939); 49 Hall of Fame votes
Dixie Walker, centerfield	18 (1931, 1933–1949) New York, Chicago, Detroit (A) Brooklyn, Pittsburgh (N)	Led National League in batting (1944), RBI (1945); lifetime .306 average; 22 Hall of Fame votes
Jesse Hill, left field	3 (1935–1937) New York, Washington, Philadelphia (A)	Lifetime .289 average (also had been intercollegiate broad jump champion)
Jack Saltzgaver, second base	6 (1932, 1934–1937, 1945) New York (A), Pittsburgh (N)	Lifetime .260 average
Woody Jensen, right field	9 (1931–1939) Pittsburgh (N)	Lifetime .285 average

Marv Owen, third base	9 (1931, 1933–1940) Detroit, Chicago, Boston (A)	Lifetime .275 average
Charlie Hargreaves, catcher	8 (1923–1930) Brooklyn, Pittsburgh (N)	Lifetime .270 average
Don Brennan, pitcher	5 (1933–1937) New York (A), Cincinnati, New York (N)	Won 21, Lost 12
Al Mamaux, pitcher- manager	12 (1913–1924) Pittsburgh, Brooklyn (N), New York (A)	Won 76, lost 67; lifetime 2.89 ERA; led National League in strikeouts per game (1920)
Johnny Murphy, pitcher	13 (1932, 1934–1943, 1946–1947) New York, Boston (A)	Won 93, Lost 53; led American League in saves four times
Willie Hershberger, backup catcher	3 (1938–1940) Cincinnati (N)	Lifetime .316 average
Eddie Phillips, backup catcher	6 (1924, 1929, 1931–1932, 1934–1935) Boston (N), Detroit, Pittsburgh, New York (A), Washington, Cleveland	Lifetime .237 average
Jimmy Moore, utility outfielder	2 (1930–1931) Chicago, Philadelphia (A)	Lifetime .254 average

*These players made up the regular starting lineup in 1932.
†A = American League; N = National League.

Jim Gleeson, who would play five years in major league outfields, four for Cincinnati, after leading the 1937 International League in doubles.

Bob Seeds, nicknamed "Suitcase Bob," probably because he played outfield for four major league teams in six years before joining the 1937 Bears, making the All-Star team (along with almost everyone else on the Newark squad), and contending for the league's RBI leadership.

Nolen Richardson, journeyman shortstop who spent 1936–1937 in the minors between major league chapters with Detroit and the Yankees (1929–1935) and Cincinnati (1938–1939).

Buddy Rosar, future Yankee, Indian, Athletic, and Red Sox catcher in twelve major league seasons.

Atley Donald, Joe Beggs, Vito Tamulis, and *Steve Sundra,* the Big Four of the pitching staff, who together won seventy-three games while losing only sixteen in 1937. The following season Donald, Beggs, and Sundra went up to the Yankees, and Tamulis moved on to the St. Louis Browns and Brooklyn Dodgers; their combined record that year was a decent 21–16, while lifetime in the majors they all had winning records for a total of 209 wins against 137 losses.

Also among the 1937 Bear "regulars" were utility infielders Francis Kelleher and Merrill May; backup catcher Willie Hershberger; and pitchers Marius Russo and Jack Fallon. The lone holdover from the 1932 champions was the tragic Hershberger, who would put a bullet in his head in a Boston hotel room a few years later.

These Bears captured first place in mid-May. They led the league in team batting average (.299), runs (890), RBI (843), hits (1,574), doubles (292), triples (80), team fielding average (.970), and shutouts (15). Their pitching staff had the top four individual records for the year.

In the postseason International League playoffs, called the Governor's Cup Series, the Bears first wiped out third-place Syracuse in four straight games. Their victim in game 2 was Jerseyan Johnny Vander Meer, who was less than a year away from his historic consecutive no-hitters in the major leagues. More than twelve thousand fans flocked to Ruppert Stadium for that game after the Bears had pulled out a 2–1 victory the day before with back-to-back two-out homers (by Gordon and Gleeson) in the ninth inning.

The Baltimore Orioles were next. In the league finals they suffered the same fate as Syracuse—a 4–0 shellacking. Only game 2 was truly close, a 6–5 squeaker. Beggs, with a one-hitter, and Keller and Seeds, with home runs, supplied the heroics.

And then the Bears came face to face with the American Association champion Columbus Cardinals, crown jewel of the St. Louis farm system. It was to be the original "farmers" versus the new kids in the fields. The defenders of the American Association's four-year winning streak in the Little World Series versus the inheritors of the last International League team to win it (the 1932 Bears). Keller versus the Columbus wonder kid, Enos Slaughter. Future major league stars versus future major league stars, head to head and toe to toe. (In addition to Slaughter, Columbus boasted Johnny Rizzo, Dick Siebert, and Max Lanier.) It was to be thunder versus thunder.

Despite the heady promise of this series, barely more than six thousand fans came out to Ruppert to see Beggs and the Bears go down, 5–3, in game 1. The following night the gate topped seventeen thousand—but the result was not much better: Columbus 5, Newark 4. Game 3 also went to the Red Birds, 6–3, and Grizzlie fans prepared themselves to wait for next year.

But then the Bears pulled off one of the great sporting comebacks of all time, insuring their place on everyone's list of top minor league teams. Traveling to Ohio, they began chipping away at the Red Birds with an 8–1 win in game 4. Beggs kept eight Cardinal hits well spread, and Keller and Gleeson each contributed three hits to the Bear attack. Game 5 saw Atley Donald hurl a three-hitter and gain a 1–0 win. And now the Columbus fans began to get the jitters. They had good cause. In game 6, little-used Spurgeon Ferdinand ("Spud") Chandler pitched the Bears to a 10–1 victory to deadlock the series. (Six seasons later, with the Yankees, Chandler would lead the American League with twenty wins, an .833 win-loss percentage, twenty complete games, five shutouts, and a 1.67 ERA.)

After crowds in excess of ten thousand at earlier games, fewer than four thousand of the Columbus faithful came out for the decisive game. They might as well have stayed home, for the Bears were on a roll and were not to be denied. Though Beggs did not have his best stuff, reliever Phil Page held the Cards close while Keller (who batted .478 for the series) led the offense. When the dust settled, the Bears had the game, 10–4, and the 1937 Little World Series, 4–3.

In his book *The Newark Bears*, Randolph Linthurst describes the homecoming of the champs: "Over 5,000 fans put their Depression concerns aside and turned out at Pennsylvania Station to welcome the triumphant Bears back to Newark, and over 50 policemen were hard pressed to restrain the enthusiastic crowd. When Chandler poked his head out of the players' special car, a brass band began playing 'Happy Days Are Here Again.'"

Newark's and New Jersey's peak in professional baseball—organized baseball–style—had been reached (though the glory days of the Negro League Newark Eagles were yet to come). The Bears did repeat as International League pennant winners the following year. Keller and Gleeson had not yet gone up to the majors, and Beggs had returned. But after twice leading the Kansas City Blues in the Little World Series (two games to one and three games to two), the Bears succumbed in the final two games. Among the Blues stars in 1938 were Eddie Joost (later to star at shortstop for Cincinnati and the Philadelphia Athletics during the seventeen-season career in the majors); Wally Judnich (outfielder, seven big league seasons, mostly with the St. Louis Browns); and Marv ("Baby Face") Breuer, who would later pitch five seasons for the Yankees.

Linthurst contrasts the Bears' 1938 homecoming with that of a year earlier: "The Bears returned to Newark with $300 apiece, loser's share in the series. Thousands had turned out to welcome the triumphant 1937 Bears home from Columbus, but only six adults, four youngsters and the players' wives were on hand when their train pulled into Newark this time. A brilliant era was coming to an end."

The Bears continued to play in Newark, with mixed results, through the 1949 season. Then, with attendance way off and financial losses mounting, the team moved on to Springfield, Massachusetts.

What happened to the Bears? The superficial answer is that television killed minor league ball and Newark was just one of the victims. But in the final year of Newark's decline as a minor league baseball power (1949), the number of minor leagues reached an all-time high of fifty-nine. A decline ensued, to be sure, but since 1959 the number of minor leagues has been notably constant—never more than twenty-two, never fewer than seventeen. And in all that time, only one has failed to finish a season. In other words, minor league baseball never died—has, in fact, enjoyed good health for a long time.

Television surely did not help the cause of minor league baseball in Newark. But there were other factors. Newark Baseball authority Larry Keefe, quoted by Linthurst, says one was the regulation banning pleasure driving during World War II. It is true that the number of minor leagues shrank to only ten during the war; however, minor league ball rebounded nicely in other places. The location of Ruppert Stadium is also mentioned as a problem—but the notion that it was "almost as easy to get to New York parks" does not hold true. The big unmentioned factor—along with television and an improving road system—was the sheer quantity of superior major league ball available to northern New Jersey fans. With the Yankees, Dodgers, and Giants almost constantly in pennant races—and often meeting one another in the World Series—it was worth the effort to battle traffic into Manhattan, Brooklyn, or the Bronx. Television, of course, made it that much easier. But it was the deadly combination of nearby, superior, and plentiful major league ball, plus television and better transportation, that did the Bears in.

THE TRENTON GIANTS

The story of minor league ball in Jersey is not complete, though, without mention of two other teams—one deserving for its excellence, the other for its persistence.

Though minor league ball died in Trenton just a year after its demise in Newark, the glory days in Trenton came much closer to the end—in 1947.

In 1947 it was sixty-three years since Trenton had seen a champion in professional baseball (Leo Smith's backbiting backers-in of 1884). The city had hosted a mediocre Tri-State League team for seven seasons just prior to World War I, followed by a barren two decades. In 1936, as the Bears were building their International League powerhouse, Trenton returned to the minor leagues with an entry in the New York–Penn League. Two years later the team moved to the Eastern League, and then, in 1939, began a twelve-year stay in the Class B Interstate League. Among the players who labored briefly for the team in the late 1930s or early 1940s were Hall of Famer and New Jerseyan Goose Goslin (on his way out); George Case (on his way up to eleven years in the majors, mostly with the Senators); Eddie Miksis (also on his way up, to Brooklyn, Chicago, and other places, for a total of fourteen seasons); Del Ennis (prior to his fourteen years in the big time, mostly with the Phillies); and Walter Alston (at about the time of his one-game, one-at-bat, one-strike-out major league playing career with the St. Louis Cardinals).

The home of the Trenton Giants, an independent club until the New York Giants bought them after the 1945 season, was Dunn Field, located at the Brunswick Circle on Route 1. Built specifically for the team in 1936, the

The 1947 Trenton Giants, winners of the Interstate League pennant, included future major leaguers Bobby Hofman, Paul LaPalme, Hal Bamberger, Andy Tomasic, Roger Bowman, and Bill Jennings. (Randolph Linthurst)

place was said to be a dream for pitchers and a nightmare for hitters (the exact opposite of Ruppert Stadium). The lights were bad and the fences were long (350 feet and 345 feet down the lines, 385 to straightaway center). Seating capacity was 3,500.

The preceding seasons gave little warning of what was about to happen. The Giants finished third in the league in 1945, drawing only thirty-two thousand for the entire season. In 1946 they fell to seventh. As the 1947 season approached, they had every reason to fear another year eating the dust of the rest of the league: the Wilmington Blue Rocks, the Hagerstown Owls, the Allentown Cardinals, the Sunbury Yankees, the Harrisburg Senators, the York White Roses, and the Lancaster Red Roses.

Manager Tommy Heath, a former major leaguer with the St. Louis Browns, could not have been optimistic at the Lakewood spring training camp run that year by the New York Giants for seven of its farm clubs. Among the 250 or so hopefuls in the camp at Ocean County Park, few of the better ones belonged to Trenton. Jack Maguire, star of the 1946 Trenton team, was there, but he was being fought over by the parent team and the higher-class San Francisco Seals. (Maguire eventually wound up with Jersey City in the International League that year and played for New York in 1950–1951.) Of the thirty-nine players on the Trenton roster the first week of April, only three—Bobby Hofman, Hal Bamberger, and Bill Jennings—would ever make it to the majors. The last two would stick for but one season each. The roster contained eleven returnees from the 1946 team, thirteen who had played for other pro teams the previous year, twelve amateurs, two men recently mustered out of the armed forces, and one player lured out of retirement.

Heath's problems were confirmed in four preseason exhibitions, two against the Montreal Royals and one each versus the Newark Bears and the Jersey City Little Giants (all International League teams). Trenton dropped all three games that were completed, giving up more than thirty runs and garnering fewer than ten. In the other contest they were trailing the Bears 4–0 when rain mercifully interceded. Fortunately for Heath and for Trenton fans, a sympathetic and influential witness was on hand for the 12–4 loss to Jersey City. He was Hall of Famer Carl Hubbell, former New York Giant great and in 1947 the organization's farm system director. Hubbell huddled with Heath and Trenton general manager Bill McKechnie, Jr., and promised to send help.

The help took the form of pitchers Andy Tomasic (late of Temple University), Phil Frick, Roger Bowman, and Paul LaPalme; catchers Nick Testa and Gene Swedler; first bagger Stan Miasek; and outfielder Roy Drews.

Dunn Field, home of the Trenton Giants, was located at Brunswick Circle on Route 1. This site now accommodates the offices of the New Jersey Lottery. (Courtesy of Trenton Public Library, Trenton)

Combining the not so old and the totally new, Heath cobbled together this opening day lineup:

Leo Niezgoda, left field

Bobby Hofman, second base

Hal Bamberger, center field

Roy Drews, right field

Bill Jennings, shortstop

Stan Miasek, first base

Wilbur Jackson, third base

Gene Swedler, catcher

Phil Frick, pitcher

But as the season got under way, it appeared that the team might be beyond help. After a postponed opener in rainy Allentown on April 30, Trenton proceeded to drop an 8–7 squeaker to the Cardinals on May 1, wasting homers by Hofman, Drews, and Jackson. The next day they lost in Sunbury to the Yankees, then went on to Harrisburg to dump a double-header to the Senators 10–1 and 10–3. A frustrated but less than prescient reporter for the *Trenton Times* wrote: "It was obvious to the 1,491 fans that the Giants lack a standout pitcher on the entire staff."

Two days later, lefty Roger Bowman engineered the team's first win of 1947, whiffing thirteen Senators along the way. Then Frick beat Lancaster's Red Roses 8–2, and Trenton went on to sweep three from Sunbury, including a May 11 doubleheader with "in your face" scores of 18–11 and 5–0.

The Giants could have done without the rest of May, though. By month's end they stood dead last—nine games behind Harrisburg. Things did not improve much through June and the first half of July. Though they rose as high as third at the end of June, mid-July saw them back in sixth with a record of thirty-six wins against thirty-five losses.

Then the amazing drive began. They won fifty-two of their last sixty-two games, taking over fourth place on July 24, third place on July 28, second place on July 29, and first place by percentage points on August 9. On a night in mid-August, at a game honoring Tommy Heath (who had played for the team after his brief stint with the St. Louis Browns), they burst the seams of Dunn Field with over five thousand paying customers. That raised their gate for the year to over seventy-seven thousand, setting a new league record.

On the first of September, before more than sixty-five hundred fans (many of them standees), they beat Wilmington's Curt Simmons. Later in the month Simmons would go up to the Phillies, pitch one complete game, win it (giving up a single run for an ERA of 1.00), and then spend the next twenty years in the majors. A fellow by the name of John Carden hurled that night for Trenton. His entire major league career had consisted of two innings for the New York Giants the previous year, in which he gave up four hits and four walks for an ERA of 22.50.

Trenton clinched the pennant the following night with a 7–0 win over Wilmington. At season's end a few days later they were 88–50 and had drawn a total of 109,164 fans to Dunn Field. In the sixth and final game of the anticlimactic league playoffs at Dunn Field, Trenton's fans set a new Interstate League attendance record by turning out 7,126 strong.

The stars of Trenton's 1947 champs were:

Andy Tomasic, who led the league's pitchers with an 18–10 record, 2.48 ERA, 24 complete games, and 278 strikeouts. Andy moved up to the New York Giants' Jersey City farm team in 1948, then made it to the parent club for two games in 1949 (winning none and losing one). Also in 1949 he won the final game played in Ruppert Stadium as the Jerseys beat the Bears.

Hal Bamberger, outfielder who led the team in batting with a .333 average and the league in triples with twenty-four. Bamberger, too, moved up to Jersey City in 1948. He played seven games for the New York club that year in an abbreviated major league career (one hit in twelve at bats).

Bobby Hofman, Trenton second baseman who would play first, second, and third, as well as catch and pinch-hit, in a supersub role for the New York Giants (1949, 1952–1957). He moved up to "A" ball with Sioux City in 1948.

Roger Bowman, pitcher who would play parts of five seasons for the New York Giants and Pittsburgh Pirates between 1949 and 1955, compiling a 2–11 record. He also moved to Sioux City in 1948.

Paul LaPalme, perhaps the most accomplished of the 1947 Trentons when he hit the big time: seven seasons (1951–1957) with the

Willie Mays (right) played briefly for the 1950 Trenton Giants before moving on to the Triple A Minneapolis Millers, where he joined Ray Dandridge (left), formerly of the Newark Eagles, and John Barnhill. (Courtesy of Newark Public Library)

Pirates, Cards, Reds, and White Sox, pitching in 253 games (winning 24, saving 14, and losing 45).

Bill Jennings, shortstop, sixty-four games with the St. Louis Browns in 1951.

There were two other big league appearances by members of the team—but not in baseball. Tomasic also played football for the Pittsburgh Steelers (a model for Bo Jackson?), while first baseman Stan Miasek played for the Chicago Stags of the National Basketball Association.

In the flush of triumph, the citizens of Trenton passed a referendum in the fall of 1947 to replace Dunn Field with a larger stadium. They hired the architect, selected the site—but never built the ball park.

Suppressing their disappointment, the team kept right on winning. Though Wilmington managed to nip Trenton by percentage points for the 1948 pennant, the Giants won the playoffs. The 1949 team finished a poor fourth but again prevailed in the playoffs.

The happy news for Trenton fans in 1950 came in the form of an ebullient nineteen-year-old black man with a funny way of catching easy fly balls and an eye-popping way of catching impossible ones. He was the "Say, Hey Kid"—Willie Mays. But Mays moved on to the Triple A Minneapolis Millers before the year was out, and the news turned bad.

Finishing fourth and going nowhere in the playoffs was the least of it. The New York Giants, looking for a more lucrative market and warming up for their own defection to the West Coast a few seasons later, sold out to local interests and bought the Sunbury franchise instead. The locals proved no more loyal to Trenton, however, moving the team to Salisbury in the off-season.

Trenton and minor league baseball were through.

THE JERSEY CITY LITTLE GIANTS

New Jersey was down to its last minor league baseball card. It was played in 1961 in Jersey City, a town known more for its persistence in baseball than for its performance. But even Jersey City had its moments of hope and glory before the curtain finally came down.

Although the Federal League had not invaded Jersey City in 1914–1915, the city's International League franchise became an after-the-armistice victim of the Federal League's war with organized baseball. What set off the chain reaction was Richmond's refusal to relinquish the International League franchise that had transferred there from Baltimore in 1915. The response of Baltimore's baseball interests, led for years by Jack Dunn, was to make an unrefusable offer for the Jersey City team and move it south. So if you wanted to say that the great Oriole teams of later in the century had some roots in Jersey, you probably could.

What the baseball wars took away, a military war restored. The official history of the International League tells the story: "World War I in 1917 brought to its wake a fresh crisis for the International. Attendance fell and club exchequers barely carried through the war. Financially feeble, the league in 1918 was compelled to reorganize as the New International. Ed Barrow, his salary halved, stepped down. Richmond, Providence and Montreal dropped out in favor of Jersey City, Binghamton and Syracuse. But Syracuse found support wanting and moved to Hamilton during the campaign. In this hectic year the International alone of all the minors completed its season."

Unfortunately, the postwar Skeeters had little more on the ball than did the prewar team. For the next fifteen years or so they just hung in there, more often than not serving up "breathers" for the league's contenders. As the 1920s drew to a close, the emergence in the league of a farm system powerhouse, the Rochester Red Wings, further diminished the hopes of the independent Jersey City club. And then the Great Depression destroyed them altogether. In 1933 the franchise departed for Syracuse.

What reportedly brought baseball back to Jersey City, in 1937, was Frank Hague, the political boss of the Democratic stronghold. He enticed the New York Giants to buy the Albany franchise and bring it south, inaugurating a fourteen-year period of farm-system baseball in the city. It was a time of great stability for the league, with not a single change until Newark moved to Springfield, Massachusetts, for the 1950 season.

In 1939 the "Jersey Giants" made the Governor's Cup playoffs for the first time under New York Giant ownership. But they lost in the first round and repeated the performance in 1940. It was not until 1942 that they got to the finals—and then lost four straight games. This seems to have caused such melancholy that it took five more years to make the playoffs again, only to lose once more in the first round. The same fate befell the team in 1949.

In 1950, when the season ended on September 10, the Little Giants had snuck into fourth place, making the playoffs by the thinnest of margins. Two days later, they began what would be their final Governor's Cup run, confronting the still powerful Red Wings of Rochester.

This was the Jersey City lineup:

Bracchitta, center field

Pavlick, second base

Stan Jok, third base (later third base, outfield, pinch hitter for Philadelphia Phillies and Chicago White Sox, 1954–1955)

Mele, right field (probably Albert "Dutch" Mele, earlier outfield for Cincinnati Reds, 1937)

Lasba, left field

Marv Blaylock, first base (later first base, outfield for Philadelphia Phillies, 1955–1957)

Sokol, catcher

Jasinski, shortstop

Roger Bowman, pitcher (see Trenton)

Andy Tomasic, pitcher (see Trenton)

Johnnie Wittig, relief pitcher (earlier New York Giants, Boston Red Sox, 1938–1939, 1941, 1943, 1949)

When Jersey City took the first game 5–4, behind Bowman's hurling and Blaylock's sixth inning two-run homer, the hopes of Hagueville soared. Then plummeted as Rochester hammered the Jerseys 10–4 in game 2. Then soared again as the team came home to Roosevelt Stadium and blasted the Red Wings 6–1, with Tomasic fanning seven and Mele driving in three runs on two hits.

But then, on what came to be known by Jersey City fans as Black Saturday and Black Sunday, September 16–17, 1950, the Red Wings took the Jerseys apart at Roosevelt by identical 6–3 scores. And so it was back to Rochester, trailing 2–3 in games and with hope dimming. The home team routed Tomasic 7–3, and the season ended for Jersey City.

So did this penultimate stint in the International League. The club had

Jersey City's Roosevelt Stadium, built during the Great Depression, served for many years as home of the city's International League entries. Fifteen Brooklyn Dodger home games were played there in 1956 and 1957. (New Jersey Room, Jersey City Public Library)

drawn only seventy thousand paying customers for the season and had lost a hundred thousand dollars. With the city raising the team's rent for Roosevelt Stadium from one to fifteen thousand dollars per year, the parent club began looking for a buyer. Throughout the fall of 1950 the *Jersey Journal* ran several stories about the on-again, off-again negotiations with a group from Ottawa. Finally a deal was struck and the Little Giants were gone.

But not for good. Even as local politics had brought a team back to Jersey City in 1937, global politics returned one in 1960. Whereas the city had Frank Hague to thank in 1937, Fidel Castro was the dubious benefactor in 1960. According to the International League's official history, "political disturbances in Cuba caused the league in mid-season to transfer the Havana franchise to Jersey City."

The team got something less than a prodigal's welcome. Sports columnist Ed Brennan wrote in the *Jersey Journal*, "They were strangers in their own hometown. [They] played in obscurity at spacious Roosevelt Stadium."

They drew only 47,715 fans in thirty-eight home games, an average of only 1,647 per game. Winning twenty-two and losing sixteen at home, they compiled an overall record of 29–27 after leaving Havana. A pitcher named Zack Monroe, who had won four against two losses for the 1958 New York Yankees, hurled the 1960 home finale for the Jerseys, winning it on a five-hitter.

If the 1960 season was mediocre, 1961 was disastrous. As the season drew near its close on September 1, the hardworking Monroe raised his record to 10–12 with a 3–1 win over third-place Charleston. But the team was submerged in seventh place with a 65–76 record, twenty-two games behind first-place Columbus. In addition to Columbus and Charleston, Jersey City had to look up to Buffalo, Toronto, Rochester, and Richmond. Only Syracuse lagged behind.

It came as little surprise, then, when the Jersey City franchise was used to open the International League's new Atlanta territory in 1962. With that, minor league baseball disappeared for good from the Garden State.

Even the old ball parks are gone now. Ruppert and Roosevelt stadiums have been torn down. Dunn Field was replaced by a Penn Fruit store, which in turn gave way to the headquarters of the New Jersey Lottery—an ironic segue from baseball to betting in this age of organized baseball's gambling angst.

THE FUTURE OF THE MINOR LEAGUES IN NEW JERSEY

It now appears that minor league baseball may be on the Garden State's doorstep once more. As we write this the state's newspapers have been full of stories about the plans of an investment banking group out of Chester named Cathedra. These stories (which erroneously report that Jersey City had a minor league team as late as 1970) at first named several possible sites for a new team—including Somerville, Bridgewater, Woodbridge, Wayne, and Parsippany. Cathedra representatives made presentations in the fall of 1988 to the authorities of some of these towns, stating the desire to build a ball park seating five to ten thousand, with easy access and plenty of parking. They refused to name the teams with whom they were negotiating to move to New Jersey. It was subsequently reported, though, that they had tried and failed to buy the Double A Williamsport Bills of the Eastern League and the Triple A franchise in Oklahoma City.

On June 20, 1989, Cathedra and Great Adventure announced an agreement to "permit construction of" a $6 million stadium on sixty acres near the Jackson Township theme park's main entrance. (Later stories reduced this field of dreams to fifty acres.) Still the Cathedra executives were silent on the team they might bring in. They said, however, that play could start at the Great Adventure site as early as the spring of 1990.

But then in late February 1990 came the disappointing news that opening day for New Jersey's new minor league team would be delayed until 1991. Still no word on where the team would come from.

Can minor league ball really make a comeback in New Jersey? Television, which purportedly killed the minors here nearly forty years ago, is still around, and better than ever when it comes to covering sports. On the other hand, the caliber of nearby major league baseball has slipped considerably since the heyday of the Yanks, Dodgers, Giants, and Phillies. Perhaps Jerseyans *would* rather come out to see live minor league ball rather than watch mediocre or inconsistent major league fare on the tube—or battle increasingly aggravating traffic to the major league ball parks.

Assuming that Garden Staters would support a team, would and could they do so with sufficient frequency to make the investment pay off for the backers? The *Trenton Times* of July 3, 1988, quotes Miles Wolff, owner of the Durham Bulls, on this matter: "Investors probably will not see a quick return on their investment," said the head man of the North Carolina team that served as a model for the movie *Bull Durham*. "A 5,500-seat stadium, selling $6 tickets, would need sellout crowds every night of the 71-game schedule for the enterprise to earn $2.34 million. At that rate, it could take more than five years for the project to pay off itself," said Wolff. "Day-to-day operating expenses and the likelihood of rain outs would delay the return on investment even further."

CHAPTER 5

An Inning in the Big Time

Newark in the Federal League

Banished to Harrisburg by the Federal League Peps in 1915, the International League Indians returned to Newark in 1916, but could not recapture their pennant-winning ways of 1913. (Courtesy of Newark Public Library)

On April 16, 1915, the *Newark Evening News* headlined: "AIR RAIDERS HIT ENGLAND AGAIN TODAY." The article revealed that aerial bombing had room for growth as a tool of mass destruction: "Zeppelins again bombed British towns, causing $150,000 property damage and injuring woman and girl." Also prominent on that front page was an analysis of President Woodrow Wilson's role in Democratic politics at home in New Jersey. In sum, he was leaving the situation "to friends who are expected to hew the line marked out." Aside from the mayhem of war and politics, the front-page news of the day ranged from official corruption to untimely death to a "virtual paroxysm of emotion" by evangelist and ex-big leaguer Billy Sunday at his new tabernacle in Paterson.

But the real news for many readers appeared beneath a headline just a little smaller than that of the war story and more prominent than the one covering the president's views on who should run for governor. "BASEBALL LID OFF AT LAST," it declared. The story described the festivities preceding the home opener of the Garden State's only universally recognized major league baseball team—the Newark Peps of the Federal League.

As the paper went to press that day, more than thirty-two thousand fans, a record for a Federal League game and not too shabby for any league, jammed the new stadium across the Passaic River in Harrison. The *New York Times* would colorfully report that "Newark and its surrounding hamlets were seized with a violent attack of baseball yesterday, accompanied by a high fever and laryngitis."

Unhappily, the Baltimore Terrapins thrashed the Peps 6–2, evening the Newarkers' record for the young season at 3–3 and dropping them into fourth place in the eight-team league behind the Brooklyn Tip Tops, the Chicago Whales, and the Kansas City Packers. But the loss did not diminish Newark's joy at finally having made the big leagues.

A YEAR EARLIER, when the Federal League launched its assault on the entrenched National League (founded 1876) and the still slightly green Americans (1901), the team that would become the Newark Peps made its home in Indianapolis and called itself the Hoosiers. Joining the Hoosiers, Terrapins, Tip Tops, Whales, and Packers for the 1914 season were the Pittsburgh Rebels, St. Louis Terriers, and Buffalo BufFeds.

In simplest terms, the Federal League challenge to organized baseball could be called a case of haves versus have-nots, though the have-nots

The 1915 Federal League Newark Peps, who finished in fifth place only six games out of first, were New Jersey's first and only major league team. (National Baseball Library, Cooperstown, N.Y.)

hardly needed charity. Whereas several wealthy men of the day owned major league baseball teams, a lot of other wealthy men did not—and some were determined to correct that deficiency. Among them were St. Louis brewer Otto Stifel and his partner, Phil Ball; Chicago restaurateur Charles Weeghman; brothers Robert B. and George S. Ward of Brooklyn's Ward Baking Company, purveyors of Tip Top bread; and most important for New Jersey, oil tycoon Harry F. Sinclair of Tulsa, Oklahoma, and his partner, Trenton-born Patrick T. Powers, then of Jersey City.

The have-nots had already tried buying their way into the major leagues, only to be rebuffed. The alternative was to lever themselves into the big time by forming a new league to compete with the majors at the turnstiles. A successful, hard-driving bunch used to making things happen, these men decided to take a chance. Their rallying cry may well have been, "If you can't join 'em, beat 'em." They had nothing to lose but money, a commodity in large supply in their ranks; together they came up with $50 million, a great deal of money at the time, to pay for players and ball parks. Though their league was gone by 1916, some used the peace negotiations with the Nationals and Americans to secure the place they coveted in the major leagues. Others, like Harry Sinclair, sold off their players and ball parks piecemeal and walked away wealthier, if disenfranchised.

But the twisting road to that end, weaving in and out of law courts and moving ballplayers around like so many chess pieces, was all in the future on that April day in 1914 when the Hoosiers, Whales, and friends first took to the Federal League diamonds.

The Federal League actually had begun the previous season as a six-team midwestern circuit, which showed its mettle by completing a 120-game schedule. But in 1913 there was no pretense of major league status. Class D was more like it—and the inability to compete for fans in four cities with big league teams almost led to the collapse of the league in mid-season. What turned it all around in the winter of 1913–1914 was the appointment of an energetic and well-connected league president, Chicago coal magnate James A. Gilmore. He convinced Stifel, Weeghman, the Wards, Sinclair, and the others that a Federal League franchise was the way to the promised land.

If these would-be moguls of baseball knew anything, they knew they could never call themselves "major league" until they staffed their clubs with bona fide major league ballplayers. The problem, of course, was that all the major leaguers were already in the National and American leagues.

"No problem," said they. "We'll buy us some major leaguers." And they did just that. Weeghman and his Whales got Joe Tinker—the front end of the famous Tinker-to-Evers-to-Chance double play combination of the Chicago Cubs. Mordecai ("Three Finger") Brown, who had won twenty games or more in each of six consecutive seasons for the Cubs despite mangling his pitching hand in a farming accident, defected to the St. Louis Terriers. Otto Knabe, star second baseman of the Philadelphia Phillies, became player-manager of the Baltimore Terrapins. Altogether, the Federal League seduced 172 players with major league experience, six of them future Hall of Famers: Tinker, Brown, Chief Bender, Eddie Plank, Bill McKechnie, and Edd Roush.

Whether they jumped to the Federal League or stayed in the National or American, players loved the soaring salaries created by the bidding war for their services. Federal League owners had reason to be pleased, too, as fans received their teams with an enthusiasm rivaling what the Nationals and Americans enjoyed. (It did not hurt that they were playing in eight spanking new ball parks, which contrasted markedly with the shabbiness of some of organized ball's emporiums.) Only the bosses of the incumbent major leagues were unhappy, and they took their displeasure to the courts, bringing suit for contract infringement against Federal clubs that signed their players.

In this atmosphere of legal wrangling, and with the sporting press taking delight in "the baseball war," the 1914 season got under way. On opening day in Baltimore, the Terrapins beat the BufFeds 3–2 before a crowd of twenty-five thousand at brand new Terrapin Park. It was the largest crowd ever to witness a baseball game at the birthplace of "The Star-Spangled Banner." A fly ball away at Oriole Park, a meager band of one thousand watched John McGraw's National League New York Giants beat the International League Baltimore Orioles in the Giants' last exhibition game of spring training, also by 3–2. A young pitcher by the name of George Herman Ruth took the loss for the Orioles.

As the season unfolded and war clouds gathered over Europe that summer of 1914, the Indianapolis Hoosiers enjoyed victory. Blessed with future Hall of Famers McKechnie and Roush, plus eventual batting champ Benny Kauff (.366), the club nosed out Tinker's Whales by one and a half games despite twenty-nine victories by Chicago ace Claude Hendrix. In addition to an exciting race for the pennant, Federal League fans were treated to a no-hitter and nearly three hundred home runs, a few more than hammered by the Nationals and more than double the output of the Americans.

MEANWHILE in minor league Newark, the thirst for good professional baseball was being slaked by the Newark Indians of the International League. Though not a major league club, the Indians had a major league owner in Charles H. Ebbets, Sr., proprietor of Brooklyn's Ebbets Field and paymaster of the National League Brooklyn Superbas. (This crew also answered to the nickname Trolley Dodgers, later shortened to just plain Dodgers.)

The main event for Newark fans in 1914 was the Indians' attempt to defend their 1913 league championship (first since 1896) under the direction of new club president Charles H. Ebbets, Jr. To repeat as pennant winners, the Indians would have to beat the arch-rival Jersey City Skeeters as well as the Baltimore Orioles and teams from Rochester, Toronto, Providence, Montreal, and Buffalo. To enjoy the confidence of their fans, they also would have to stay clear of the gamblers, whose growing penetration of the national pastime would culminate five years later in the Black Sox scandal of 1919. The Ebbetses, father and son, swore to keep the gamblers out of Weidenmayer's Park, the Indians' home field. The park carried the name of prominent Newarker Gus A. Weidenmayer, who also was a stockholder in the club.

The Indians held spring training that year in Columbus, Georgia, coming north to a refurbished Weidenmayer's Park to play a final exhibition game against the New York Yankees. Emphasizing the Ebbetses' commitment to Newark, the team found its park equipped with new lockers, a new press box, and new box seats for better-heeled fans. But it was to be a tough season. The Indians got off to a slow start, struggled through the summer, and arrived at mid-September with a 56–83 record that mired them in sixth place. They could take little comfort from noting that the cellar housed the Skeeters, better known as the Pests to Newark sportswriters and fans. Cooler weather must have agreed with them, though. They proceeded to win most of their remaining games, nearly thwarting Providence's drive to snatch the International League pennant from Rochester, and rising to fifth place in the bargain. The season ended with a split doubleheader at Jersey City's West Side Park, laying one last loss on the well-swatted Skeeters (106 defeats for the season). When the Ebbetses tallied the books for the season, they found themselves eighty thousand dollars in the red.

BY CONTRAST, when the bosses of the Federal League assessed their first season in the fall of 1914, they had reason to feel good about their performance in relation to organized ball. Certainly they had fielded a respectable product, causing considerable fan defection from the other circuits. (National and American League attendance dropped from 6.36 million in 1913 to 4.45 million in 1914; Federal League clubs outdrew the entries of the other leagues in some cities, most notably Chicago, where Tinkers's Whales proved far more popular than the Cubs.)

But it had been a difficult season financially for the Federals, as well as for the Nationals and Americans (and an absolute disaster for International League clubs, which had to compete with the Federals). The Federals had poured money into the new ball parks. Buying players had been expensive for the Federals, though hardly less so than holding on to players had been for the Nationals and Americans. (A lot of top players found their salaries doubled, even tripled, in 1914.) And then there was the cost of lawsuits. On the income side of the ledger, meanwhile, Federal games conflicted with those of the established leagues (including the American Association and the International League) no fewer than 264 times.

For Newark, though, all this had a positive side. Federal League officials, with an eye on a bigger share of the lucrative New York metropolitan market, wanted to put a franchise in the Bronx or Newark, or both, in 1915. The best candidates for transfer were the undersubscribed Kansas City Packer franchise and the deep-in-debt Indianapolis Hoosier club (the latter proving that athletic success does not guarantee a fat bank account).

And so for several confusing weeks in the 1915 preseason, Newark had not one but two major league teams. Or at least it did not know which of the two it was going to get. Or it was not sure it was going to get any at all. The *Newark Evening News* had to cover two spring training camps, the Hoosiers-cum-Peps in Valdosta, Georgia, and the Packers-cum-Peps in Marshall, Texas.

The road to this strange juncture began when league officials pulled Kansas City's franchise and sold it to Harry Sinclair and Pat Powers for twenty-five thousand dollars. But citizens of Kansas City suddenly developed an attachment to the team that had not been evident at the turnstiles during the season. They wanted to keep the team and took their case to court, succeeding in getting an injunction against the sale. Someone then suggested sending the Indianapolis team to Kansas City so that the Packers could come to Newark. People of more direct mind said that they should just send the Hoosiers to Newark and leave Kansas City alone. This solution snagged on the fact that Indianapolis had already sold its two best players—batting champion Kauff and ace hurler Falkenberg—to the Tip Tops. Sportswriters opined that the Tip Tops would never relinquish Kauff and Falkenberg, and that Sinclair and Powers would not take the Hoosiers without them. So the Kansas City solution remained a possibility, and Newark sportswriters kept covering both spring camps.

But the owners proved more practical than the writers gave them credit for. At a meeting at the Biltmore Hotel in New York only two weeks before opening day 1915, they agreed that the Tip Tops would keep Kauff and Newark would get Falkenberg. Everyone departed more or less happy.

While all this was going on, the question of a ball park for the former Hoosiers or the former Packers was being resolved. Three sites emerged as "possibles"—one at the corner of South Orange Avenue and Boylan Street, where semipro ball was being played; a second in the Weequahic section; and the third at the Harrison Oval in Harrison. Midway through January 1915 the sale of the South Orange Avenue tract spurred rumors it would be home to the Newark Feds. In the end, the Harrison site was chosen, but not before Sinclair and Powers threatened to take their show to the Bronx. One Bronx location considered during that squeeze play was the future site of Yankee Stadium. (The Yankees, only recently renamed after years as the Highlanders, were still playing at the Polo Grounds.) What saved the day for Newark was a combination of Sinclair and Powers getting the terms they wanted in Harrison plus the opportunity to play Sunday ball in New Jersey (New York State was still enforcing its "blue laws" against professional sporting events on the sabbath).

There still remained the challenge of getting a ball park built in time for the season. The construction schedule seems incredible today and was thought next to impossible even then: groundbreaking did not occur until March 1 and the Peps' home opener was scheduled for April 16. Powers, who had been president of the International League, took charge, driving his contractors relentlessly. He installed arc lights to keep crews working through the night, well before they became a fixture of night games.

The 1915 Peps shaped up as a team that could repeat its pennant-winning ways of the year before despite the absence of Kauff. In addition to getting Falkenberg, McKechnie, Roush, and the rest of 1914's champion Hoosier squad, Sinclair and Powers had purchased three other quality players: Herman ("Germany") Schaefer, a switch-hitting first baseman from the Washington Senators; Ed Reulbach, a right-handed pitcher from the Brooklyn Superbas; and Chester ("Chick") Brandom, another rightie hurler who had labored the previous year for the International League's Buffalo team.

In a baseball era abounding with colorful nicknames, Chick and Germany had teammates called "Whoa Bill" (Phillips, the manager), "Kaiser" (pitcher George Kaiserling), "Jap" (outfielder Albert Scheer), and "Newt" (Harry Billiard, another pitcher). "Mose," "Trout," "Hunnie," "Tex," and "Whitey" were pitchers Earl Moseley and Fred Trautman, first bagger Emil Huhn, catcher George Textor, and outfielder Gilbert Whitehouse. And of course the team had a "Lefty" (southpaw pitcher Harry Moran). Everyone else made do with his given name.

Starting for the Peps in their home opener on April 16, 1915, were right fielder Vinnie Campbell, who would lead the team in batting; third baseman McKechnie, who would finish the season managing the team; center fielder Roush; captain and second baseman Frankie LaPorte; first baseman Schaefer; shortstop Jimmy Esmond; left fielder Scheer; catcher Bill Rariden; and pitcher Falkenberg. Except for the pitcher's slot and first base, this lineup generally would start for the Peps throughout the season, with Huhn taking over at first and Schaefer playing a utility role. For all the hoopla over who would have Falkenberg, he contributed relatively little to the Peps' success. It may have been an omen that he hit much better than he pitched that opening day, getting two of the Peps' six hits but giving the Terps thirteen in return.

April proved a happy month for the Peps. After splitting their first home series with Baltimore, they took three of four from Brooklyn and two of three from Buffalo to spend the last few days of the month in first place. Rariden was leading the team's hitters with a .360 average and the Kaiser was 3–0 on the mound. On May 6, the Federal League turned its first triple play, a rare one indeed because it began in the Brooklyn outfield. But baseball took a backseat to world affairs a day later, when a German submarine sank the British ocean liner *Lusitania* off the coast of Ireland, resulting in a loss of 1,198 lives. Among the dead were 128 Americans, and the United States was drawn a step closer to entering World War I.

Losing two of three to the St. Louis Terriers early in May dropped the Peps to third, but they drove back into second by taking three in a row from the Whales. The rest of the month saw them oscillate between second and fourth, losing four to Kansas City and three more to St. Louis for an overall record of 20–17. On Memorial Day, they played the first of what may stand as the most unusual doubleheaders of all time. In a

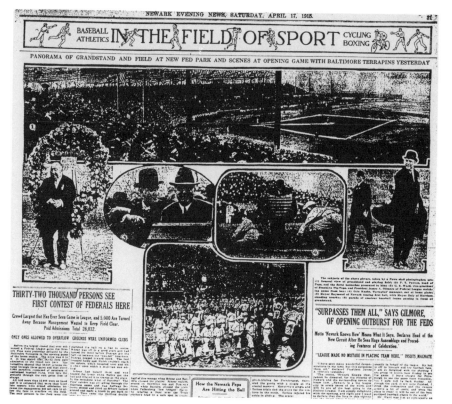

The *Newark Evening News* of April 17, 1915, heralded record attendance at the home opener of the Federal League's Newark Peps.

Amateur teams paraded before a record crowd at the
Newark Peps' home opener, as team members looked on
from the infield. (Courtesy of Newark Public Library)

move to maximize holiday attendance in their most populous market, Federal League schedulers decreed that Newark would play Brooklyn twice each holiday. Furthermore, they would play one game in each city. So on May 31, 1915, the Tip Tops trooped to Newark for a morning game and the Peps repaid with a visit to Brooklyn for an afternoon contest. To maintain the perfect symmetry of the day, both teams won 5–3 on their home grounds.

Campbell had taken over team batting honors by this time with a .346 average, while Moseley (3–1) and Moran (7–4) led the pitchers. Across the river at Weidenmayer's Park, the Indians had finished May with a 9–16 record that earned them last place in the International League (which now had a Richmond franchise replacing the Baltimore Oriole club that had been demolished at the turnstile by the Federal League Terrapins the previous season).

The Peps opened June with a pair of wins over the Terrapins, who ended up being Newark's biggest patsies by dropping seventeen of twenty-three contests between the two teams. But Brooklyn and Buffalo proved tougher, each taking three of five from the Peps, and the Terriers terrorized Newark with a four-game sweep. That put the Peps below .500 (26–27) and in sixth place for the first time. Sinclair and Powers said, "Whoa, Bill!" to manager Whoa Bill Phillips, handing the reins to McKechnie.

McKechnie hardly ignited the league in his first two weeks as manager. June ended with the Peps in fifth place at 33–33, having dropped a pair to the Whales, who hovered just above them in fourth. Campbell was the league's third-best batter at .350, while Moran's team-leading mound record stood at 7–5. Earlier rumors that the International League would move the Newark Indians to Harrisburg proved true, with the first game in its new home scheduled for July 2. And to make matters worse, the club was being sued for $1,750 in back rent by the Reliable Improvement Co. of Newark. The Indians decamped with a 25–26 record, not far from being the best in town.

July got under way for the Peps with a two-game sweep of Brooklyn and five wins in seven games with Baltimore. During the fifth game of the Terrapin series, the Federal League experimented with cut-rate prices—five cents in the pavilions and fifty cents in the grandstand. (The *Newark Evening News* was then selling for three cents a copy.) Judged a grand success when eighteen thousand bought tickets, the idea was picked up by Brooklyn three days later.

A split of four games with Buffalo, capped by Moseley's three-hit shutout, brought Newark to four games over .500 on July 15. Two days later the Peps failed to solve the Packers, ultimately escaping from Kansas City with one victory in four games thanks to another three-hit shutout by Moseley, his second in four days. Then two close losses to the Rebels of Pittsburgh reduced the Newarkers to .500 once again, and they appeared to be a permanent fixture in fifth place. As the Peps won one and tied one in a Sunday doubleheader the next day, the excursion steamer *Eastland* capsized in the Chicago River, drowning 1,718. The city went into mourning, and no baseball games were played for two days. No lives were lost later that week when a German submarine sank the U.S. cargo ship *Leelanaw* carrying flax from Archangel on Russia's Pacific coast to Belfast. But war inched a bit closer to the United States.

As July 1915 drew to a close, an umpire named Corcoran had reason to wish he had chosen a gentler line of work. In the first game of a doubleheader between Kansas City and Brooklyn, Packer manager George Stovall became enraged at one of Corcoran's calls and punched him. Not to be outdone, manager Lee Magee of the Tip Tops did the same in game two. Magee probably was still irritated over an incident a few days before in St. Louis. A sheriff with orders to grab a star outfielder who had jumped a National League contract waited until the eighth inning of the doubleheader's second game to do so. Brooklyn dropped both contests. The Peps meanwhile finished the month at 49–44, thanks in large measure to a three-game sweep in St. Louis, coupled with splits elsewhere. They continued to own fifth place, however. Campbell, still leading the team in batting, had slumped to .321 and twelfth in the league, while Moran continued to top the pitching staff with an 8–6 record.

News from other leagues arrived early in August. There was a plan in organized baseball to buy a large Georgia estate where all the teams could conduct joint spring training. And the troubled Jersey City Skeeters of the International League, bereft of their longtime rivals in Newark, were rumored to be moving to New London, Connecticut.

The Peps put together an eight-game winning streak over Chicago and Kansas City. It culminated on August 9 with a doubleheader victory over the Packers and elevation to second place on a record of 56–44, just one game behind the first-place Whales. (In those days, newspaper rankings did not include "games behind," which let winning percentage determine position.) The Peps' streak included three consecutive extra-inning games of twelve, sixteen, and thirteen frames.

The next two weeks saw the Peps on a roller coaster, sliding as far as fourth, climbing back to second, slipping to third, soaring into a tie for first at mid-month, then dipping twice to third and rebounding to first before settling into second on August 24. They won seven and lost six in the period, as Campbell stabilized his average at .319 (tenth in the league) and Reulbach took over as team mound leader with his twelfth victory against seven defeats. Both Reulbach and Kaiserling turned in two-hitters during the dog days.

On the Rio Grande at August's end, U.S. troops attempted to protect the citizens of Texas against raids by Mexican bandits. The abdication of President Porfirio Díaz in 1911 had thrown Mexico into a revolution from which it had not yet emerged. Competing armies and bandit gangs stormed across the landscape, with the bandits, at least, respecting no borders. An odd convergence of the Mexican Revolution and the baseball war occurred a few months later when a group of Mexican baseball people applied to organized baseball for a sanctioned league south of the border. Seeking any small psychological advantage over their Federal League challengers, the moguls of organized baseball agreed to meet with the Mexicans while still proclaiming no interest in peace talks with the Federals.

The Peps, unfortunately, had seen the best of their season in August with their brief stay in first place and their high-water mark of fourteen games over .500. They hit that mark again on September 2 with a 9–1 win over Buffalo, but then the long slide began. A three-game losing streak and a seven-game losing streak, mostly to Brooklyn, drove them down to five games over break-even at 67–62 and into fourth place. They rebounded to eight games over but failed to escape fourth, slipped, then battled to eight games over again at season's end, landing in fifth for their trouble. Some other teams simply were playing outstanding ball.

September 1915 was full of war news, both in and out of baseball. On September 1, Germany promised not to sink passenger liners without warning. Four days later it torpedoed the Allan Lines' *Hesperian* without a word. On the third, a detailed rumor about a baseball peace plan surfaced. The Federal League, it went, would open the 1916 season as a third major league under the National Commission (organized baseball's governing body). In return, the Federals would withdraw from Chicago and St. Louis and would not invade New York. The status of Newark and Baltimore was unresolved.

On September 6, Newark and Brooklyn played another of their home-away doubleheaders, but there was no symmetry in this one: the Tip Tops took both ends, 5–1 and 1–0. And on the tenth, Albert Goodwill Spalding died. Spalding had been a towering figure in baseball—as a player, a manager, and an executive. He began his playing career in 1865 with the Forest Citys, one of the early professional teams. He helped organize the National League in 1876. A shrewd businessman, he saw the commercial possibilities in baseball and exploited them, building two successful companies—A. G. Spalding & Bros. and American Sports Publishing.

President Gilmore of the Federal League challenged organized ball to a tripartite World Series. Organized ball cut him dead. A few days later, the *New York Times* headlined "20,000 JAPS SEE BALL GAME," going on to report that a baseball team from the University of Chicago had defeated one from Waseda University by a score of 5–3. The month closed with the news that Newark would host the 1916 Amateur Athletic Union track and field championships, and that the Great Allied Offensive in the West had begun and twenty thousand Germans had been taken prisoner.

A few days into October, the Federal League concluded its second season. Table 3 points to some interesting differences between baseball in 1915 and today. For instance, there were fewer homers then and far more triples. This might be due to that era's larger ball parks, acceptable to fans less enthralled than today's with the long ball. There also were more complete games pitched, perhaps because relieving had not yet become the highly refined specialty it is today.

Fifth-place Newark finished only six games out of first. (In the National League that year, second-place Boston finished seven games behind Philadelphia.) Had the Peps made up another of their rainouts, they might have tied for fourth with the Packers. If both teams had played their full 154-game schedules, the Peps might even have taken fourth all alone. Chicago, St. Louis, and Pittsburgh could have finished in a half dozen different orders had Chicago and Pittsburgh played all their games, as St. Louis did. Why were so many games left unplayed? One reason could be that there was no place to go—no World Series to play—after finishing first. Another could be that making up games was not so easy in that pre–air travel, pre–night game era.

Newark's strength clearly lay in pitching (see Table 4). The staff finished first in earned-run average and was the only Federal League mound crew to reach one hundred complete games. Ed Reulbach, in his eleventh professional season at age thirty-two, led the staff with a 20–10 record.

TABLE 3
The Federal League's 1915 Season

	Wins	Losses	Percentage	Batting Average	Home Runs	Triples	Doubles	Complete Games	Strikeouts	Earned Run Average
Chicago	86	66	.566	.257	50	77	185	97	576	2.64
St. Louis	87	67	.565	.261	23	81	199	94	698	2.73
Pittsburgh	86	67	.562	.262	20	80	180	88	517	2.79
Kansas City	81	72	.529	.244	27	66	200	95	626	2.82
Newark	80	72	.526	.252	17	80	210	100	581	2.60
Buffalo	74	78	.487	.249	40	68	193	79	594	3.38
Brooklyn	70	82	.461	.268	36	75	205	78	467	3.37
Baltimore	47	107	.305	.244	36	53	196	85	570	3.96

Newark's leading statistics are in italics.

TABLE 4
The Newark Peps' 1915 Season

	Games	Innings Pitched	Won	Lost	Earned Run Average	Batting Average	Home Runs	Runs Batted In	Errors
Reulbach	33	270	20	10	2.23				
Moran	34	206	13	10	2.54				
Moseley	38	268	16	16	1.91				
Kaiserling	41	261	13	14	2.24				
Falkenberg	25	172	9	11	3.24				
Seaton	12	75	3	6	2.28				
Campbell (right field)						.310	1	44	2
Roush (center field)						.298	3	60	10
Rariden (catcher)						.270	0	40	21
Scheer (left field)						.267	2	60	9
Esmond (shortstop)						.258	5	62	54
LaPorte (second base)						.253	2	56	32
McKechnie (third base)						.251	1	43	19
Huhn (first base)						.227	1	41	16
Schaefer (utility)						.214	0	8	7

Lefty Moran, a youngster of twenty-four, was second at 13–10 in his fourth season as a pro. Moseley, who won sixteen but dropped just as many, had a sparkling 1.91 earned-run average, best in the league. He clearly had a case against the team for nonsupport. Falkenberg compiled a mediocre 9–11 record prior to his trade to Brooklyn for Tom Seaton.

At bat, the Peps led the league in doubles but could do no better than fifth in average and were dead last in home runs, popping only seventeen while the league-leading Whales hammered three times as many. Vinnie Campbell, twenty-seven, who broke into professional ball with the Chicago Cubs in 1912, led the Peps in batting at .310, good for sixth in the league. His runner-up was Edd Roush (.298), who at twenty-one was just beginning his Hall of Fame career. A Hoosier through and through, Edd was born in Indiana and had never played pro ball anywhere else until coming to New Jersey. Bill McKechnie, at twenty-seven, had a better year managing than playing, hinting at the talent that would get him into the Hall of Fame. He batted only .251, but took over a 26–27 team and guided it to a 54–45 record the rest of the way. In the field, Bill Rariden tied for the league lead in errors by catchers.

In October 1915 President Wilson announced his engagement to Mrs. Norman Galt, a widow. The former Edith Bolling would one day guide the stroke-impaired hand of her husband in signing official documents as he watched his hopes for the League of Nations go down to defeat in the Senate. On October 20, New Jersey voters rejected a state constitutional amendment to give women the vote. The president came home to vote yes, whereas his fiancée told the press she was against it.

On the baseball front, the Boston Red Sox clobbered the Phillies in the World Series, four games to one. The Cubs and the White Sox played a series for the championship of Chicago. A keeper of injury statistics announced that there had been fifty-nine deaths attributed to baseball in the season just concluded. And on October 26, lights for night baseball were tested at the Washington Park field of the Brooklyn Tip Tops. (New York sportswriters refused to go along with the Ward brothers in promoting their bread through their baseball team; by common agreement, they referred to the Federal League's Brooklyn team not as the Tip Tops but as the BrookFeds.)

The no-news news of the month was that U.S. district court judge Kenesaw Mountain Landis, future commissioner of baseball (1920–1944), once again delayed ruling on the suit brought by the Federal League against organized baseball the previous January. This time he said he would not rule "until at least December."

THE FEDERAL LEAGUE'S ANTITRUST SUIT

When the Federal League filed its antitrust suit against the National League and its eight teams on January 5, 1915, both sides hoped Judge Landis would move the affair along to a speedy conclusion. Instead, he brought it to a speedy beginning and no conclusion at all.

Landis called for initial hearings on the suit just six days after its filing. Curious spectators packed the courtroom to watch some of the highest-priced legal talent in the land argue the case. The total cost of the suit in the end was said to have run about $10 million. The testimony was seemingly endless, often vitriolic, and sometimes downright silly. One newspaper headline on a story about some Federal League testimony proclaimed, "TWO BALL PLAYERS TRADED FOR DOGS." The dogs, it turned out, were hunting animals owned by a player, who sold them to the manager of a team that subsequently traded the player.

What the Federal League wanted was for the court to dismiss all suits brought by organized baseball against players who had jumped contracts to play in the new league. In effect, this would release ten thousand major and minor league players from their contracts, creating a salary free-for-all that many thought would destroy professional baseball. Judge Landis stood among those who feared for the future of baseball should the Federal League prevail. But he seems also to have found some legal validity in their case. All this added up to his unannounced decision to delay ruling until the matter got settled out of court. Although never saying as much, Landis probably signaled his intent early on by questioning the jurisdiction of his court in the case.

Though Landis then proceeded to sit on the suit throughout 1915, activity in other courts continued. In one case that set a precedent dangerous to organized baseball, a judge ruled that the St. Louis Terriers could keep Armando Marsans because his contract with the Cincinnati Reds was not binding. But 1915 saw much more jockeying for position in the newspapers than in the courts. At various times during the year the following stories appeared:

- Organized Baseball announced it would reduce the size of its rosters, thereby throwing many players out of work. (The cut players could not be absorbed by the troubled minor leagues without equivalent cuts farther down the ranks.)
- The Federal League announced it would slash rosters to twenty, but

organize the cut players into a high-quality minor league to compete with the American Association and International League.

* Organized baseball said it would turn the American Association into a third major league and staff it with better players than the Federal League.

* The National League New York Giants tried to lure leading slugger Benny Kauff away from the Brooklyn Tip Tops, and appeared on two occasions to have succeeded. But the Tip Tops hung on. The Feds kept trying to snare top players.

* Federal League owners took to saying that O.B. (organized baseball) stood for "Organized Bluff."

* Organized baseball moguls retaliated by calling the Federal League "the Lunchroom Circuit" (after the restaurants of Whales owner Weeghman) and "the Flapjack Circuit" (after the flour-based interests of the Tip Tops ownership).

In November, the women's suffrage movement suffered when the voters of New York, Massachusetts, and Pennsylvania defeated proposed amendments to their state constitutions. A Swiss military statistician calculated that "the war to end all wars" had so far cost five million lives. And Robert B. Ward, co-owner of the Tip Tops and a major force of the Federal League, died.

The remaining owners of the insurgent league met on November 10, declared their Kansas City franchise to be "in forfeit," and announced that the Packers would play in New York in 1916. The proposed site of their field was at 145th Street and Lenox Avenue in Manhattan. Spokesmen for the league were cagey about who would own the New York franchise, but Harry Sinclair was not. "I will own it," he said, reminding one and all that when he bought the Indianapolis franchise, he was buying the rights to New York.

In the offices of professional baseball, the fiscal results of 1915 had been tallied. Only four American League teams appear to have made any money, and either three or four National League clubs finished in the black, depending on which report one reads. Two Federal League franchises—Chicago and St. Louis—made money, but only a very little. Federal League ball definitely had hurt organized baseball at the box office for the second year running. But the truth is that professional baseball as a whole had been hurting for at least four years.

"What's wrong with baseball?" some writers were asking. No one really knew, but worsening economic conditions had to have been part of the problem. The cost of living was going up each year and many feared economic depression. Add to this the growing gloom of the war in Europe and the instability on the Mexican border, and baseball men realized that continuing their feud could lead them all to bankruptcy. Conditions were ripe for peace in baseball.

Newspapers reported that peace was in sight after a December 14 meeting in New York between representatives of the National and Federal leagues. It was said that Phil Ball of the St. Louis Terriers would be allowed to buy the St. Louis Cardinals, that Charles Weeghman would be sold the Chicago Cubs, and that Harry Sinclair and George Ward would get American League franchises. But when American League owners joined the party the next day, they brought with them some different ideas. Three days before Christmas 1915, in Cincinnati, the baseball peace treaty finally was signed. Its major provisions were:

- Weeghman buys the Cubs.
- Ball buys not the Cardinals, but the St. Louis Browns of the American League.
- Organized baseball reinstates all players who jumped to the Federal League.
- Federal League owners assume responsibility for the contracts of their players, but can sell them (except the Whales and the Terriers) to the highest bidder.
- Organized baseball reimburses the Wards four hundred thousand dollars for the loss of the Brooklyn opportunity.
- The Federal League withdraws its lawsuit.

There were reports in the midst of all this that Harry Sinclair would buy the New York Giants. But it never happened.

And what of the Newark Peps? Among the fifty-nine Federal Leaguers picked up for the 1916 season by the National and American Leagues were nine members of the Peps, including the traded Falkenberg.

Edd Roush went on to the most illustrious playing career of the nine. He spent sixteen more years in the majors, all of them with either the New York Giants or the Cincinnati Reds, toiling for both in 1916. He compiled an enviable lifetime batting average of .323, hit a high of .352 in two seasons, and led all National League batters twice. He also led the league once each in doubles and triples, and played in a World Series. He was elected to the Hall of Fame in 1962.

Bill McKechnie had most of his big league playing career behind him when he played for Newark in 1915. Like Roush, he wound up with both the Giants and the Reds in 1916, then spent two years with the Pittsburgh Pirates and was done. What got him into the Hall of Fame, also in 1962, were the twenty-four years he spent managing in the majors—for the Braves, Pirates, Reds, and Cardinals. He managed 3,650 games (seventh on the all-time list) and won 1,898 of them (eighth). He took his teams to four World Series over a span of fifteen years and came away with victories twice.

Ed Reulbach, like McKechnie, was on the far side of the hill by the time he arrived in New Jersey. He went to the Boston Braves in 1916, winning seven and losing six, then tailed off to 0–1 in 1917 before hanging it up. But in a fine thirteen-year career in the majors, he compiled a record of 185–104 and an earned-run average of 2.28. He played in four World Series, winning two games and losing none.

Bill Rariden joined the Giants in 1916, staying for three seasons, then wrapped up a twelve-year big league career with a couple of summers in Cincinnati. He had a lifetime batting average of only .237, but he must have been a "Mr. October" of his day, hitting .281 in two World Series.

Emil Huhn went on to play two undistinguished seasons with Cincinnati, compiling a mediocre .229 lifetime batting average.

Herman Schaefer, too, spent only two more years in the majors, 1916 with the Yankees and 1918 with Cleveland. But he had played professional ball since 1900, owned a respectable lifetime batting average of .257 in the majors, and could look back on playing in two World Series.

Tom Seaton finished up a six-year big league career with Chicago, going 10–10 for the combined 1916–1917 seasons. His career totals were far superior, at 93–64.

Earl Moseley never fulfilled the promise of his Federal League–leading earned-run average. He slipped to 3.89 with Cincinnati in 1916, compiled a record of 7–10, and was gone from the majors.

Cy Falkenberg had been at his best with the 1914 Hoosiers, leading the Federal League in strikeouts (236), shutouts (9), games (49), starts (43), and innings pitched (377). He returned briefly to the majors with the 1917 Philadelphia Athletics, adding two wins and six losses for a career record of 129–123.

Scheer, Esmond, Campbell, LaPorte, Kaiserling, and Moran were seen no more in the majors.

No one associated with the Peps became better known in ensuing years than Harry Ford Sinclair. He seems to have forgotten about baseball, instead devoting his energies and fortune to building a great petroleum-based empire. As the 1916 baseball season opened in April, Sinclair was incorporating Sinclair Oil & Refining Co., a consolidation of some earlier firms he owned or had an interest in. In the next eighteen months, he spent over $13 million building oil pipelines from fields in Oklahoma and Texas to refineries in the Midwest.

But it was not until 1922 that Harry Sinclair moved to center stage on the national scene. It was then that the infamous Teapot Dome scandal of the Harding administration broke. Sinclair and Edward L. Doheny were accused of taking bribes, deceit, and attempting to defraud the government in connection with leases their companies had obtained on federal lands. Although Harding's secretary of state, Albert B. Fall, was convicted of taking a ten-thousand-dollar bribe from Doheny, both Doheny and Sinclair won acquittal on charges of attempt to defraud.

As for his interest in the Peps, Sinclair seems to have made out well in selling three player contracts to the Giants, a couple to Cincinnati, and a few more to other teams for good measure. He also got ten annual payments of ten thousand dollars each from organized baseball for the stadium he and Pat Powers had built in Harrison.

That ball field, which was known in Harrison as Federal Park, had a colorful post-Peps history. In 1917 and early 1918, with the United States finally a combatant in World War I, the grounds became a camp for soldiers—first the 113th Regiment, 829th Division, later "the colored troops from New York." Starting in May 1918, both the Giants and the Yankees played some of their "home" games there. On July 27, 1918, seven thousand fight fans saw Jack Dempsey dispatch Fred Fulton there in 18.8 seconds of the first round of a world heavyweight championship bout. They paid ten dollars for ringside seats, two dollars for general admission. When the Bears became Newark's entry in the International League after the war, they occupied Federal Park until Ruppert Stadium was built across the river.

The park burned down in 1923. Today the land, bordered by Second, Third, Middlesex, and Burlington streets, contains a park-and-ride lot serving the nearby station on the PATH line between Newark and New York, and a new warehouse.

IF THE FEDERAL LEAGUE episode left few marks on New Jersey, it influenced the national game, and perhaps the social fabric of the country, in ways both quirky and portentous.

The damage to the fortunes of the International League Baltimore Orioles caused the sale of Babe Ruth to the Boston Red Sox, starting that legend of baseball on his circuitous route to "the House That Ruth Built" in New York. (Financial troubles also lay behind Ruth's departure from Boston: owner Harry Frazee, whose first love was the stage, needed money to fund yet another marginal undertaking. He eventually made it big by bringing *No, No, Nanette* to Broadway.)

One of the most durable and enduring of major league ball parks was built by the Federal League. Today it goes by the name of Wrigley Field, a legend less for its elegance, which is considerable, than for its long and lonely holdout against night baseball. When the Federal League and organized baseball negotiated their peace and Charles Weeghman bought the Cubs, he cobbled together a team that was half Cubs and half Whales, and then ensconced the combination in his new ball park. The Wrigley name came later.

The basic contentions of the lawsuit heard by Judge Landis kept cropping up until organized baseball could ignore them no longer. The reserve clause, which bound a player to a club until the club said otherwise, eventually fell—and free agency became the law of the ball field.

A fledgling players' union, the Baseball Player's Fraternity, proved powerless in the 1914–1915 baseball war. But in its rubble were lessons for generations of ballplayers and ballplayers' agents yet to come. The lessons were not overlooked.

PRESIDENT WILSON married Edith Bolling Galt as 1915 drew to a close. General Francisco Villa quit Mexico's revolution. The British began evacuating Gallipoli. And Germany's Austrian allies sank yet another ship, the *Ancona,* with more loss of American lives.

The nation had emerged from a war about territory in a game to face a war about territory in the world.

CHAPTER 6

Glory in the Shadows

The Negro Leagues Flourish in New Jersey

The 1946 Newark Eagles, champions of the Negro Leagues. (Courtesy of Newark Public Library)

When a muscular, broad-shouldered, pigeon-toed, intense black man stepped to home plate on April 18, 1946, nearly five shameful decades of "whites only" organized baseball came to an end. The batter was Jackie Robinson. But the location was not Ebbets Field in Brooklyn. Nor was "Dodgers" the name emblazoned across Robinson's chest.

Robinson wore the uniform of the Montreal Royals, the International League farm team of the Brooklyn Dodgers. And the place was Roosevelt Stadium in Jersey City, home of the New York Giants' International League club. New Jersey once again provided the stage for a pivotal event of the national pastime.

Robinson moved on the following year to the parent National League club (though he had not played his last in New Jersey). Paterson's Larry Doby needed a few weeks more to hurdle the color barrier in the American League by joining the Cleveland Indians. Other black men followed, first in an excruciating trickle and finally in a flood.

But that's just the happy ending of a story that had more ups and downs than a well-juiced spitball. It was, to be sure, a saga stained by ugly racial prejudice, with all the resulting pain, humiliation, deprivation, and lost opportunity. But black baseball also gave a certain joy to the game (surely not inspired by money) that may be gone forever, an inventiveness that blazed a trail for whites, and a measure of athletic prowess largely unrecorded and unheralded but amply reflected in today's black major leaguers.

There is perhaps no better year to take up the tale than 1886, and no better place than Jersey City.

THE POPULATION of the United States in 1886 stood somewhere between 50 and 60 million. Blacks, including many of the 4 million slaves emancipated twenty-three years earlier, accounted for about 10 percent of the total. The great majority continued to live in the South, where Reconstruction was nearly ten years dead and the "black codes" kept blacks in the basement of society.

The North still had relatively few blacks. The National League—a decade old, at the pinnacle of baseball, and domiciled entirely in northern states—had none. But the Western League, Eastern League, and International Association, all part of organized baseball under the National Commission, could claim a combined total of four. Among these was George

W. Stovey, southpaw hurler of the Eastern League's Jersey City entry. He was New Jersey's first black professional baseball player.

In his definitive work on the Negro Leagues, *Only the Ball Was White*, Robert W. Peterson says that Stovey's win-loss record for 1886 is unavailable. John B. Holway, in *Blackball Stars*, says he won thirty. Against the yardstick of hits yielded per batters faced, Stovey finished second in the league in 1886, giving up only 177 hits in facing 1,059 batsmen. In other words, opponents batted an anemic .167 against him. Peterson points out that Stovey's performance may have been even better by modern standards. In those days walks counted as hits on a batter's record and it was "one . . . two . . . three . . . *four* strikes, you're out, at the old ball game."

A year later, Stovey joined another early black star—Moses Fleetwood ("Fleet") Walker—on the Newark (formerly Jersey City) Little Giants of the International League (the Eastern League renamed; a warning must be given here of the difficulty the reader will encounter in keeping track of the multitude of league and team names that follow. Major league fans of today may have trouble remembering that the Baltimore Orioles were once the St. Louis Browns. They may find it difficult to correctly trace the westward migration of the Philadelphia Athletics. But those tasks are simple compared to keeping track of teams and leagues before the turn of the century. Baseball was then in its formative stages, a wobbly and somewhat shapeless affair, groping for its place on the U.S. scene. The only things of any substance were the ten-year-old National League and its four-year-old rival, the American Association, with their handful of teams. Elsewhere, teams would disband after one season, a half season, a few games, or no games at all. Switching towns, leagues, and names was commonplace. Leagues, too, disbanded and changed names practically overnight. Adding to the confusion are many cases of totally different teams and leagues using the same names at different times. In the Negro Leagues alone Newark had three different teams in two different leagues. One of the leagues, the Negro National League, was on its second go-round when Newark joined. The other league, which included the Newark Browns, survived but one season.)

Stovey, whom Peterson calls "the first great Negro pitcher," had a 33–14 record in 1887, leading the Newark club to a fourth-place finish. Playing outfield when he was not pitching, he batted .255. Walker, who had been the first black major leaguer three years earlier with the Toledo Blue Stockings of the American Association, caught and batted .263.

Stovey and Walker did more than enough to lay to rest the question that racist skeptics kept repeating for the next fifty years as an excuse for barring blacks from organized baseball: are there any black men talented enough to play alongside the best white men? It was another 1887 International League black, though, who made the question as ludicrous as did the Robinsons, Dobys, Mayses, Aarons, Gibsons, Brocks, Winfields, Goodens, and Jacksons of later years. He was Frank Grant, star infielder of the Buffalo Bisons. In leading Buffalo to a second-place finish, he batted .366, best on the team, and topped the entire league in doubles, triples, and home runs. He stood only five feet, seven and a half inches tall and weighed but 155 pounds.

If the fans of New Jersey in 1887 witnessed some inspiring moments for blacks in baseball, they also experienced one of the uglier racial incidents in the history of the game. It happened in Newark on July 19, when the Chicago White Stockings of the National League came to Newark for an exhibition game. Hall of Famer Adrian Constantine ("Cap") Anson, Chicago manager and unabashed racist, threatened to pull his team if Stovey pitched for Newark. Stovey did not; Newark won anyway. Later that year, Anson protested the proposed move of Stovey to the New York Giants. Unfortunately he prevailed.

Newark's fourth-place finish in 1887 evidently proved unsatisfactory to fans, owners, or both—for the team never saw opening day in 1888.

New Jersey was not deprived of top-flight black baseball in 1888, though. For by then the Cuban Giants, based in Trenton but playing many "home" games in Hoboken, were going strong. (Here another caution on team names: the Newark Little Giants and the Cuban Giants are but the first of a number of teams named "Giants" that the reader will encounter. Blame the National League New York Giants, dynasty of the era, after whom everyone seemed to want to name their team.)

The Cuban Giants, probably the first team of black baseball professionals to draw salaries, had started life on Long Island, New York, in the summer of 1885 as the Babylon Athletics. The players all worked as waiters at a resort hotel there. The following season the team landed in New Jersey's capital and acquired a new name, both thanks to Walter Cook, generally described in accounts of black baseball simply as a "capitalist of Trenton." He may have come from the rubber-manufacturing Cooks, or the brickmaking Cooks, or most likely from the ceramic-producing Cooks, who in the same era sponsored Cook's East Trenton Potters, an amateur baseball team.

Cook's apparent strategy in renaming the team neatly summarizes the status of black Americans barely twenty years after the war to set them free. No longer slaves, they remained inferior people in the view of most whites. Even in the North, they commonly could not eat in the same restaurants or stay in the same hotels as whites. Whites presumably would not come out to see them play baseball either. Cook evidently thought that casting them as foreigners might diminish these prejudices, easing their difficulties with food and lodging and making them acceptable opponents of white teams.

For a time the strategy worked. In 1887, the Cuban Giants rebuffed the newly formed League of Colored Base Ball Clubs (LCBBC) and the Eastern League in order to continue playing lucrative Sunday games in Hoboken and Brooklyn. (Both the LCBBC and the Eastern League were recognized in the minor league under the National Agreement governing organized baseball, which at the time prohibited Sunday ball.) The Giants "barnstormed," scheduling games against major and minor league professional teams as well as amateur clubs. They played the world champion Detroit Tigers that year, losing a heartbreaker by a score of 6–4 on a ninth-inning error after leading 4–2 in the eighth inning. They also took on collegiate opposition including Princeton, Yale, Amherst, and Penn.

Two players thought by historians of Negro baseball to be among the all-time greats played for the Cuban Giants: pitcher Billy Whyte and catcher Clarence Williams. Stovey also labored briefly for the Trenton team before joining Jersey City. As stellar as these players may have been, though, their pay was abysmal. Pitchers and catchers got eighteen dollars per week, infielders fifteen dollars, and outfielders twelve dollars—less than half of what white players got.

In 1889, the Cuban Giants joined the Middle States League. Though still based in Trenton, they played home games in other New Jersey cities, most frequently Hoboken. A second all-black team—the New York Gorhams—joined them in the Middle States League along with white or mixed teams representing Harrisburg, Lancaster, Reading, York, and Philadelphia. Harrisburg won the pennant.

A year later everything changed. The team had a new hometown, York, and a new name, the Monarchs. The league was renamed Eastern Interstate, and then confused things even further by folding in mid-season. The following season saw the erstwhile Cuban Giants of Trenton playing as the Big Gorhams of Ansonia in the Connecticut State League, which disbanded in midsummer.

A few more summers would pass before black teams and black individuals would totally disappear from organized baseball. (The Acme Colored Giants of Celeron, New York, closed the era of minimal, controlled, incident-marred semi-integration in 1898.) But the Cuban Giants called it quits with the white leagues after the 1891 season, preferring to market their talents strictly as barnstormers. They survived well into the first decade of the 1900s, though the exact year of their demise is unknown. All historians of Negro baseball, especially of the early years, face the same frustration: spotty record keeping. With teams and leagues coming and going as they did, with nonleague exhibitions often the mainstay of a season, and with sparsely staffed black newspapers the only regular chroniclers, it is little wonder that records of black baseball are full of gaps. This certainly has complicated the cause of getting the stars of black baseball their rightful spots in the game's Hall of Fame. Beyond doubt, though, New Jersey's Cuban Giants cast the mold for the great black teams of the era of total segregation, 1899–1946.

AS THE CENTURY TURNED, the black population of the United States had grown to about 9 million, with 90 percent still living in the rural South. Black professional baseball, however, like its white counterpart, operated almost entirely in the North. Though the North was hardly a paradise for the black man, freedom and opportunity fairly abounded there by comparison with the South.

The Philadelphia Giants, arguably the outstanding black team of the first decade of the twentieth century, began to play in 1902. They joined five existing professional black teams, including the original Cuban Giants (now the Genuine Cuban Giants), the Cuban X Giants of New York, the Norfolk Red Stockings, the Chicago Unions, and the Columbia Giants, formerly the Page Fence Giants of Adrian, Michigan. The 1906 Philadelphia squad, which Peterson calls "probably the best black team in the early years of this century," included former Cuban Giants Sol White and Bill Francis. (Sol White's thirty-nine-year career as player, manager, coach, and business manager included stints not only with the Cuban Giants and the Philadelphia Giants, but also with the Genuine Cuban Giants, Cuban X Giants, Page Fence Giants, Columbia Giants, Lincoln Giants, and Quaker Giants—not to mention the Newark Stars, about which more later.)

Black teams continued to proliferate until a second attempt at an official black league was made in 1906. This one fared better than the stillborn League of Colored Base Ball Clubs in 1887, but it died nonetheless at the end of the season. The cause seemed to be chronic underfinancing, which drove some teams to quit at mid-season and made the league fair game for hustlers: the owners, mostly white, had little compunction against skipping scheduled league games if more lucrative opportunities to stay afloat presented themselves. Such was the hard-scrabbling world of black baseball, and it probably contributed to the early demise of a third try at creating a league in 1910.

Despite the fragility of some of the early Negro Leagues, many of the teams proved exceptionally durable, notwithstanding the occasional need to defer paychecks and pass the hat at games. One of these teams— bearing the unlikely name of Bacharach Giants—wrote New Jersey's next great chapter in black baseball.

THE ATLANTIC CITY BACHARACHS

Atlantic City, in 1916, was at the height of its popularity as a summer resort, especially for the rich and the famous. Thomas Edison came there to fish, Broadway stars to play. A promotional retrospective on the city put it this way: "If a theater-goer had attended consecutively every Broadway tryout in Atlantic City from 1901 to 1935, he would have spent nearly four months in his seat, 24 hours a day."

For the struggling Duval Giants of Jacksonville, Florida, Atlantic City might well have seemed a place where fans, money, exposure, and acceptance might come more easily. There are two different versions of how that opportunity developed.

The first version has it that Atlantic City black politicians Tom Jackson and Henry Tucker lured the team northward. The name had to change, of course, and what more fitting solution for a couple of pols than to call it after the reigning power, Mayor Harry Bacharach (a name made more famous by his son, Burt). The second version, reported by John Holway, asserts that it was Mayor Bacharach himself, on a visit to Florida, who saw the Duvals play and invited them north. Donn Rogosin, in his book *Invisible Men*, agrees with Holway's version, adding that the mayor put the team on the city payroll.

Did Atlantic City meet the ballplayers' financial expectations? Well, sort of. Peterson quotes star first baseman Napoleon "Chance" Cummings comparing Jacksonville and the Jersey resort: "It was pretty informal [in Jacksonville] and we didn't make much—we just got peanuts. But we were working other jobs, too, you know; I had this job in a grocery store, but I wanted to be a ballplayer. . . . We got a contract [in Atlantic City] for

$250 or $300 a month, and you were supposed to get that money every thirty days. Well, at that time, sometimes you made the money and sometimes you didn't."

If Atlantic City did not always provide for the team, the team certainly did not shortchange the town. The Bacharachs represented Atlantic City for fourteen seasons, six as members of the Eastern Colored League, which broke up in 1928, and one as a founding member of the American Negro League (not to be confused with the later Negro American League). What killed the American Negro League after one season and finally stopped the Bacharachs was the Great Depression.

But what a team it was! In 1920, the inaugural year of the successful first Negro National League, the "associate member" Bacharachs played the American Giants of Chicago for the loosely defined national championship. The clubs split four games in a series terminated under circumstances that contemporary reports leave unclear. Earlier that season, the Bacharachs had had the distinction of appearing in the first all-black game ever played at Ebbets Field. "Cannonball" Dick Redding beat the Lincoln Giants 5–0.

A year later, the American Giants again came east and again deadlocked the Bacharachs, this time four games to four. The rivalry continued in 1922, when the Bacharachs paid a postseason visit to Chicago, losing 1–0 in a memorable twenty-inning marathon.

The Atlantic City team then helped found the Eastern Colored League in 1923, finishing fourth that year and in 1924 and 1925. But in 1926, the Bacharachs took the pennant and brought New Jersey its first World Series (the Negro World Series had begun in 1924). Among the team's stars were shortstop Dick Lundy, widely regarded as the best at his position in the 1920s. Many thought Lundy the peer of the great John Henry Lloyd, called "the black Honus Wagner." (Lloyd, a past and future Bacharach, was with the Lincoln Giants that year, batting .342 at age forty-two.) Also on the 1926 Bacharachs were hot-tempered Orville H. ("Ghost") Marcelle, who Holway in *Blackball Stars* says was "considered the slickest fielding third baseman in black history"; Chaney White, speedy and hard-hitting center fielder; first baseman Chance Cummings; and pitcher Rats Henderson. Lundy and Marcelle may have rivaled any shortstop–third baseman combination in the history of the game.

The inaugural Negro World Series in 1924 had pitted the famed Kansas City Monarchs of the Negro National League against the almost equally renowned Philadelphia Hilldales of the Eastern Colored League. The Monarchs (later to be Jackie Robinson's first professional team) beat the

The Chicago Defender, October 6, 1926, proclaims the Atlantic City Bacharachs' lead over Chicago's American Giants in the third Negro World Series. Chicago won the series, five games to three. (Courtesy of Lawrence Hogan)

Hilldales five games to four. A year later, the same teams contested with a far different result: Hilldale 5, Monarchs 1. Then the Monarchs gave way in the West to Chicago's American Giants, the Hilldales surrendered the East to the Bacharachs, and the 1926 Negro World Series—Giants versus Giants—was on.

There seems to be some doubt about the location of the opening game on October 1. Peterson puts it at Shibe Park, then the Philadelphia Phillies' ball park. The *Philadelphia Inquirer* of October 2, 1926, has it at Bacharach Park in Atlantic City. The nod has to go to the *Inquirer*, then as now reliable enough to know what was happening, or not happening, in its own backyard.

Some games of the 1926 Negro World Series were played in Shibe Park, though, and one in Baltimore too. The custom in black baseball was to spread series games around, for some good reasons. First, Negro League teams were somewhat nomadic as a rule since most were tenants of white major league teams. They could use the ball parks only when the landlord teams were on the road, provided the landlord did not come up with a better offer from an evangelist or a prizefight promoter. This, however, seems not to have been the case in the 1926 World Series; all of Chicago's games were played at the team's home field, and Atlantic City had no major league landlord to contend with.

A second reason for moving the games around—and probably the main factor in 1926—was simple economics. For contestants with small hometown parks—a description fitting the Bacharachs—playing "home" series games in available major league parks in other cities (and sharing the larger gates) could make good fiscal sense.

Peterson notwithstanding, the first two games of the 1926 series were played in Atlantic City, the third in Baltimore, and the fourth and fifth at Philadelphia's Shibe Park. The other five were played in Chicago. (While the four different ball parks of the 1926 series may strike us today as two too many, it hardly sets the record for the Negro League classic; that goes to the 1943 series, which used six locales for seven games.)

In these early days, the winner of the series was the first team to take five games. In the 1926 series, it took ten games to get a winner. The first game was a 3–3 tie, called at the end of nine innings due to darkness; a similar fate befell the fourth game, a 4–4 deadlock. (On the subject of darkness and lights: baseball buffs know that the first night game in the major leagues was played in Cincinnati in 1935. But the Kansas City Monarchs introduced portable lighting five years earlier, with other Negro League teams quickly following suit. These teams had to play as many games as possible to make ends meet. Toting portable lights in their buses, they might play a day game in one city, then move on to another, set up their lights, and play a night engagement. However, night games were still unknown in 1926.)

After the Chicagos earned a 7–6 win in the second game of the 1926 series at Atlantic City, history was made in Baltimore on October 3. Claude ("Red") Grier, pitching for Atlantic City, hurled the first Negro World Series no-hitter. (Thirty years and five days later, Don Larsen of the New York Yankees would pitch the first and only no-hitter in the World Series of Organized Baseball.) Grier, who had been chased from the mound in game 2 by the American Giants and also lost game 8, had a brief and largely undistinguished professional career. It would end after a lone additional victory the following season. Sadly, his moment of glory earned but a paragraph and a box score in the *Inquirer*, while Grover Cleveland Alexander's four-hit, two-run World Series of Organized Baseball performance the same day for the St. Louis Cardinals against the New York Yankees received a lengthy recounting, replete with photographs. True, Alexander faced the likes of Ruth, Gehrig, Lazzeri, and Meusel that day. But the American Giants confronting Grier were tough players too. They included lifetime .300 hitter Dave Malarcher, one of the top half dozen third baggers in Negro League history; Floyd ("Jelly") Gardner, a line-drive hitter and one of the fastest men in baseball; and Jim Brown and Jimmy Hayes, who batted .335 and .328, respectively, that season.

Before leaving the East, Atlantic City took a 2–1 series lead with a 5–3 win in the second game played at Philadelphia. But the baseball proverb that "home cookin' wins games" came true in Chicago. The American Giants took four of five games to win the series 5–3. The turning point came in the first game at Chicago when the home team broke a 4–4 tie with two out in the ninth.

Though the Bacharachs brought the series to Atlantic City again the following year, their opponents were the same and so was the final result. After dropping the first four games, the Jersey shore team battled back to even, only to lose the final contest, 1–0. Oddly enough, a Bacharach pitcher—Luther "Red" Farrell—hurled the Negro Leagues' second no-hitter in the fifth game of the series.

A year later, in 1928, the Eastern Colored League was gone. The Bacharachs, Holway recounts, "were not doing well at the box office—their park, a former greyhound track on South Carolina Avenue, was padlocked by the sheriff before one game because they owed back rent." They continued to play, however, finishing near the bottom of the ill-fated American

Negro League in 1929. Although the Bacharachs were still around in the mid-thirties, the heyday of baseball in Atlantic City was over.

This account cannot depart the Jersey Shore resort, however, without mentioning Whitey Gruhler. At a time when few white newspapers or sportswriters paid much attention to black baseball, Gruhler celebrated it in the sports pages of the *Atlantic City Press*. Lawrence Hogan, professor of black history at Union County College and an authority on black media, noting that Atlantic City had no black newspaper, says that Gruhler's "reportage is especially noteworthy for its extent and sympathetic quality."

A cynic might say that Gruhler, with no major league team in town to distract him, only followed the journalist's urge to report what was at hand. But he did it both lovingly and eloquently. An oft-quoted passage from one of Gruhler's columns during World War II sums up his argument for opening organized baseball to blacks: "We are fighting a war—the most terrible war in all history. We are spending billions of dollars. Our youth is shedding barrels and barrels of blood. Every day is one of heartache and tragedy. And what are we fighting for? Freedom and democracy. But some of us seem to have forgotten that freedom and democracy are the human rights for which we fought the Civil War."

THE HALL OF FAME AND BLACK PLAYERS

What do the following people have in common?

        Bell, James ("Cool Papa")

        Charleston, Oscar

        Dandridge, Raymond ("Hooks" or "Squatty")

        Dihigo, Martin

        Foster, Andrew ("Rube")

        Gibson, Joshua ("Josh")

        Irvin, Monford Merrill ("Monte")

        Johnson, William J. ("Judy")

        Leonard, Walter F. ("Buck")

Lloyd, John Henry

Paige, LeRoy ("Satchel")

You could say they all were vastly underpaid for their labors in the Negro Leagues, relative to white baseball stars of the day with comparable skills. That would be true (though Satchel Paige is said to have made a fair amount of money).

What really sets them apart is that they alone—out of perhaps three thousand men who played in the Negro Leagues—have been accorded a place in the Baseball Hall of Fame at Cooperstown, New York. (This excludes the likes of Jackie Robinson, Roy Campanella, and others who started in the Negro Leagues but played long enough in the majors to earn their Hall of Fame niches the conventional way.) Observers and students of segregated black baseball believe that the eleven men named above should be joined in the Hall of Fame by many others from the Negro Leagues.

Three of the men on the list shared something else: the Garden State as a place of employment in baseball. Dandridge and Irvin toiled for the Newark Eagles—a team that not only brought the World Series to New Jersey, but also won it. Lloyd was the star of an earlier era. Born in Florida in 1884, he began his professional career as a catcher for a club too poor to own a mask or chest protector. Wisely switching to shortstop, he played for the great Lincoln Giants (originally of Nebraska but later of New York) and the Chicago American Giants of the days just before and during World War I. Some call Lloyd the best of all Negro League players, and almost no one disputes his claim to the shortstop slot on the all-time Negro League team.

By the time Lloyd got to Atlantic City and the Bacharachs in the 1920s, people were already calling him "Pop." He was playing much less shortstop by then, his aging body better suited to first base. What he proved especially good at in those years was teaching younger players as a coach and manager. Peterson tells us that when "he retired from big-time Negro baseball in 1931, Lloyd became a janitor in the post office in Atlantic City. . . . He declined offers to manage the Newark Eagles and the Baltimore Elite Giants and spent the rest of his life as a sort of foster father to the children of Atlantic City."

Though he retired from top Negro League baseball in 1931, Lloyd played semipro ball until age fifty-eight in 1942. His latter-day team was the Atlantic City Johnson Stars, which also boasted Luther Farrell, an Atlantic City policeman after his years with the Bacharachs and his no-hitter fame. Commissioner of the city's Little League for a number of years, Lloyd was honored in 1949 by having a community ball field named for him. Another testimonial was planned for him on the very day in 1965 when his wife found him dead of arteriosclerosis, just a month short of his eighty-first birthday.

ON AN OVERCAST and muggy mid-August day in Atlantic City in 1989, Donald Trump's Castle Casino proffers, as always, cool dry air, bright flashy light, and the seductive possibility of hitting it big in a hurry. As an added attraction this summer, an even million dollars presses against the insides of a huge Plexiglas cube in the main lobby, waiting to be claimed by a lucky patron in a few weeks. Across the way in the marina, the sleek, white *Trump Princess*, worth considerably more than the greenbacks in the cube, sits docilely at her moorings—as though brooding about her owner's professed desire to trade up to something larger. Nearby, equally sleek but in a midnight-blue finish that seems an inch deep, rides the *Mystique,* out of Guernsey. Dozens of other, smaller yachts—poor cousins at perhaps at mere one hundred thousand dollars a copy—contribute to the enormous floating wealth of the marina.

A few blocks away, within sight of Trump's casino and yacht, sits a dilapidated old ball field. Few people give it more than a disinterested glance on their way to or from the excitement of the casino. Along the first-base side of the brick grandstand the corrugated roof peels back like the lid of a sardine can. Broken or missing windows stare vacantly at the passing traffic. Doors and window frames need paint, but the windowsills lack nothing in the way of empty pint booze bottles. Paper and plastic trash decorates the overgrown weeds between the grandstand and the street. No sign declares the name of this place. But something about it tells the visitor that it might be the place they once dedicated to the man many consider the greatest black ballplayer of all time.

Looking out toward center field from the highest row in the middle of the little grandstand, the visitor has trouble conjuring the salad days of this place. It would be easier if there were a scoreboard out there with POP LLOYD FIELD in big letters across the top and a stone-and-brass monument, like those in Yankee Stadium for Ruth and Gehrig, listing his accomplishments. At the very least the place should have a sign out front that tips passing gamblers to the fact that it honors a great man named John Henry Lloyd. And it should be getting the kind of care that tells people Atlantic City still remembers and cares about the great ballplayer who once cared about the place and its kids. The place simply should not be sitting there decaying in the shadow of such opulence.

DANDRIDGE AND IRVIN, by contrast to Lloyd, played most of their Negro League careers in New Jersey—and so enjoyed glory days there. (By 1940, the black population of the country had grown to 13 million people, 25 percent of whom lived in Newark and other cities of the North. Negro League teams, all domiciled in the North, welcomed a growing base of fans throughout the 1930s and 1940s.)

Dandridge got in on the ground floor. When the Negro National League, which had folded in 1931, was reincarnated in 1933, the Detroit Stars were reborn, too. Dandridge, up from Virginia, was there. The league had a rough year, failing to complete its second-half schedule. The Stars evidently fared worse than most, for the following year they were among the missing.

Although a new team, the Philadelphia Stars, entered the league in 1934 (winning the pennant, in fact), they do not seem to have been a new version of the Detroit Stars. Rather, the roster of the 1933 Detroit Stars apparently scattered, with Dandridge winding up on another new team, the Newark Dodgers. (A few years earlier, Newark had been represented by the Newark Stars, probably the old Wilmington Potomacs and not a member of any big-time Negro League. Another black Newark team of this era was the 1932 Browns, which the Depression killed along with its league, the East-West, after less than a season.)

The Dodgers lasted just two seasons (1934–1935), compiling an overall record of twenty-eight wins against fifty-five losses. They finished dead last in both halves of the 1935 season. Dandridge suffered along. Meanwhile, a club called the Eagles, from Brooklyn, had joined the Negro National League in 1935, managing to play close to .500 ball. When the 1936 season opened, the Eagles had replaced the Dodgers in Newark. Thus began a reign of thirteen years during which the Newark club finished worse than fourth in the league only once and won the pennant twice. In addition to Dandridge and Irvin, the Eagles enjoyed the services of Larry Doby

(1943–1947), Don Newcombe (1944–1945), and a group of leading candidates for the Hall of Fame should the doors ever open again to Negro League stars: catcher Raleigh ("Biz") Mackey, first baseman George ("Mule") Suttles, and shortstops Dick Lundy, Willie Wells, and Dick Seay.

Dandridge, according to Monte Irvin and many others, was the best all-around third baseman ever to play the game. With overall batting averages of .319 in the Negro Leagues and .318 in the top white minors, Dandridge also is arguably the most deserving black player who never made the majors. Holway sums up the poignancy of his situation: "[He] was just young enough to get his hopes up and just old enough to have them dashed." He finally made it to the high white minors with the Triple A Minneapolis Millers of the New York Giants organization at age thirty-five in 1949. He hit .359 that year and was voted the league's Most Valuable Player the next.

Dandridge also managed to miss the World Series year of 1946 in Newark. Like many black players of the era (including Campanella, Gibson, and Wells), Dandridge played part of his career in Latin America. Starring at various times for teams in Mexico, Cuba, Puerto Rico, and Venezuela, he spent the 1946 season in Vera Cruz, batting .323 and stealing twenty-four bases. When a touring all-star team of white major leaguers passed through, he hit .455 against them.

New York Giants fans of the 1950s will remember Monte Irvin patrolling the outfield (1949–1955) along with Willie Mays, Hank Thompson, Bobby Thompson, and Don Mueller. But it was in Newark with the Eagles, at shortstop and third base as well as in the outfield, between 1938 and 1948, that Monte earned his way into the Hall of Fame.

Born in Columbia, Alabama, Irvin moved to New Jersey as a child and became, in the opinion of many, the state's greatest schoolboy athlete. Though others would say that Olympians Marty Glickman and Carl Lewis deserve at least a share of the honors, Irvin's credentials are awesome: All-State in football, basketball, baseball, and track for three consecutive years. Among other trophies on his shelf is one for winning the state javelin competition in 1936 with a throw of 192 feet, 2 inches.

After playing for the amateur Orange Triangles as a youth in the mid-1930s, Irvin joined the Eagles at age nineteen in 1938 at a salary of $150 a month. He first made the showcase East-West All-Star game in 1941 as a third baseman, Dandridge having gone South. When he next appeared in the Negro League classic, it was in 1946, as an outfielder. He also played outfield for the East Stars in 1947 and 1948.

Young Monte Irvin, nineteen years old and fresh from a four-sport All-State career at East Orange High School, gazes from Newark Eagles' dugout in 1938. (Courtesy of Lawrence Hogan)

At home with the Eagles in 1946, though, shortstop Irvin teamed with second baseman Larry Doby in what might have been one of the best double-play combinations of all time, fielding and hitting considered. Much to the dismay of many baseball experts, particularly Negro League authorities, Larry Doby thus far has made the Hall of Fame neither as a Negro League star nor as an American League standout. In fact, Doby has been notably unsuccessful in winning any awards or honors. The closest he came in his major league career was second to Yogi Berra in the balloting for American League Most Valuable Player in 1954 (230 votes for Berra, 210 for Doby, 203 for Doby's Cleveland teammate Bobby Avila).

But Doby is remembered with much admiration and not a little awe by Paterson and Newark fans who enjoyed his performances in the 1930s and 1940s. Coming north from Camden, *South Carolina,* as a child, he became the finest athlete ever to attend Paterson's Eastside High—and certainly a contender for the title of New Jersey's best ever. An outstanding football running back until a bad knee forced him to quit, he concentrated on baseball and began playing semipro with the Orange Base Ball Club, whose home was the Grove Street Oval.

Doby probably will be best remembered as the American League's first black player. This is far from insignificant—especially, as is generally agreed, because Doby's easygoing personality was not as well adapted as Robinson's to the trials of breaking the color line. But those who knew him and saw him play believe he should be remembered—and appropriately honored—for much more.

DURING A RARE recognition of black baseball, a "Salute to the Negro National League" at Irvington High School in June 1989, former Eagle outfielder Bob Harvey reminisced about Dandridge, Irvin, and his heady days in Newark: "Every time we won, this cop would come take me home on his motorcycle. But I never saw him when we lost." Harvey rode more often than not: from opening day of 1944 until mid-season of 1947 (final standings were not published after that), the Eagles won 114 and lost 70. In the pinnacle year of 1946, they won 47 and dropped only 16.

Discovered by a Philadelphia scout for the Eagles while playing semipro ball in his native Cambridge, Maryland, Harvey had come up to Trenton for a tryout and made the Newark team when "I hit a few out of the park."

Newark Eagles team bus. In an era of segregated public transportation, Negro League teams traveled long distances in cramped team buses and even private automobiles. (Courtesy of Lawrence Hogan)

Also at the Irvington testimonial were Patricio Athelstan Scantlebury, the last Negro League player to move up to the major leagues (pitching nineteen innings for Cincinnati in 1956), and Charlie Biot, another former outfielder for the Eagles. Biot, who played for the Newarks in 1939 before moving on to the New York Black Yankees and Baltimore Elite Giants, remembered postseason All-Star play against white major leaguers: "George Case was the fastest man I ever saw. I was playing center in a 1940 All-Star game when he hit a single through the middle. I was a little slow coming in for it, and by the time I brought my arm up to throw, he was sliding into second."

Biot described Case accurately: in eight full seasons with the Washington Senators and one with the Cleveland Indians, he led the American League in stolen bases no fewer than six times. Biot also remembers Case, who later coached baseball at Rutgers, for a bit of color-blind camaraderie: "Case was one of the first to try a glove with the last two fingers combined. In those days we'd leave our gloves on the field when we came in to bat, and one time Case told me to try his new glove if I wanted to. I did, but I didn't care for it."

Born and raised in East Orange, and still making his home there after seventy-one years, Biot also recalled being a teammate of future New York Yankee third baseman Billy Johnson (1943–1951, with time out for World War II). Montclair native Johnson and Biot played together at Bloomfield Tech.

Harvey reminisced at the 1989 Irvington High event about the postseason games between Negro League and major league All-Stars: "More often than not we'd beat them. We thought that was funny, with them making all that money and us playing for so little." Rather than bitterness, the words seemed to convey a rueful sense of having been born too soon. Harvey had no doubt reflected upon this just weeks earlier, when the original copy of his first professional contract was returned to him. Calling for a salary of $350 per month, the contract was among boxes of other Eagle records found by a crew demolishing the former Crawford Street home of Eagle owners Abe and Effa Manley.

Effa Manley, born in Philadelphia to a black father and a white mother of German extraction, met Abe, twenty years her senior, at the 1932 World Series. They married and in 1935 organized the Eagles in Brooklyn, bringing the team to Newark in 1936.

In owning the Eagles, Abe was pursuing a lifelong fascination with baseball. What allowed him this indulgence was his profits from "the numbers," a game he seems to have controlled in Newark, at least among the black citizenry. In this he was hardly unique among Negro League owners of the day, the legendary Gus Greenlee of Pittsburgh being another outstanding example. Rogosin says that "the entire 1937 Negro National League was run by the numbers boys."

Abe seems to have enjoyed the team hugely. He attended every home game, sat in the dugout, often traveled with the Eagles to away games. It was his hobby, his toy.

To Effa, though, the Eagles were a business. "She ran the team," recalls Harvey. Virtually everyone else who mentions Effa Manley says approximately the same. Peterson describes her as a beautiful "lady of positive opinions [who] was prone to offer unsolicited advice to other owners in league meetings and sometimes took a hand in the proceedings on the field."

She was a hard woman with a dollar, too. Though the Dodgers' Branch Rickey set a precedent of sorts by paying nothing to the Kansas City Monarchs for Jackie Robinson, Effa Manley extracted compensation from Cleveland's Bill Veeck for Larry Doby. It was a ridiculously small amount (fifteen thousand dollars) in light of Doby's great talents, but it was infinitely more than other Negro League owners got for sending "franchise" players to the majors. "If he'd have been white," she said, "they'd have given me a hundred thousand."

Even Effa got nothing, though, when Rickey signed Don Newcombe for the Brooklyn Dodgers in 1946. Thereafter Effa stepped up her outspoken criticism of major league raids on Negro League talent. She ultimately won a round against Rickey, legally blocking a contract that would have taken Monte Irvin to the Dodgers, on the grounds that Rickey had failed to negotiate with her.

Lawrence Hogan repeats a well-worn tale about Effa Manley and money: "It seems that Monte asked Effa for half of the $5,000 paid for his contract by Horace Stoneham of the New York Giants. She turned him down. Years later she showed up at a Negro League alumni affair sporting the fur stole she had bought with the money. When Monte caught sight of her, he walked up and said, 'Isn't that me you're wearing?'" (Effa's financial acumen extended beyond baseball. The New Jersey chapter of the National Association for the Advancement of Colored People recognized her talents when it elected her treasurer.)

Under Abe's easy hand and Effa's sharp eye, the Eagles finished with the league's second-best record in 1936, 1937, 1939, and 1941; fourth in 1938; and third in 1940, 1942, 1943, and 1945. All of which was prelude to 1946.

The season opened on May 5, a Sunday and Newark Eagles Day by city

Effa Manley, on the dugout steps at Ruppert Stadium, was co-owner of the Newark Eagles. She and husband Abe brought the Eagles to Newark. (Courtesy of Lawrence Hogan)

proclamation. The site was Ruppert Stadium, down in the meadows on Wilson Avenue, home to both the Eagles and the International League Bears (the stadium and the Bears both belonged to the New York Yankees). The opposition was the Philadelphia Stars, a team that had finished just a game behind the Eagles in 1945.

The day proved a bright omen for the Eagles. Larry Doby streaked home to break a scoreless tie in the sixth, and the hosts went on to win despite the absence of big Don Newcombe. "Newk," a native of Elizabeth, had just signed with the Dodger organization following an outstanding rookie year with the Eagles in 1945. In addition to Doby, the nineteen-member Eagles of 1946 included Irvin (who formed the double-play combo with Doby); first baseman Lennie Pearson; third bagger Pat Patterson; outfielders Bob Harvey, Jimmy Wilkes, and John Davis; pitchers Leon Day, Max Manning, Rufus Lewis, and Len Hooker; and catcher Leon Ruffin. Biz Mackey, a premier catcher in his own playing days and Roy Campanella's mentor, managed.

Ronald Murphy served up the bats for the Eagles that year. "I took Newcombe's brother's place," he recalls. He also remembers getting paid twenty-five or thirty cents a game. "But I didn't care about the pay because they gave me a uniform. . . . I'd go with them to Yankee Stadium when they played the Black Yankees and to the Polo Grounds when they played the New York Cubans, and I'd get to be on the field where the big leaguers played. . . . I even went on the road with them, all through Ohio . . . sometimes the players would give me money for soda and candy."

Murphy says it was tiring for the players, though. "They'd play a Friday night game and a Saturday day game in Newark, then go to New York for a Saturday night game, then right back to Newark for a Sunday double-header." Even in the black big leagues, the scrambling for paying audiences never ceased.

Playing a two-half format, with a playoff if the half seasons produced different winners, the Eagles took the first half handily with a record of 25–9. Streaks of nine straight and fourteen of fifteen helped. Irvin led the league for the half with a batting average of .409 and Doby contributed a solid .339.

The second half of the 1946 season turned out even better for the Newark team. Their record was 22–7 as Doby raised his batting average to .348 and Irvin finished at .395. Up in Montreal, meanwhile, Robinson was winning the batting crown of the International League with a .349 average. During this second session, the Eagles sent Doby, Irvin, Ruffin, Pearson, and Day to a two-game East-West All-Star series. (These Negro League

All-Star games actually drew more attention and were more important showcases for black players than was the Negro League World Series. The first game that year, in Chicago's Comiskey Park, drew more than forty-five thousand fans.) Doby and Irvin got half of the East's four hits in the first game as the West All-Stars prevailed 4–1. In the second game, at Washington's Griffith Stadium, Doby had two hits and scored two runs in helping the East even the record for 1946 with a 5–3 victory.

As the Eagles were taking the Negro National League title, the Kansas City Monarchs were topping the Negro American League. And so, on September 17, 1946, a New Jersey team went to bat in a World Series for the first time since the feat was accomplished by the Newark Bears of 1938. The place was neither Newark nor Kansas City, but the Polo Grounds in New York City. Nearly twenty thousand fans attended the night contest. Leon Day and Kansas City's Hilton Smith locked up in a pitching duel, with Day striking out six and Smith wiffing eight before both departed with the score at 1–1 in the sixth inning. Satchel Paige, relieving Smith, beat out an infield hit in the seventh and scored the winning run in a 2–1 Monarch victory. Mackey threw fifteen players, including himself as a pinch hitter, into the contest. Harvey and Davis each contributed two hits to the Eagles' attack; Doby, with a hit and two stolen bases, scored the Eagles' lone run.

The Eagles came home to Ruppert Stadium two nights later for game 2, receiving a tumultuous welcome from their fans. Fighter Joe Louis, fresh from the twenty-third consecutive defense of his heavyweight title at Yankee Stadium the evening before, threw out the first ball. (The following day, Louis's invincibility was shattered in a golf match at Newark's Hendricks Field. Pairing with top black pro Theodore Rhodes, he lost to the team of Maurrie O'Connor, a Hendricks pro, and former state amateur champ Myron Friedman.)

Game 2, played before 9,787 fans, saw the hitters put the pitchers in the shade. With the score tied at 1–1 entering the sixth inning, Willard Brown slammed a three-run homer for the visitors. But an inning later, Newark plated six runs, led by a two-run homer off Doby's bat. Paige came on in relief again but failed, giving up four hits in the inning. Newark prevailed by the score of 7–4.

Though the *Newark Evening News*, New Jersey's premier paper of the day, ran stories on each of the 1946 Negro World Series games, top baseball billing was reserved for a National League race drawing to a close finish. Brooklyn and St. Louis both lost on the final day of the regular season, ending in a dead heat. In the first ever major league playoff series,

St. Louis won two games to one and went on to meet the Red Sox in the World Series of Organized Baseball.

When the Negro World Series moved on to Blues Stadium in Kansas City, hitting continued to dominate pitching. In game 3 on September 23, another night contest, Kansas City walloped Newark 15–5. The Monarchs teed off on Hooker for four runs in the second inning and iced the game with seven more in the eighth. As Kansas City pounded out twenty-one hits, Pearson got three of Newark's seven and Irvin spoiled a double with two errors.

In game 4 at Kansas City the following night, Newark countered with a hitting-pitching combination that produced an 8–1 victory. Rufus Lewis earned the win on a four-hitter, striking out six and walking no one. Newark scored four runs in the fifth, then touched up reliever Paige for three more in the sixth. Irvin clouted a solo homer over the 350-foot marker in left field to end the scoring in the seventh. The series was deadlocked at two games apiece.

The show then departed for Chicago's Comiskey Park, where Kansas City turned the tables on Newark by a 5–1 score. Although the Eagles outhit the Monarchs 10–9, Hilton Smith managed to spread the damage around. Manning took the loss for Newark. And then it was back to Newark, the Eagles on the brink of oblivion in the seven-game series. Game 6, on Friday night, September 27, at Ruppert Stadium, was the first to get space on the lead page of the *Evening News'* sports section. Baseballs flew around and out of Ruppert Stadium, starting early. Willard Brown chased Leon Day in the first inning with a three-run blast to key a five-run outburst. Newark got four back in their half of the inning on three walks and two singles by Pearson and Ruffin. Then Hooker kept the Monarchs in check while his teammates got two in the second on Irvin's home run and two more in the fourth on Pearson's round-tripper. Irvin again closed the scoring for the Eagles, clouting his second homer of the game and third of the series. Kansas City got two more on a late four-bagger of their own, but finished on the short end of a 9–7 score. The series was tied again, this time at three.

So down to the seventh game it came. It was Sunday, September 29, and for the first time it was daylight at Ruppert. Wilbur Lewis hurled for Newark, giving up eight hits while his teammates managed but three off Hilton Smith. Fortunately for Lewis, the Eagle defense was airtight that day, the opposition's just porous enough. In the first inning, Pat Patterson was safe on an error by the Monarch second baseman. He moved up on a walk to Doby and scored on Irvin's single to right. That held up until the sixth, when Kansas City's Johnny O'Neill cracked one over the left-field fence. But Newark promptly broke the tie in the bottom of the inning when Doby and Irvin walked on eight straight balls and Johnny Davis doubled them home. A half inning later, the Monarchs drew nearly even by manufacturing a run on three singles. It was Newark 3, Kansas City 2.

After a scoreless eighth, Kansas City mounted a last-ditch rally. With one man out, the batter laced a "gapper" to left-center that looked like a double to everyone in the park except center fielder Wilkes. Cutting it off in the gap, he fired a strike to Doby at second to nail the sliding runner. And a good thing, too, for the next batter also singled and the one after that drew a walk. But Lewis engineered a popup to Doby for the last out. The team from Newark was the champion of blackball.

The *Evening News* covered the Eagles' victory on its first sports page—above the fold, no less. It was a shining moment for Doby, Irvin, and company, for the city of Newark, and for the state of New Jersey. But in the background the final bell had begun to toll for the Negro Leagues. Robinson, Newcombe, and Campanella had already departed for organized baseball. Doby would cross over in another half season, jumping directly from the Eagles to the Cleveland Indians. In all, sixteen blacks would play in organized baseball in 1947.

As team after team in organized baseball added blacks to their rosters (and desegregated their stands), black fans inevitably began to drift away from the Negro League teams. The Newark Eagles, playing home games at Ebbets Field when the Dodgers were away, drew only two thousand fans to a midsummer Sunday doubleheader in 1947. Their deficit for the year was twenty-two thousand dollars. Even the champions of the two Negro Leagues lost money in 1947.

After struggling through 1948, the New York Black Yankees, the Newark Eagles, and the Negro National League all failed to see opening day in 1949. The Black Yankees were gone for good. The Eagles departed for the Negro American League and Houston, a town still more than a decade away from major league status. The revamped Negro American League hung on for two more seasons, surviving as a developer of young black talent for organized baseball. But eventually black ballplayers just turning professional joined teams in organized baseball's minor leagues.

Blackball was gone—unlamented for the racism it reflected, but honored by the talent it had nurtured. Newark and Trenton and Hoboken and Atlantic City and Jersey City had seen some of its most important moments, and had helped keep it alive until the barriers of prejudice finally fell.

CHAPTER 7

The Common Denominator

Amateur Baseball in the Garden State

New Brunswick's turn-of-century Union Athletic Club assumes a classic team pose. James Clelland is standing second from right. (Authors' Collection)

How James Clelland came to wear a baseball uniform at the turn of the century is not known. What is known is that the young New Brunswick man was born in Liverpool, England, had a Scottish father of strict Calvinist upbringing who probably never played a frivolous game in his life, and served with his two brothers in the Spanish-American War. His duty in that conflict brought him as close to the enemy as Athens, Georgia. It was there that the Clelland boys sustained their single wartime injury: brother Bill was hit in the eye with a missile—a baseball.

Like many other New Jersey men of his era, James Clelland was a member of an amateur baseball team, the New Brunswick Union Athletic Club. He proudly posed for the team's first photograph in a uniform probably ordered from the Sears, Roebuck catalogue.

It is doubtful that Clelland knew much about earlier New Brunswick teams—Liberty, Star, Hopeful, or the all-black team of the 1860s. But he may have crossed the Raritan River to Highland Park in 1890 when a touring all-girl team faced the New Brunswick Athletic Club. (He may even have heard that Rutgers' athletic director had denied them the use of its Neilsen Field when he heard that women were going to play. His reason could not have been concern for the quality of play, for Rutgers' own ball team sported a mediocre record at the time.)

Clelland certainly knew of the major league squads. It was the era of Rube Waddell, Walter Johnson, Cy Young, Ty Cobb, Nap Lajoie, and Honus Wagner; the birth of the American League and the World Series; booming attendance and heavy press coverage. Being a ballplayer, even if just on a hometown nine, was a pretty heady experience.

Although James Clelland's father had been a baker like his father before him, James found the opportunities in the burgeoning New Brunswick–area factories more appealing. When he grew too old to make the Union Athletic Club's first nine, his mechanic's job at nearby Milltown's Michelin plant kept him close to the game in another way.

Michelin, the French tire maker, had moved into Milltown in 1907, taking over what was left of the Meyer Rubber Company plant and making the small community almost a "company town" until it departed in the spring of 1930. It was a great company town, however, for anyone who wanted to participate in sports. Michelin built a community center, where bowling and basketball were played. It sponsored cross-country and multievent track teams. And it let the local baseball team, then called the Crescent Athletic Club, use its hall for meetings and its Michelin Field for games. Crescent regularly played teams in the nearby industrialized country towns of Old Bridge, Spotswood, and Helmetta and was regarded as fairly competitive.

Because so many Crescent players worked for Michelin, and in gratitude for the use of the Michelin facilities, the team eventually changed its name to the Michelin Athletic Association. By 1916, populated with players with names like Swifty, Pop, Lefty, Sticker, and Bunk, the team was making a mark in New Jersey baseball. Upward of three thousand people, more than the entire population of Milltown, regularly filled the stands at Michelin Field to watch the team take on other top teams from the state and beyond. It was a tough field. The left-field fence was a mere 550 feet down the line. Straight-away center was so far away that its grass was rarely mowed, creating search missions by outfielders that only fans of today's Wrigley Field ivy could appreciate.

The team reached its peak in 1918–1920. It competed against some of the better teams of the era and had enough local stars to keep the crowds filing in. Best of all was Albert ("Ab") Hermann, Milltown-born pitcher and slugger who had been a standout at New Brunswick High School and would be the only native of the town to go on to the majors (two years with the Boston Braves, 1923–1924). In 1918 Hermann hit .406 for Michelin while his brother Carl, also known as "Sticker," hit .350.

Carl was behind the plate in 1918 when batterymate Howard ("Swifty") Evans pitched against a team from the Brooklyn Navy Yard. The Brooklyn boys had a few "ringers" in the lineup, including one Charles ("Casey") Stengel, who went one for four against Evans. Although Swifty had a no-hitter going for six innings, the team lost by a single run.

Clelland was still a Michelin man when the famous House of David team from Michigan came to town in 1919. The Midwest baseball players, known for the beards every player sported, showed up two hours late but managed to blow out the Milltown team 6–1. The Philadelphia Colored Giants had no such success later that season, falling to the Michelin squad.

Eventually other diversions of the 1920s conspired to kill top-caliber baseball in Milltown. Occasional appearances by semipro teams, a House of David exhibition against a pickup team, a "donkey baseball game" with local dignitaries playing softball astride reluctant burros sponsored by the Fire Department, itinerant circuses, and special displays occupied Michelin Field until 1952, seventeen years after Clelland died. Then another New Jersey amateur baseball movement took over the Michelin

The 1920 Michelin Athletic Club, pride of Milltown, poses before a fence-sitting crowd prior to a Michelin Field contest against House of David of Michigan. Ab Hermann, the town's only major leaguer (Boston, NL, 1923–1924) is standing third from left. (Milltown Historical Society)

By 1952 Michelin Field hosted less experienced but no less enthusiastic ball teams. Co-author Pavelec (center) whistles "Take Me Out to the Ball Game" to inspire his Milltown Lions Little League team. (Authors' Collection)

grounds—the Little League. On the Milltown Lions Club Cubs of that year, proudly posing for his first team photograph, was Clelland's twelve-year-old great-grandson (and coauthor of this book).

ALL OF NEW JERSEY'S early teams were strictly amateur until the lure of professionalism changed the baseball landscape in the 1860s. College teams aside, at least 130 amateur baseball clubs were active in New Jersey between 1855 and 1860, with Newark alone accounting for 36 junior and senior organizations. Jersey City had 42.

The Civil War did little to reduce enthusiasm for baseball in New Jersey. No better evidence exists than the 1862 tour of the Philadelphia Athletics. More than fifteen thousand watched Philadelphia prevail in a game at Hoboken. *Wilke's Spirit of the Times* said the contest awakened "the old furor for the game that marked the years 1857, 8 and 9 [and] did more to advance the interest and popularity of the game in that city than five ordinary seasons' play would have done." Later trips to Philadelphia by New Jersey clubs included some benefit matches for the United States Sanitary Commission, aiding the wounded of the war.

The war did help to kill off cricket, though. Between 1845 and 1860, the sport had been extremely popular in New Jersey, with two dozen top clubs playing each week. By 1864 there were only a half dozen cricket clubs in Newark, Orange, Paterson, and Trenton, once the centers of the game.

What fueled the growth of baseball, by contrast, was a combination of support by the newspapers, a reservoir of competent players, a flood of young immigrants who wanted to be included in the "national game," and an increasing tendency to associate ball clubs with other activities such as church, school, and job.

The trades began to create teams in the 1860s. In Newark, saloonkeepers of the Fourth Ward played their counterparts in the First Ward. Traders' Express Company complained that their loss on July 4, 1870, at the hands of the rival New Jersey Express Company had occurred with "the assistance of some outside parties." They refused to continue play unless "legitimate employees" were used.

The mix of white-collar and blue-collar players varied according to team. Early clubs, including the Newark Knickerbocker Antiquarians and the Jersey City Hamiltons, were made up of merchants, managers, lawyers, doctors, clerks, actors, and "petty professionals." Mixed blue- and white-collar clubs included the Newark Base Ball Club, the Newark Adriatics, and the Newark Lafayettes. The Newark Base Ball Club, the state's oldest team (organized in 1855), had skilled craftsmen, small shop proprietors, clerks, and bookkeepers of moderate wealth. The Adriatics were primarily jewelers, merchants, and professionals. The Lafayettes had men from the building and leather trades, along with some clerks and merchants.

In the summer of 1860 the Brooklyn Resolutes traveled to Bergen County to play the Mechanics of Jersey City. Open gambling by spectators and their foul language so upset the Resolutes' president that after his team was defeated he reluctantly gave up the game ball and refused to speak to the Mechanics' captain. A few days later he wrote a scathing letter to the *Jersey City Daily Courier and Advertiser* denouncing the crowd and accusing the Mechanics of unfairness and interference with his players. A series of point and counterpoint letters appeared in the newspaper for days afterward.

Despite gamblers and garbage-mouths, amateur baseball continued to flourish in the state, as demonstrated by the list of major amateur teams in Table 5 and the years they began to get a mention by the sporting press.

Fan behavior had not improved by 1866 when the Eurekas of Newark beat the Kearneys of Rahway 45–6 for the championship of New Jersey. The furor caused by gambling and fan interference persuaded the losers to avoid the usual postgame rituals and climb into the clubhouse via the windows to retrieve their street clothes. In a more sedate if remote event that year, the Actives played Irvington on October 3 at the Sussex County Fair Grounds in Newton for a gold ball trophy. A year later, the Belle Vue and Galaxy clubs of Bordentown introduced new excitement to New Jersey baseball. The teams were composed exclusively of young women.

New Jersey formed its own State Baseball Association in 1867, but it never built the kind of strength needed to combat the professionalism sweeping the game in the state. At its fourth annual convention at Library Hall in Elizabeth on November 9, 1870, only ten of thirty-one member clubs sent delegates. The next day the amateur Resolutes of Elizabeth won the New Jersey championship in a poorly played game. Princeton University could have claimed the cup because it had won every game played that year versus New Jersey clubs, but it declined the title.

In 1871 the nation's all-amateur teams withdrew from the National Association of Base Ball Players and formed their own organization. A March 1872 meeting in New York had seventeen clubs represented, including seven from leading colleges. F. B. Wood of the Champion Club of Jersey

TABLE 5
Major Amateur Baseball Teams in New Jersey

Team	Location	Year Press Took Note
Olympic	Paterson	1864
Americus	Newark	1864
Pioneer	Newark	1865
Alpine	Alpine	1865
Alert	West Orange (Seton Hall)	1865
Enterprise	Camden	1865
Mount Holly	Mount Holly	1865
Burlington	Burlington	1865
Kearney	Rahway	1865
Hopeful	New Brunswick	1865
National	Morristown	1865
Union	East Orange	1865
Eureka	Newark	1865
National	Jersey City	1865
Irvington	Irvington	1865
Resolute	Elizabeth	1866
Logan	Lambertville	1866
Columbia	Bordentown	1866
Penn Railroad Club	Camden	1866
Atlantic	Trenton	1866
Mohican	Hightstown	1866
Neptune	Shrewsbury	1866
Bergen	Bergen	1866
Champion	Jersey City	1866
Excelsior	Paterson	1866
Friendship	Beverly	1866
Monmouth	Hoboken	1866
Palisade	Englewood	1866
Princeton	Princeton	1866
Randolph	Dover	1866
Seaside	Long Branch	1866
Union	Camden	1866
Mystic	Paterson	1868
Oneidas	Bloomfield	1868
Hudson City	East Newark	1868

City was elected president, becoming the first chief executive of the first National Association of Amateur Base Ball Players. But this organization was never able to function with any kind of strength. It died a quiet death in 1874.

Amateur ball was still attractive, however. On Friday, September 24, 1875, ten thousand attended the New York–area amateur championship game in Hoboken. Chelsea beat the Flyaways 18–4. The size of the crowd was proof, according to the local press, that "the interest in professional ball playing has faded out and that those who like to see the game played earnestly and honestly flock to see the amateurs play as this was the largest crowd that assembled at any game this season." The next day a thin crowd watched the professional Mutuals beat the Athletics at the same site.

ALONG WITH NEWARK, Paterson, and Camden, Trenton showed early and strong interest in the game. Its baseball story is illustrative of the sport's acceptance and growth in a single city.

As early as 1867 different sections of Trenton were competing against one another, with outside teams occasionally coming to town. The first great game in the city was between the Trenton Atlantics and the Philadelphia Athletics on July 4, 1867. The field was east of the Delaware-Raritan Canal between Hamilton and Greenwood avenues. Trenton was shockingly beaten 67–8. The Trenton nine were Colwell, catcher; Treadwell, pitcher; Laing, first base; Beasley, second; Headley, third; Lear, shortstop; Lawton, John May, and Dumont in the outfield. The game was followed by a banquet presided over by Trenton mayor Alfred Reed, future president of the State Baseball Association.

The Trentons won fifty-one of fifty-four games played in 1871. By 1876, there were additional clubs, including the Red Stockings, the Marions, and the Resolutes. Early in the 1880s, the state of amateur baseball in Trenton advanced further with the creation of the Catholic Young Men's Association of South Trenton. Some members of this group helped staff the first Trenton professional team in the Eastern League, 1883–1885. A Trentonian, Patrick T. Powers, managed the team and went with it when it was sold to Jersey City. It was also during this time that other Trenton-born players were making their marks. Notable were "Silent" Mike Tiernan, who played for a dozen years with the New York Giants, and William O. Gilbert, another Giant.

Industrial league baseball also flourished in Trenton, as in Paterson, Newark, and Jersey City. From 1887 until 1895, the Trades League was the focus of baseball attention in the city. Cook's East Trenton pottery, the Equitable, the Delaware, the Enterprise and Ott & Brewer's potteries, Wilson's woolen mill, Peter Fell's, and the Walton brickyards fielded teams. Only bona fide workmen of the respective establishments could play. No alcohol was sold and no salaries were paid, but the gate receipts were distributed to the players. They became what New Jersey fans have since called semipro teams. The John A. Roebling's Sons Company fielded a team at about the time they were constructing the cables for the Brooklyn Bridge, the structure that would make Brooklyn versus New York a logistically simpler baseball competition.

In 1895 the Young Men's Christian Association (YMCA) started a Trenton team that became one of the best amateur squads in the East. Originally playing only local amateur nines, it eventually took on both National and American League teams in exhibitions as well as the Cuban Giants and Cuban Stars, the top black teams of the day.

Getting ever more serious, Trenton interests created the Delaware Valley League under the presidency of Thomas F. Waldron. Teams included the YMCA, Waldrons, Bowmans, American Bridge Company, Morrisville (Pennsylvania), and Lambertville.

With competition and numbers of fans booming, Colonel Lewis Perrine, president of the local transit company, was inspired to apply for a franchise in the professional Tri-State League in 1907. When it was granted, he created a first-class field conveniently (and profitably) situated at the end of his trolley line. From then until the demise of professional baseball in Trenton nearly half a century later, the city would be a center of both the amateur and paid versions of the game.

In Hoboken, "old-time baseball" was mostly a memory by the 1890s. An 1893 history of the city observed, "All of the old Elysian fields have been swept away in the march of the demand for building lots." Irvington did hold a reunion of the old-time greats in 1897. On hand were Charles Sweasy, Rynie Wolters, Mike Campbell, John Farrow, and Stockman, the shortstop who jumped to the Excelsiors. The townsfolk loved it as much as modern fans love to watch "old-timers" games. But things were changing.

At the turn of the century, New Jersey minor league professional teams were getting most of the attention not siphoned off by the major league teams across the rivers in New York and Philadelphia. Amateur squads continued to come and go, some gaining great popular followings, some quickly disappearing.

The esteem in which the amateur game was held may have been reflected by a game played in October 1912 at the Englewood Field Club. As reported in a history of the town:

> A novel baseball game was played on the Field Club grounds for the benefit of the hospital, between the lawyers and the doctors. The legal profession was represented by Messrs. Wortendyke, Zabriskie, Harry Ward, Mattocks, Demarest, Huckin, Ellis, Mackay and Foster. Their opponents, who appeared in operating gowns and antiseptic turbans, were Drs. Holmes, Bradner, Haring, Sullivan, Phillips, Proctor, Edwards, Wyler, Ruch and Van Dyke. Dr. Haring, who practiced medicine before baseball had entered the mind of man, made a gazelle-like home run amid wild applause. Mr. Wortendyke did a marathon, surprising those who knew him only in his dignified capacity. The hospital treasury was enriched $210 by the game.

THE COLLEGE SCENE

The earliest baseball teams consisted of "gentlemen" seeking manly, active pursuits to provide both recreation and a modern American male cachet. It is hardly surprising, then, that college men of the mid-nineteenth century looked on baseball as a worthy pastime.

Princeton students had been playing a version of town ball on campus as early as 1761, and the activity occasionally got them into difficulty with the faculty. In 1857 a cricket club and two baseball clubs were formed at Princeton, the latter playing the old "Connecticut game." A graduate recalled: "It was not the modern scientific game, but baseball, nevertheless, in its rudimentary stage. We made occasional records in this game, too, though they were never published. W. L. Rankin, '60, made one on the side of my head one day with a bat while I was catching behind him, by carelessly swinging around with bat extended after he had missed and I had caught the ball. The bat was probably of very soft wood, so I recovered."

When the growing popularity of the game required a more appropriate playing area, the "pasture" of the back campus was chosen. A standing committee was created to "remove all bricks, stones and other obstructions on the ground which were liable to cut the feet and impede the operations of the energetic club."

In the fall of 1858, three boys from Brooklyn got off the train at Princeton Junction packing balls and bats and experience in playing the hot new form of the sport, the New York game. Their arrival launched the history of modern college baseball in the United States.

The young men were Lewis Ward Mudge, H. S. Butler, and Henry L. Sampson, all of whom had played for the Star Club of Brooklyn. On March 14, 1859, they formed the Baseball Club of the Class of 1862, Nassau Hall (the Nassau Club). Expenditures were slight, amounting to $9.43 in the first year for bats, balls, and other equipment. Monthly dues of ten cents and an annual fee of fifty cents were augmented by fines for swearing (ten cents) and arguing with captains or umpires (five cents). Players expressing an opinion of a play before the decision of the umpire was given were fined three cents. Matches were held weekdays at noon and on Saturday afternoons.

On October 22, 1860, the Nassau Club played its first game with a team other than another Princeton squad. Invited by Mudge's former prep school preceptor at the Bloomfield (N.J.) Institute, Dr. E. D. Pierson, Princeton class of 1859, to play a team of college graduates in Orange, New Jersey, they journeyed north. With the score 42–42, the game had to be called due to darkness. Captain Mudge also tried to arrange a game with Rutgers but was informed that Rutgers was still playing town ball.

In the first year of the Civil War, college baseball activity slowed. But by 1862 action picked up again, and the Nassau Club played two games with the Stars of New Brunswick, winning each and thus carrying off the New Jersey state championship. The first game was played September 24 at Princeton and won by the home team 22–16. A Princeton account described Mudge's first at bat in the second contest, held in New Brunswick on October 11: "Their pitcher seized the ball and swinging his hand behind him as if in an effort to dislocate his shoulder, put his head between his legs—almost—and running furiously, discharged the ball some yards away from the home base. After repeating this action an indefinite number of times, our worthy captain, who was batting, at last got a ball that suited him and set a good example by a fine hit."

In 1863 the Nassau Club played two Philadelphia clubs, beating the Olympics and losing to the Athletics. A later rematch with the Athletics

Princeton's Nassau Base Ball Club of 1860, the first collegiate team playing under New York Rules in New Jersey. Captain Mudge is fourth from right. (Princeton University Library)

was won by Nassau in Princeton. Apparently the university's attempt at field grooming had not been successful, as a Philadelphia newspaper commented:

No one but a topographical engineer could describe that ground. To get to 1st base you ran up a hill, ran down to 2nd base, up to 3rd base and home base. The right field played at the top of a hill, the centre field at the bottom and the left field in a gully. To the Nassau players, who had been accustomed to and had overcome the difficulties of fielding on such a ground, the irregularities were of no account, but the effect was terrible on the Philadelphians, while the weakening feeling of playing on empty stomachs also told heavily against them. The Athletics, however, always play a good uphill game, and this was decidedly up hill and down hill too.

The Princetonians also played in Brooklyn that year, paying their own expenses and beating the Resolutes, Excelsiors, and Stars. They were beaten by the Atlantics, the U.S. champions. The significance of these contests seemed lost on the student body of Princeton, however. Said a contemporary commentator, they "preferred to write an essay for [the student literary magazine] than to know flies on the diamond."

In the spring of 1864, eighty-eight men were playing on clubs at Princeton. After commencement, the Nassaus went to Philadelphia to play and be beaten by the Athletics. On July 4, they beat the New York Mutuals in Hoboken, and on the fifth, they lost to the Stars in Brooklyn. On the sixth, they were beaten again by the Atlantics. On the seventh, they were beaten by the Eurekas.

In the fall they organized into a team known as the Champions of '66. Their first outing was Princeton's first intercollegiate athletic contest, a game against Williams College played in Princeton on November 22, 1864. The handsomely uniformed Williams team, which had played intercollegiate contests since 1859, when it had met Amherst in the first recorded game (under Massachusetts rules) between colleges, was none too happy with its defeat at the hands of what one player later described as "country jakes who merely pulled off their coats and played in shirt sleeves." Better spirits prevailed immediately after the contest, however, when the teams and their supporters adjourned to Mercer Hall and partook of a meal that included wild duck, snipe, chicken's tongue, lobster salad, fried oysters, and plum pudding. After dining the teams retired to enjoy speeches, cigars, and singing.

On May 5, 1865, Princeton met Rutgers for the first time, beating them 40–2. Rutgers could manage to field only eight men. After the game Rutgers challenged Nassau to a return match the following Saturday, but it was not accepted due to the Greek examinations that the Princeton students were preparing for.

Princeton baseball has long tried to establish that its pitchers were the first to throw the curve ball in competition, claiming that F. P. Henry, class of 1866, pitched curves in the fall of 1863 when the Nassau Club faced the Philadelphia Athletics and won by a score of 29–13. The *New York Clipper* reported: "In this match slow pitching with a great twist to the ball achieved a victory over swift pitching."

But the possibility of baseballs curving in flight was recognized as early as 1856, when *Porter's Spirit of the Times*, critiquing an amateur pitcher's fast and straight delivery, said: "It is questionable, however, whether his style of pitching is most successful, many believing a slow ball curving near the bat to be the most effective."

Stronger evidence than that supporting Henry's claim suggests that E. Davis, Princeton class of 1870, was pitching curve balls in 1866, two years before A. J. ("Candy") Cummings, then with the Brooklyn Excelsiors, supposedly invented the pitch after analyzing the curving flight of clamshells skipped across a pond.

Davis had prepared for Princeton University at the Edge Hill School in Princeton, where he was captain of his team. Attending games of Princeton University teams made him determined to excel in baseball when he matriculated there in 1867. During the preceding summer he practiced by bouncing a ball against a brick wall. He noticed that when a twisting ball struck the wall, it bounced back with an opposite twist created by the rotation of the ball. He therefore attempted to give the ball a downward twist so that a batter, hitting it, would send it directly upward, where it could be easily caught. He did not think about putting a curve on his pitches to prevent a batter from hitting the ball.

When Davis began to pitch in games, however, he soon began trying to curve pitches in toward the batters to make them hit the ball on the handle of the bat, thus dissipating their power. His "inshoot" pitch became legendary on campus, and he became pitcher of the first nine of the Nassau Club because few could hit his curves. During the winter students would gather in the long hall at the west end of North College to watch him practice and to try to catch his strangely curving pitches. But a rule newly instituted in the spring of 1868 required a straight-arm delivery, causing

Davis to quit baseball in his sophomore year. His legend never had a chance to develop.

The year 1868 was significant for Princeton baseball in another way, too: financial support came from outside the team for the first time. A subscription was taken among all the students and the team was sent, after commencement, to New England, where they faced Williams, Harvard, and Yale. That fall Princeton defeated the Philadelphia Athletics, an event whose outcome was overshadowed by the fact that the newly appointed president of the university, Dr. James McCosh, attended the contest. His presence and strong support of athletics in general did much to further sport in Princeton.

In 1869, when Princeton faced Rutgers in the celebrated first intercollegiate football game, the Tiger team featured four of its baseball players, including football captain W. S. Gummere, class of 1870 (a Trenton ballplayer and later chief justice of the New Jersey Supreme Court), and baseball captain W. H. Buck, also in the class of 1870.

After a brief lull, baseball enthusiasm rebounded at Princeton in 1873, with strong performances in games with Yale and Harvard. The Elizabeth Resolutes, New Jersey's entry in the first professional league, challenged the Princetons to a May 24 game. The Resolutes fielded their brightest stars, including Doug and Art Allison, John Farrow, Hugh and Mike Campbell, and still lost 6–2. Worse things were to come for Elizabeth, whose losing ways led to its departure from the pro league before season's end.

Princeton's disastrous 1874 season was quickly forgotten the following year as attention focused on the new secret weapon, "Mac" Mann and his curve ball. With Mann hurling, Princeton lost to the Philadelphia Centennials—but the 2–1 score was almost unheard of in 1875, and the sporting world focused on Princeton's upcoming contest with the Brooklyn Atlantics. Mann pitched again and Princeton won 3–2. The victory put the team at the top of U.S. baseball—but the attention may have been too much. Two days later, Princeton faced Yale and lost 14–4. Then the team lost to Harvard because it became "rattled." All was forgiven in the next contest, however, when Mann pitched a no-hitter and the team beat Yale 3–0. Then in a battle of the "parabolic" pitchers, Mann faced Hartford's Candy Cummings, recently acquired from Philadelphia and the pitcher generally credited with "inventing" the curve ball in 1864. It was no contest. Hartford won 15–1.

Earlier that season a Burlington team traveled to Princeton to play the university nine. At first base for the visitors was a Mr. Fenimore, undoubtedly of the local family that was related to Burlington-born James Fenimore Cooper, son of the founder of Cooperstown, New York. Princeton won 6–2. Burlington played Princeton twice more that season, winning 9–2 and 11–8, with first baseman Fenimore scoring one run in each contest.

Mann's arm finally succumbed to the strain of pitching every game of the 1875 season—eleven in the spring, five in the fall—and the team suffered. But in 1876 the baseball world had a new focus—the fledgling professional National League—and college ball took a backseat. Mann was now at first base for Princeton and the team went through a half a dozen pitchers trying to replace him in the box. He tried a comeback in the Yale game but could not control the ball and gave it up for good. The team went 10–6 on the season.

In May 1879, Princeton played two contests with Harvard in which the Cambridge nine insisted on using an 1876 graduate named Tyng who was both a pitcher and catcher. (He is also given credit by some baseball historians for introducing the catcher's mask, although an earlier Harvard man, Fred Thayer, gets the usual nod.) Tyng rotated duties with another named Alger, class of 1879. The combination, listed together in the box score like Siamese twins, struck out ten, allowed two bases on balls, and gave up three wild pitches (in this category divided into one for Tyng and two for Alger). Princeton, however, was too much for Harvard, Tyng and Alger. It won 5–2. The following day, Harvard turned the tables and won 8–2, but according to a Princeton source, "only with the assistance of the protested old-graduate, confidence restoring, never-wear-out pitching and catching machines, one useless without the other, and Harvard lifeless without both." (Mr. Tyng showed up again in June 1882, when he caught for the New York Stock Exchange team that lost to Princeton 9–4. He went hitless.)

The subject of player eligibility, manifested in the Princeton-Harvard contests that May, led to the forming of the American College Baseball Association on December 6, 1879. Original members included Amherst, Brown, Dartmouth, Harvard, and Princeton, with Yale entering the following year. The rules limited eligibility to students who had been in a department of the university for an entire year and excluded men who had played in professional games. Princeton sustained no damage from the new rules, emerging as champion in 1880 with a record of 16–5.

At the winter 1881–1882 meeting of the American College Baseball Association the subject of financial support to players was broached. A new rule was adopted: "Any student who had been pursuing a course of study through the entire collegiate year and whose college expenses are in no way borne by any man connected with baseball interests shall be eligible for the college nine. Any student who shall play on a professional ball nine and receive pay therefore shall not be eligible."

The rules did not yet prevent playing against professionals though, and Princeton continued to be a favorite competitor of the top pro teams. In 1881 Princeton had a significant schedule against major league teams, including Detroit (one win); the Philadelphia Athletics (two wins); the New York Metropolitans (two losses); the Washington Nationals (two losses); the New York Giants, with their stars Kelly, Brouthers, and Farrel (one loss); Providence (one loss); and the Atlantics of Brooklyn (one win, one loss).

By the spring of 1883, however, the faculty of Princeton had passed a resolution limiting the absences from class of members of the team to five days per term and prohibiting games with professional teams. The faculty obviously felt that the morals of the student players were being corrupted by games with professionals. The five-day limit effectively prevented the team from playing any practice games out of town, and many good amateur teams would not, therefore, schedule Princeton because a return game would be impossible.

But a Princeton man knows how to bend the rules when necessary. Captain J. S. Harlan, class of 1883, later told how he was able to exercise a little "law on order":

When the rule was passed forbidding play with professionals, I indulged in a diplomatic maneuvre, which was entirely successful. After some correspondence, I got hold of a baseball nine out of a patent pill manufactory in New Jersey. They were non-professionals, and on the whole, were fairly decent fellows.

I told the captain just before the game started of our troubles arising out of the rule against professional games, and that I desired him and his men to make a suitable demonstration, explaining to him the thought I had in mind. I had previously sent complimentary tickets to the Faculty, telling them that I had succeeded in getting a non-professional nine for a practice game.

Many of the Faculty came. I presume they never saw such an exhibition of ruffianism as those good fellows gave us. The pitcher came out in a red undershirt, and with one shoe off; and the way they howled and quarreled among themselves, and with the umpire, and

Beneath "Coogan's Bluff," the Princeton University student body celebrates the June 17, 1899, victory over Yale for that year's collegiate championship at the Polo Grounds in New York. (Princeton University Library)

with me, was astonishing. The result was so convincing that when I appeared at the next Faculty meeting, with a copy of the rules adopted by the professional league, parts of which forbidding swearing, card playing, gambling, and boisterous conduct, etc. I carefully read, the Faculty unanimously rescinded the rule made a few weeks before. The result was that the practice games with professionals again became possible, and Princeton made an excellent record for the season.

It was a record that might have been spoiled on June 1 when Princeton expected to play a championship game with Harvard in Cambridge. When the Tigers' uniforms could not be found, the team had to play in their street clothes. Harvard graciously agreed to call the contest an "exhibition" and rescheduled the real game for a later day.

In 1887 the existing college baseball association was abandoned and a quadrangular league was formed among Yale, Harvard, Columbia, and Princeton. Columbia dropped out the next year. But Princeton and Columbia would play again—with at least one of their games standing as a baseball milestone.

SETON HALL is the second oldest college team in the state. Its club team, called the Alerts, was competing as early as 1863, when, on October 22, it beat Fordham 20–16 at Seton Hall. It was the first intercollegiate game ever played in New Jersey.

Nearly a half century later, in 1910, the Hall could boast of two players in the major leagues: John Ferry with the Pirates and Billy Burke with the Boston Braves. Later, Kevin (Chuck) Connors graduated from the West Orange team to the Dodgers, the Cubs, and television fame on "The Rifleman." Now players such as Rick Cerone and Craig Biggio continue the representation. Among other Pirate baseball claims to fame: an undefeated season in 1942 (11–0) following an 18–1–1 performance in 1941. The team has played in four College World Series: 1964, 1971, 1974, and 1975.

Rutgers had club teams in the 1860s but did not have an official team until 1870, when it won one game and lost two. One of those losses was to Princeton by the shocking score of 47–7.

Early in this century, Rutgers boasted Paul Robeson, class of 1919, as its

Catcher and football All-American Paul Robeson (second from left) talks with the 1918 Rutgers University varsity baseball coach as teammates look on. (Rutgers University Library)

catcher. Robeson was the first black football player at Rutgers and two-time football All-American. A Phi Beta Kappa in his junior year, he became class valedictorian. His class predicted that by 1940 he would be governor of New Jersey and "the leader of the colored race in America." Instead he went on to become a celebrated actor, singer, and staunch supporter of Soviet communism.

Rutgers' finest hour may have been when it beat the once mighty but declining Newark Bears of the International League on April 12, 1947. Then called the Chanticleers, they scored five runs in the eighth inning, when ten batters came up to make the final score 7–4. Among the highlights of recent years was future Dodger, Indian, and Chicago White Sox Jeff Torborg's .537 batting average in 1963, a year the catcher also had a 1.000 slugging average. At the end of the 1989 season the all-time Rutgers record stood at 971–932–19.

The New York Knickerbockers' last clubhouse on Elysian Fields was just a few years old when organized baseball began at Stevens Institute of Technology, the college named for the Stevens family of Hoboken and situated on grounds once the homestead of the clan. From 1873 until 1893, the Stevens nine was a club team. It did not become a formal college squad until 1906. The student body in 1873 stood at just seventy-five, so fielding a team was not easy. Like all sporting groups associated with Stevens, it used the old St. George Cricket grounds at Tenth and Clinton from 1874 until the college built a new athletic field in 1907.

For the club, success was not always easy to come by. A comment in the *Link*, Stevens's magazine, cited the plight of the team in 1890: "It is owing to the lack of funds that necessitated our playing the various athletic club nines in the immediate vicinity of New York and as in almost every instance they depended on professionals for their batteries, it is not surprising that they often worsted us."

When the boys gave up the team in 1893, a final comment was offered in the college's publication:

Baseball during the season of 1893 was prolific of a series of complications which finally culminated in its abolition as a representative game at Stevens. The players who manfully stood by it during its decline showed not only a laudable patriotism for the game but also an exceptional proficiency in it, reflecting great credit on themselves and their college. The result of the season's work from the standpoint of games won was satisfactory, but the policy of professionalism, which the absence of pitching ability forced the management to adopt, reached against the game which has long threatened to lose its hold in the preference of well-wishers of Stevens' athletics. It is hoped that the continued growth of the Institute may at some future date make it possible for Stevens to assume her old stand as an exponent of the beauties of the National Game.

Another attempt was made to introduce a club in 1905. Its success caused baseball to be adopted as a college sport the following year. The *Link* observed: "Many thanks are due those men who by their diligent and persevering work on the improvised and inadequately equipped practice grounds at Castle Point made it possible for baseball to be taken under the wing of the Athletic Association."

In 1907, the new team got a new baseball field but had to look elsewhere for a batting practice site. Around 1912, the team used the Holland-American piers on Fifth Street for practice, and later the roof of the navy building. In 1947, the field house was built and a year-round batting cage became available.

In a quest for immortality, or perhaps because of a lack of dexterity, Stevens's catcher Cummings, class of 1895, was the first anywhere to throw to bases without removing his mask. But the true high spot of Stevens baseball was the occasion of Dave Garcia's perfect game, pitched against Pratt in 1971. It was his first varsity start.

One of the minor heroes of college baseball near the turn of the century ultimately became a major hero in another field. Neither accomplishment occurred in New Jersey, but the state unknowingly provided a pivotal bridge.

A University of Pennsylvania pitcher-turned-outfielder, Pearl Grey, tried to recapture his collegiate glory on an Orange club team in 1897. Born in Zanesville, Ohio, in 1856, the young man had a Garden State ancestor—a Dane named Robert Zane, who first emigrated to England and then followed William Penn to North America and New Jersey in 1678. Pearl and his brother first played baseball for the semipro Capitols of the Columbus (Ohio) City League. Pitcher Pearl was recruited by the University of Pennsylvania and there became an outstanding hurler. But when the baseball rules changed in 1893, lengthening the distance from the mound to home plate, he became an instant pitching has-been. Fortunately he could hit, and like Babe Ruth after him, he shifted to the outfield. After graduation in 1896 he went to New York City to pursue a career as a dentist.

But all pull and no play was making Pearl a dull boy, so he signed to play ball with the Orange Athletic Club in East Orange. His career there was so impressive that in 1900 a New York sportswriter wrote, "Doc Grey is famous for making home runs when needed."

Young Dr. Pearl Grey had ambitions other than dentistry and baseball, though. Unlike his brother Romer, who as "Reddy" Grey made it to the majors in 1903, Pearl chose that year to adopt a new first name, Zane, and write his first book, *Betty Zane*.

As Zane Grey, the author, he managed to include three popular tributes to baseball among his long and distinguished list of credits: *The Short Stop* (1909), *The Young Pitcher* (1911), and *The Red-Headed Outfielder and Other Stories* (1920). Drawing on his own memories of playing baseball in New Jersey as the century ended, he wrote in 1909 that "ball playing is fight all the time. . . . Every man for himself! Survival of the Fittest! Dog eat dog!"

THOUGH FOOTBALL had far overshadowed baseball on college campuses by the 1930s, baseball still was achieving sports milestones. One such event occurred on May 17, 1939, when the Princeton-Columbia game at Baker Field in Manhattan was televised, with Bill Stern providing the commentary. The broadcast took place three months before the first telecast of a professional game. Princeton won in ten innings, 2–1.

More recently, New Jersey college baseball has earned some important postseason honors. Seton Hall's Owen Carroll (1977), Rutgers' Matt Bolger (1982), and Glassboro State's Michael Briglia (1990) have been named to the American Baseball Coaches Association Hall of Fame. Glassboro State's 1978 and 1979 squads won the National Collegiate Athletic Association (NCAA) Division III championship, as did Ramapo College in 1984 and Montclair State in 1987. Top individual player honors have gone to four-time NCAA Division III All-American John Deutch, a Montclair State outfielder; 1989 National Junior College All-American pitcher Wayne Masters, also of Montclair State; and All-American outfielder Dennis McCaffrey of Brookdale College.

New Jersey college baseball players attending schools around the country are on view each summer in the Atlantic Collegiate Baseball League, an off-season circuit with headquarters in Park Ridge. The league includes teams in Teaneck (the New Jersey A's) and North Plainfield (the Pilots).

Of all New Jersey four-year colleges only Caldwell College, a school recently converted from an all-women's institution, does not field either a varsity or club baseball team.

THE OLYMPIANS

On a beautiful late afternoon on the last day of July 1984, in a baseball stadium belonging to a team with Camden roots and that once called Brooklyn home, a New Jersey college player, Seton Hall pitcher Pat Pacillo, stood with new teammates watching flags, balloons, and a marching band, and listening to John Williams's Olympic Fanfare. It was music heard frequently that summer in the town three thousand miles from the Hoboken site where a Brooklyn team played the first match game of baseball. The Los Angeles Olympics were in full sway, and the event in Dodger Stadium was the opening of the demonstration competition of the good old American game. Pacillo's team represented the United States in a seven-day tournament designed to demonstrate baseball's attractiveness for full-fledged Olympic competition.

As the infield and much of the outfield filled with the eight competing teams and other participants in the opening ceremonies, an image filled the giant Diamond Vision screen before more than fifty thousand spectators. The huge electronic face was many times taller than the five foot five body to which it belonged, that of Hamilton Township's Dick Case, executive director of the U.S. Baseball Federation (USBF), the Trenton-based national governing body of amateur baseball in the United States.

In his first encounter with organized baseball, Case had not made much of an impression. The uniform the adolescent was given by the Amsterdam, New York, youth baseball officials fit his slight body so poorly that, as he puts it, "The front only spelled 'Amster'!"

Today, Case and his dynamic sports organization orchestrate U.S. involvement with amateur baseball around the world. It is common to see his face on the Dodger Stadium Diamond Vision Screen during the Olympics, or to watch him shake hands with the president of the United States, or to observe his hurried strides through Cuban or Nicaraguan streets as he tries to set up matches for his country. His innate sense of politics puts him at ease whether dining with Nicaraguan leader Daniel Ortega or "talking baseball" with former ballplayers Fidel Castro and George Bush.

For most of the 1980s, first from the Hamilton Township headquarters

Prior to 1984 the gold medal contest between Japan and the United States at Los Angeles' Dodger Stadium, U.S. Baseball Federation's Dick Case is flanked by Olympian Cory Snyder and Marty Stutka, representative of the French Baseball Federation. (United States Baseball Federation)

and now from a new home just inside the Trenton border, Case and the USBF have been laying the groundwork for making baseball an Olympic sport. The federation is one of three dozen national governing bodies for amateur sport recognized by the U.S. Olympic Committee under the guidelines of the Amateur Sports Act of 1978. It is one of only two headquartered in New Jersey (the other being the United States Equestrian Team). The USBF also is one of the founding members of the International Baseball Association, the worldwide governing body of the amateur version of the sport.

Beneath the USBF umbrella are thirteen other baseball organizations, which retain their autonomy but derive their international representation through the USBF. As diverse as amateur baseball itself, they include: American Legion Baseball, Dixie Baseball, YMCA's of the United States, National Police Athletic Leagues, National Baseball Congress, National Collegiate Athletic Association, National Association of Intercollegiate Athletics, National Federation of State High School Associations, National Junior College Athletic Association, American Baseball Coaches Association, Little League Baseball, Inc., American Amateur Baseball Congress, and Pony Baseball. Surprisingly missing from the list is another Trenton-based amateur baseball association, Babe Ruth Baseball, which Dick Case headed for years before he came to the USBF.

The Amateur Athletic Union (AAU) also remains outside the USBF, a legacy of the AAU's change of status following Congress's passage of the Amateur Sports Act of 1978 and its apparent unwillingness to give up control of certain activities. The AAU's Junior Olympics regularly features baseball competition, causing some confusion when the USBF calls on potential corporate sponsors to support its own sanctioned Olympic Games participation.

But the USBF has not let these glitches disturb the course of baseball evolution. From a public awareness perspective, its responsibility for fielding the U.S. Olympic baseball team is most significant. The federation must select the team, train it, transport it to and from training sites and the Olympic site itself, and act as liaison between the team and the International Baseball Association. Although the Olympic Games are scheduled every four years, the work involved with fielding the U.S. team is almost continuous.

The team competes in the Intercontinental Cup Games, World Championships, Goodwill Games, Pan American Games, and the Olympic Games themselves. In preparation for international competition, the national team trains at the USBF's new training site in Millington, Tennessee, and plays in a series of games across the country against top-flight teams both domestic and international. A U.S. junior team is built from players on the four regional finalists in the Olympic Festival held during years between Olympics.

The USBF also issues the only official sanctions for international play by any U.S. amateur baseball group or individual regardless of situation. Under the Amateur Sports Act of 1978, every U.S. group must be sanctioned by the USBF in order to go abroad to play or to invite a foreign team to the United States for competition.

Freelance international competition is a constant problem for the federation. A bad situation resulting from a poorly planned or executed nonsanctioned event can damage years of effort by the USBF or its member organizations. The new participation by the USSR in the sport in the era of *glasnost* has caused more than one nonsanctioned U.S.-versus-USSR baseball game to make unwanted ripples in the field of international baseball competition.

Finally, the federation also gains national reputation with its awards programs, including the Golden Spikes. This award goes annually to the outstanding amateur baseball player in the United States. The USBF hopes that one day it will have the cachet of amateur football's Heisman Trophy. The USBF also bestows the Golden Diamonds to the outstanding amateur junior player, coach, and woman of the year.

THE SENIORS

From his restaurant in Point Pleasant Bob Delahant helps keep boyhood baseball dreams alive for the state's former ballplayers. Strictly amateur, the Over Thirty Baseball League of New Jersey fields twenty-six teams during a twenty-two-game season. Players must be over thirty, and although the average age is thirty-five, there is at least one player over sixty who shows up on a regular basis.

One can decipher the state of mind of the participants as well as the geographical spread of the senior game by reading the names of other like associations around the country: the Senior Men's Baseball League, Jericho, New York; the Roy Hobbs Baseball Association, Woodlands, California; the Over Forty Baseball League, Metairie, Louisiana; and the Fountain of Youth League, St. Louis, Missouri.

In the not-so-senior category, a league for eighteen-and-over players functions in Union and Essex counties. This Eastern State Baseball League is composed primarily of home-for-the-summer college players and a few noncollege diehards of all ages. Its team roster includes the Clifton Indians, the Cory Angels (Jersey City), the Dumont Athletic Club, the Jersey City Rangers, the Jersey City Trojans, the Montclair Eagles, the Newark Sharks, and the Summit Anchors.

The Metropolitan Baseball League, featuring a mix of ex-college and ex-professional players in the northeastern part of New Jersey, has as its resident superstar Jim Bouton, the former Yankee pitcher, sportscaster, author, and moundsman for the Little Ferry Giants. Other teams include the Hackensack Troasts, the Moonachie Braves, the North Bergen Cardinals, the Saddle Brook Colonials, the Teaneck Merchants, the Waldwick Senators, Clifton AAMCO, the Clifton Phillies, the Elmwood Park Orioles, the Haledon Pioneers, the Montclair Indians, the Verona Express, and the Wayne Athletics.

A KIDS' GAME AGAIN

A most significant portent of the future of amateur ball, not only in New Jersey but across the country as well, appeared in September 1908 in the *Newark Evening News*. In an article titled "Base Ball for Boys," the Newark paper reviewed a new movement that had begun in Trenton, where city leaders had organized a Junior Base Ball League for boys. The effort had resulted in 153 teams of about a dozen boys each competing for championship prizes. The *Evening News* observed that:

> This "boys' movement" has taken such a firm hold in Trenton that last week 6,000 citizen attended an athletic meet near that city, given for the benefit of the movement, and $1000 was netted with which to promote and maintain the Base Ball fields and other playgrounds next year. And the beauty of it is, that there has been clean, harmless Base Ball under reliable auspices, the boys have been kept out of danger, mischief and immoral associations, and the police records show a very marked decrease in the number of juvenile arrests. Not a single arrest for disorder was made during the entire summer at the ball grounds, though many hotly disputed points had to be settled.

Ken Hyde of the Teaneck Merchants prepares to deliver a pitch in the 1989 Metropolitan Baseball League Game. This league combines college, ex-college, and ex-professional players in summer competition in northern New Jersey. (Courtesy of Robert W. Hyde)

After noting that "an American boy can no more be separated from Base Ball than he can from the dinner table when he's hungry," the paper suggested a future problem: "Trenton seems to have successfully solved the problem of what to do for the boys, and is now trying to find out what to do for the girls."

Of course, the boys of Trenton were just recapturing the game that had been wrested from their youthful counterparts sixty years earlier. In the 1840s and 1850s, the men who took over the sport made it a point to diminish attention to the "childish" form of the game lest their own activities be thought of as less than manly. The National Association of Base Ball Players (NABBP), for example, tried to ignore the junior players. Though some senior players, such as Dr. Daniel L. Adams of the Knickerbockers, were in favor of granting full voting rights to any junior (under twenty-one) teams that applied that year, others did not want to play with individuals they considered children. These objectors worried that the junior teams were so numerous they would "over-rule those improvements that did not chime with their ideas of the game." They believed the juniors did not truly understand the sport and that they quarreled too much at matches. The 1858 convention of the NABBP settled the matter by allowing junior clubs to attend meetings but not vote.

A letter writer to *Porter's Spirit of the Times* calling himself "Infant Ball Player" wrote in protest of the snub. He stated that boys wanted "to keep up the points of the game which require the utmost physical exertion, and the exercise of skill and strength combined." He suggested the senior players wanted "to make the game a means of showing off their figures in fancy dresses, and their wealth in fancy dinners." He went on to ask that "the boys have a say in regard to this game, which they have always played, and which most of you [adults] have only just now taken out of their hands—unless you have no other way of showing the world that you are not children, except by refusing to have anything to do with boys." The *Spirit of the Times* suggested that junior clubs simply form their own group, which they did in 1860.

Nonetheless, boys playing base ball in the last half of the nineteenth century were considered to be mimicking the adults, not the other way around. The *Newark Daily Advertiser* wrote, "There is not an urchin in Newark" who did not belong to a club that emulated a senior club. The article lauded "that little republic of baseball," where "the child of wealth is seen playing with the youthful ragamuffins from some neighboring alley, and the magic ball passes swiftly from the pretty hand of the patrician boy to the soiled fist of the little plebeian."

Thirty-one years after Trenton began its boys baseball movement in 1908, a new program began in Williamsport, Pennsylvania. There on June 6, 1939, twenty-nine-year-old Carl Stotz created the Little League. His structured program for boys between nine and twelve received increasing attention over the next few years, not only in his state but in others as well. By 1947 Stotz felt he had enough teams to hold a state tournament and, with an eye toward expansion, invited an all-star team from the Hammonton, New Jersey, Little Big League to play the winner. In 1949 the tournament was officially called the Little League World Series and was won by that year's Hammonton team. It would be two decades before a New Jersey team would again come out on top. In 1970, Wayne took the honors, followed in 1975 by Lakewood.

In 1951, a new organization was formed in Hamilton Township to give a baseball home to boys who had outgrown Little League. Babe Ruth Baseball, whose headquarters have since moved to Trenton, first established leagues for thirteen- to fifteen-year-olds. In 1952, it held its first World Series in Trenton, which was won by Stamford, Connecticut. It took until 1956 for a New Jersey team to win the finale, when Trenton took the championship in Portland, Oregon. Other New Jersey teams finishing number one have been: Trenton again in 1962, Ewing Township in 1970, and Cherry Hill in 1989.

League officials expanded the program in 1966 by adding a league for sixteen- to eighteen-year-olds and in 1974 by introducing its Babe Ruth Prep League for thirteen-year-olds. In 1984 it entered Little League turf and formed its Bambino Division for players twelve and under. Rutherford won the sixteen–eighteen World Series in 1981. Among current major leaguers who have played in the state's Babe Ruth League are Dodger Orel Hershiser (Cherry Hill East), California Angel Bill Schroeder (West Windsor), and White Sox Dave Gallagher (Hamilton).

Babe Ruth League records include a couple of players who lived just a few miles from baseball's birthplace on the Elysian Fields: in the thirteen-year-old World Series of 1983, George Mendoza of West New York struck out twenty-three batters. In the thirteen–fifteen World Series of 1961, Englewood hit a record twelve home runs, three by Al Levithan (also a record).

The barriers erected by men against boy ballplayers have long since been breached. But what of New Jersey girls? Each year Peter Watson, a Summit resident who administers the Howell Living History Farm in Hopewell, recreates a town ball game as originally played in Camden and gives girls a chance to play along with boys and men. On a field near the

The 1947 "Little Big League" team from Hammonton, New Jersey, arrives in Williamsport to play as the first non-Pennsylvania team in the fledgling Little League, founded there in 1939. The 1949 Hammonton team won the championship in what by then was called the Little League World Series. (Carl E. Stotz)

Hoboken Dems' pitcher Maria Pepe gets instruction from her coach in the 1972 Little League appearance that marked the beginning of end for institutionalized discrimination against female players in youth baseball program. (Courtesy of photographer, Jack Johnston, *Newark News*, 1972)

site's farmhouse, Watson runs the games by rules that preceded Alexander Cartwright's innovations in 1845. Players run to their stakes, are "soaked" with thrown balls for outs, and wait their turn as thirteen other team members take their turns batting at the Mercer County Park Commission facility.

Girls playing any form of the game creates little stir these days. But in 1972, baseball's birthplace experienced a real shock when the Young Dems of Hoboken, a Little League team, sent its pitcher to the mound. It was the beginning of the end of an evolutionary process that may have started in 1867 when the two all-female clubs of Bordentown took the field. Or when ever-surprising Ed Barrow, who had introduced Honus Wagner to the world, sent Elizabeth Stroud (using the name Lizzie Arlington) to the mound in Newark in 1898.

In 1972, in Hoboken, Maria Pepe went to her windup, threw her first pitch, and thereby broke the rules of Little League, Inc. After a few appearances, the outcry and pressures to remove her from the game reached the point that Little League powers threatened to revoke Hoboken's charter in the league. The controversy eventually went before the New Jersey Supreme Court, where a judgment was rendered determining that Little League rules discriminated against females. The ensuing storm of publicity across the country, followed by other court cases, eventually persuaded Little League, Inc. to petition Congress for permission to change its charter to allow girls to participate. Too late for Maria Pepe, who was over the age limit by the time the matter was finally settled. But she and the Young Dems of Hoboken had written another first for the New Jersey town. Today almost seven thousand girls play Little League ball, and a girl made it to the Little League World Series in 1989. For that we can thank Maria Pepe, her parents, her coach, her teammates, and Hoboken baseball—again.

CHAPTER 8

Getting Down to Business

New Jersey Firms Turn Diamonds into Gold

Classic ceramic work, now in the New Jersey State Museum, is one of two baseball vases created in 1876 by Isaac Broome of Ott & Brewer Company of Trenton. Its mate was presented to the Detroit Wolverines, winners of 1887 National League pennant. (The Brewer Collection, New Jersey State Museum)

When Jack Armstrong, the National League's starting pitcher in the 1990 All-Star game, stepped to Wrigley Field's mound, no more than a handful of people knew of the intimate connection he had at that very moment with New Jersey. It was not just that Armstrong was Jersey-born (Englewood), Jersey-resident (Neptune), and Jersey-educated (Rider College, before transferring to the University of Oklahoma). The fact was, as he looked to the catcher for his signal, his feet stood on a small patch of New Jersey soil and he held in his hand a baseball that had been prepared for play by an umpire's deliberate massage in a glob of New Jersey river mud.

He may also have been one of dozens of players in the major leagues whose feet were shod with spikes supplied by one of two New Jersey–based sporting goods manufacturers. Watching his every move at home via TV were tens of millions of fans who would soon see a commercial offering the 1990 All-Star game program to anyone who sent off a few dollars to a Trenton, New Jersey, address, and would see, after a rain delay, the Wrigley Field grounds crew try to dry the field with shovels full of New Jersey clay.

At the height of the New York Yankees' 1950s dynasty, WPIX-TV telecasts used to commercially extol "Baseball and Ballantine," promoting both the sport and its connection with a New Jersey–brewed beer. Many similar connections exist in the 1990s between baseball and New Jersey firms, as they have from day one of the modern game.

Perhaps the first to make money from an interest in baseball was New Jerseyan Colonel John Stevens when he collected fares from the New Yorkers, who increasingly came to his Hoboken pleasure ground to play the game. But others were there at the start, too. Prominent among them was a Hoboken hotelier named McCarty, whose establishment on the edge of Elysian Fields was the favorite after-competition watering hole for baseball and cricket players. From earliest times, McCarty's was the usual Hoboken destination for the New York Base Ball Club and the Knicker-bockers, starting in 1845 and continuing for some years afterward. His connection with the Elysian Fields was such that he seems to have been able to collect an annual fee (ten dollars) for the fields' use and for the construction of clubhouses. Undoubtedly, the money spent on postgame festivities more than compensated McCarty for any expense on his part.

Like the ferries and hotels, the railroads made money from baseball, transporting teams and fans across the state for regular contests. At the game sites, owners of horse-drawn wagons regularly picked up fares. Resorts such as Spring Lake, Lakewood, Allaire, Absecon, Pleasantville, and

199

Cape May were sites for major league spring training camps and were able to push their seasons back into March, long before the normal influx of tourists.

In the 1890s, New Jersey's legendarily lenient incorporation laws attracted firms connected with the sport. These included A. G. Spalding Brothers and even such teams as the New York Giants and Pittsburgh Pirates.

Trenton pottery makers, traditional supporters of baseball even into this century, sought promotional recognition at the 1876 centennial celebration with the creation of two unique ceramic baseball trophies. They were described two years later in a book on ceramic art:

A pair of vases in parian [a china made distinctive by its soft, ivorylike tint] designed to illustrate the national game of baseball. . . . Round the foot of each vase, and standing on the supporting pedestal, are arranged three figures of base-ball players, modelled after a thoroughly American ideal of physical beauty, embodying muscular activity rather than ponderous strength. . . . A series of clubs belted round with a strap ornaments the stem of the vases, and some exquisitely wrought leaves and berries are woven round the top. The orifice is covered by a cupola or dome, composed of a segment of a base-ball, upon which stands an eagle.

The pieces got mixed reviews at the 1876 exhibition and were separated in the 1880s. One was given to the National League in 1887, to be awarded to the league champions. The Detroit Wolverines won the pennant that year and presumably were given the trophy. In 1988 it was found in the Detroit Historical Museum by Ellen Paul Denker, an art historian working for Lawrenceville, New Jersey's Lenox Inc., which was preparing a traveling exhibition of distinctive American ceramics. She was instrumental in reuniting the missing vase with its partner, which had found its way to the collections of the New Jersey State Museum in Trenton. Later that year the American Wing of the Metropolitan Museum of Art displayed the New Jersey State Museum's vase along with its long missing partner in its exhibition "American Porcelain: 1770–1920." The *New York Times* declared them to be "show stoppers." Today the two pieces are widely considered to be "great monuments in American ceramic art."

Future baseball business opportunities might have been responsible for a development in Princeton in the spring of 1897. Many in Princeton (at least those who were baseball fans) were pleased by the sounds coming from the back campus. The crack of the ball against the bat was a sound they loved, and it occurred no more frequently than when shortstop G. H. Butler, class of 1898, stepped to the plate. Butler batted .422 that year and contributed ten home runs to the Tigers' cause.

But there was another baseball-related sound on the Princeton campus, one that was less pleasing: the thunderous roar of Professor Hinton's marvelous pitching machine. It was a device Abner Doubleday would have loved. Hinton's machine was actually a small, smooth-bore cannon mounted on two wheels that the ingenious professor had modified to fire baseballs rather than cannonballs. With the addition of curved metal prongs, or "fingers," the ball was given a variety of spins as it left the muzzle to mimic the pitches of the day. A slight adjustment in the amount of black powder used as a charge modified the speed of the delivery.

Staring down the barrel of the professor's invention may have helped Butler in 1897, but the cannon evidently was not on the practice field the following spring, for Butler saw his fortunes change drastically. Although elected team captain, he resigned later in the season for reasons unrecorded. His average fell 168 points from the previous year. What became of the Hinton machine is unrecorded as well.

Sporting goods companies were established early in New Jersey, led in 1892 by the prestigious firm of Albert G. Spalding. The former pitcher and would-be athletic equipment baron capitalized his firm at $4 million. After buying out his major competitors, Reach and Wright & Ditson, he set about trying to corner the baseball equipment market. Although the firm eventually moved its offices out of New Jersey, its corporate roots remained for decades. The Spalding baseball, or one manufactured by one of its subsidiaries, would be the one batted about in the majors until well into the 1970s.

Today dozens of large and small equipment firms provide everything from the uniform numerals made by Morris Plains' Miracle Grip Lettering, to the bases supplied by General Sportcraft in Bergenfield, to the Ace brand bandages of Franklin Lake–based Becton-Dickinson and the Red Cross adhesive tape of New Brunswick–headquartered Johnson & Johnson. The athletic shoes of Adidas USA, headquartered in Warren, and PONY Sports & Leisure of Rutherford are worn and endorsed by countless college athletes and major leaguers. And before leaving the state in 1989, the MacGregor company of East Rutherford provided a variety of equipment to baseball, including the official ball for Little League and Babe Ruth baseball and the glove used by major leaguers.

Of course major leaguers are supplied their gloves for free by these manufacturers, but when the user-purchased gloves of amateur ball-players around the country have seen better days, John Golomb, the self-styled "sports doctor" of Rocky Hill, restores them to mint condition. Golomb will repair a glove, totally rebuild it, or replicate any vintage mitt from scratch. A highlight of his business came when he reproduced a glove exactly like that worn by Robert Redford in *The Natural* for a fan of the film. From $7 to replace a lace to $60 for a complete overhaul to $175 for a vintage replica, Golomb's services have kept him busy and extended the lives of hundreds of "old favorites" for players around the country.

A more prosaic supplier servicing the national pastime is the Partac Peat Corporation of Great Meadows. The Warren County firm digs and bags New Jersey soil and ships it to ball parks throughout the United States, where it becomes pitching mounds, batting boxes, running paths, infields, and edge of outfield warning tracks. Partac's "Beam Clay" brand of Jersey dirt has been used in professional stadiums since 1922. Today, more than fifty professional ball yards are really little islands of New Jersey. They include Wrigley Field, the Astrodome, Dodger Stadium, Yankee Stadium, Shea Stadium, Milwaukee County Stadium, Three Rivers Stadium, and Toronto's Exhibition Stadium.

A patch of the Garden State is the setting for action on more than two hundred college fields as well—from home-state Princeton and Seton Hall to the universities of Miami and Hawaii. And when things get wet in the pros or at the colleges, Partac's "Diamond Dry" sops up the problem. In addition to its use in the 1990 All-Star game in Chicago, the drying agent came to the rescue at the 1979 World Series in Pittsburgh and the 1983 Fall Classic in Milwaukee and St. Louis. Altogether a dozen major league clubs keep it on hand to combat mud.

Mud is what matters, too, in the most intriguing New Jersey baseball-business connection. Each year, before the season starts, the office of Major League Baseball arranges to ship a single coffee can packed with about fifteen pounds of New Jersey creek mud to each of the twenty-six big league teams throughout the country. For more than fifty years the mud has come from the same source and has served the same purpose—to remove the shine from new baseballs in preparation for play, a task accomplished by the umpiring staff prior to each contest. In half a century, not a single ball has been thrown, hit, or caught in major league baseball that was not baptized in this singular Jersey ooze. But ask for information about the company, the product, or its source and officials will suggest you write your questions in a letter, which will be forwarded to and

John Golomb, self-styled "Sports Doctor," repairs baseball gloves and other equipment from around the country in his Rocky Hill workshop. (John Golomb)

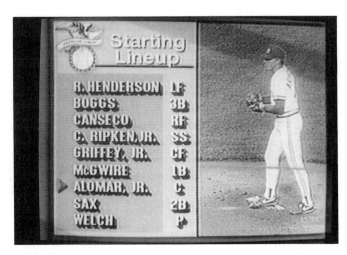

Millions watched as New Jerseyan Jack Armstrong stood atop the mound of Garden State soil to begin the 1990 Major League All-Star Game in Chicago's Wrigley Field. Later, viewers saw New Jersey clay being used to dry up the bullpen after more than an hour of rain delay. (Reproduced with permission of Major League Baseball. Copyright 1990 by MAJOR LEAGUE BASEBALL.)

"possibly" (but, it is hinted, probably not) answered by the mystery mud masters.

What is known is the product's name: "Lena Blackburne's Baseball Rubbing Mud." What is guessed is that it comes from the bed of the Pennsauken Creek. The rest of the story is muddy.

There *was* a Lena Blackburne, although he was born Russell Aubrey Blackburne in Clifton Heights, Pennsylvania, in October 1886. By the time he was twenty-four he had acquired two additional names, Slats and Lena, and enough ability to play infield for the Chicago White Sox. Blackburne stayed with the Sox for five years and then slipped from major league view until 1918, when he played for Cincinnati's National League team. (He, thus, was not in the Windy City to muddy his name in the following year's Black Sox scandal.)

In 1919, Blackburne showed up for the start of the season with the National League Boston Braves and by midsummer was with the Phillies. He played his position well and was ranked fifth in not allowing runs to score by virtue of his fielding ability. But it was a different story at the plate. At year's end he had batted only .199 with the Philadelphia squad.

The 1919 Phillies finished forty-seven and a half games out of first place, so Blackburne's batting problems were of minor consequence. Apparently, though, he found time to become acquainted with the surrounding territory. He might even have gazed into one or more creeks on the Jersey side. Somehow he got to know what mud was. When he returned to the majors with the White Sox in 1927, first as a pinch hitter, then as a player-manager in 1928, he introduced his Jersey mud baseball rubdown to the majors. Blackburne's uniquely refined product replaced the competing glop and eventually found its place with every major league team. It even found a place of recognition in the Hall of Fame, where a tin of Lena Blackburne's Rubbing Mud is on permanent display.

When Blackburne died in 1968 in Riverside, New Jersey, his name continued to represent him in the game. Who exactly mines the river mud today is unclear.

From the mud below, the history of the baseball business in New Jersey soars to the very heavens. Although not strictly speaking a business, an enterprise known as Baseball Chapel in Bloomingdale orchestrates a nationwide involvement with church groups and major league baseball teams. Trips to big league games incorporate a precontest chapel or Bible study with members of both teams in attendance.

At a slightly lower altitude, the earth's ionosphere has been saturated with broadcasts of baseball games controlled from New Jersey for more than six decades. It began in 1921 with the first "subway World Series" between the Yankees (playing in the Polo Grounds because the "house that Ruth built" had not been built yet) and the New York Giants. In a field-level box seat with a live telephone in his hand was *Newark Sunday Call* sports editor Sandy Hunt.

On the other end of the line, atop the Bamberger's department store building in Newark, was the staff of radio station WJZ, with Graham McNamee recreating the game from Hunt's play-by-play calls for the benefit of a national audience listening at home and at department store radio displays, linked by KDKA of Pittsburgh and WBZ of Springfield, Massachusetts. The following year the same two teams met, but radio audiences were treated to a new experiment by WJZ—a live mike at the ball park. Listeners heard not only Grantland Rice's stirring descriptions but also the actual crack of the bat and the roar of the crowd and even the loud voice of legendary umpire Bill Klem when he called balls and strikes.

Today Secaucus is the corporate headquarters of a distant descendant of WJZ, which ultimately became New York's WOR radio. Its New Jersey–based television offspring, WWOR-TV, is the flagship television station of the New York Mets, whose noncablecast games are seen nationwide via "superstation" transmission.

Those radio broadcasts of long ago are not lost to the vastness of space, however, thanks to a small firm in Clifton. Danrick Enterprises offers audio tapes of classic baseball broadcasts of the past. From game 3 of the 1936 World Series to the 1990 interleague competition, Danrick keeps the sounds of radio baseball alive.

Sharp Electronics in Mahwah provides TV monitors for closed-circuit delivery of every pitch, hit, and catch to fans who spend much of each game queuing up for refreshments or souvenirs beneath the stands at Shea Stadium. In arenas such as Toronto's Exhibition Stadium, giant TV displays manufactured by Sony USA, based in Park Ridge, bring glimpses of the contests to those who stay seated.

Other firms use electronics for delivering news of baseball. Jackson Township's Alan Stein is developing "1-900-Go Team-1," a pay-per-call highlight service for diehard Yankee fans. In Jersey City, just a few miles south of Elysian Fields, SportsTicker, Inc. transmits "real-time" baseball scores and breaking events directly from ball parks around the country. Editors at its Jersey City news center create broadcast-quality copy that is transmitted via satellite to radio and television stations and via computer terminal and printer to other users of the service. The company covers all major and minor league action and has customers in the United States, Canada, South America, and Japan.

SportsTicker is a service of Telerate Sports, Inc., whose owner, Dow Jones & Company, Inc., enters into the baseball news business at other times as well. Its more familiar product, the *Wall Street Journal*, includes scores of World Series games on its front page, which is transmitted to its satellite printing plants around the country from a parabolic dish on the grounds of its South Brunswick facility.

SportsTicker is the successor of Western Union's original Baseball Ticker, which was launched in 1909. Just three years earlier, West Orange–based Thomas Edison (whose first real job was with Western Union in 1868) created the first film about baseball with a story line. His 1906 *How the Office Boy Saw the Ball Game*, was a tale about a young man escaping from work to get to a ball game, only to find his boss sitting in the next seat.

Edison's motion pictures were frequently blamed for the decline of attendance at pro ball games in the late 1890s, but enough fans came to the contests at the parks in Columbus, Toledo, Milwaukee, Pittsburgh, Cleveland, Boston, Washington, and Philadelphia to keep another enterprising Ohioan in greenbacks. Harry Mozley Stevens, born in England but a resident of Niles, Ohio, had found that there was money to be made in selling scorecards to the fans in the stands. Pre-Stevens scorecards had been slips of paper, insubstantial and often incorrect, with no attention paid to changes in batting order. Stevens formalized the cards by printing them on heavy stock and by allowing room for keeping score. Later, Stevens augmented scorecard sales with offerings of sandwiches, pie, ice cream, peanuts, and soda. His big break came when he was offered the opportunity to handle all the concessions at New York's Polo Grounds in 1894. Before he took the leap, however, he offered his partner in Pittsburgh a chance to come along. That partner, Ed Barrow, declined, stating he'd rather stick to baseball. Stick he did, managing the Paterson team in the Atlantic League and Newark in the International League, then becoming the International League's president, field manager of the Boston Red Sox (where he converted Babe Ruth to the outfield), and finally the major architect of the development of the New York Yankee dynasty of the 1920s. His management achievements ultimately earned him a place in baseball's Hall of Fame.

Harry Stevens went to the Polo Grounds, introduced the hot dog, and built the Harry M. Stevens company, now located in Cranbury, New Jersey.

Cranbury-headquartered Harry M. Stevens company has supplied baseball parks since the late nineteenth century with everything from hot dogs to beer to official programs. This 1899 program was sold to the faithful who journeyed to the Polo Grounds for the Princeton-Yale contest pictured on page 180. (Harry M. Stevens, Inc., Cranbury)

There, in a brand new (1988) corporate office and warehouse facility, the company is looking toward its second hundred years of baseball involvement. It is the concessionaire for Shea Stadium, the Houston Astrodome, and maintaining its baseball Giants' connection, Candlestick Park in San Francisco. It also services Fenway Park in Boston, whose resident Red Sox are in part owned by the Stevens parent company. In addition, Stevens's subsidiary companies provide souvenirs, do facility maintenance, and manage luxury boxes.

Around the state smaller companies provide a delightful variety of "official" major league products. In Vincentown, JKA Specialties markets celluloid buttons featuring major league players. In Carlstadt, Cliff Engle Sweaters manufactures knitwear with team logos. A Vernon firm with the unlikely name of the Congruent Machine Company, Inc. manufactures logo-bedecked pocket flashlights. MDV, R&D Marketing, Inc. of Atlantic Highlands produces soft wall hangings celebrating major league teams.

All these products appear in the Major League Baseball Officially Licensed Merchandise Catalogue, one of the many printed baseball materials distributed by Trenton's Hibbert Group, whose Pro Sports Center is the destination of all those "P.O. Box 90, Trenton, New Jersey 08561" promotions seen on World Series and All-Star game telecasts.

A division of this corporation, the Hibbert Company, a well-established Trenton printing and marketing firm, ships thousands of All-Star game and World Series souvenir programs, media guides, instructional videotapes, and even baseballs. It also produces and distributes Major League Baseball's own Annual Report, which tells the financial world just how healthy the professional game really is.

Other New Jersey companies tie into baseball via the promotional route. Morris Plains' Warner-Lambert Company, for example, promotes its Rolaids antacid with a program called "the Rolaids Relief Man Award," given to the outstanding major league relief pitcher each year.

Throughout the state a growing number of small baseball collectible shops has sprung up. Catering to thousands of collectors of anything to do with baseball, some operate out of garages, others, such as the J&C Baseball Dugout in Brick Township, have full-fledged and constantly expanding retail space and make hundred-dollar deals day after day.

New Jersey baseball collector shows range from the semiannual Meadowlands show, to Atlantic City casinos, to church basements. They occur throughout the year and keep the game of the past alive for generations who never saw the greats of the golden age of baseball.

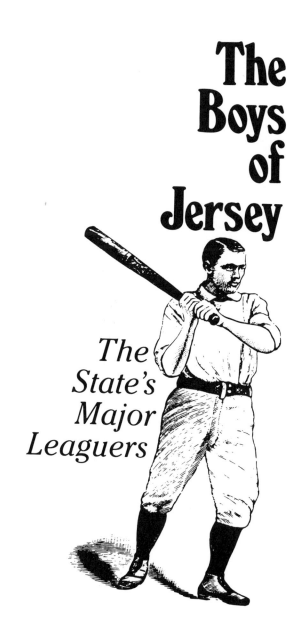

CHAPTER 9

The
Boys
of
Jersey

The
State's
Major
Leaguers

John Henry Lloyd (Courtesy of Newark Public Library)

Through the end of the 1989 season, about five thousand men had toed the rubber and hurled a baseball homeward at least once in a major league baseball game. Another seventy-six hundred or so had batted (not including pitchers unless they regularly pinch-hit or played other positions).

Of the 7,600 batters, some 190 claimed New Jersey as their place of birth, or about 2.5 percent of the total—not bad since the average for fifty states would be 2.0 percent. It is true, of course, that when the National League threw out its first ball in 1876, many of today's states were not even states yet. (The citizenry of these nonstates—Alaska, Arizona, Hawaii, Idaho, Montana, New Mexico, North Dakota, Oklahoma, South Dakota, Utah, and Washington—probably had better things to do than play baseball in 1876.) And since baseball as we know it got started in Jersey, you might say that the state should have sent more people to the big leagues than places that host surfing championships or thousand-mile dogsled races.

New Jersey has done better with pitchers than with batters, delivering 155 or so native sons to the majors—a bit above 3 percent of all who have pitched in the bigs. Perhaps not surprisingly, the state's catcher contribution is also larger than average.

The big question, inevitably, is: Who were the best of these Garden State natives? With malice toward none and sympathy for all who get short shrift in the next few pages, we hereby offer our choices for the All–New Jersey team (see Table 6). (We got lots of statistical help from *Total Baseball*, edited by John Thorn and Pete Palmer.)

With the exception of William Robert ("Sliding Billy") Hamilton, we've restricted the first team to those who played the bulk of their major league ball after the turn of the century. Our justification for this is that some strange rules held sway in the early days: four strikes to the out, fifty feet from mound to home, spitballs allowed. Not that all these rules changed on January 1, 1900. But that is as neat a dividing line as any other we might have chosen.

Three of the selections were automatic: if Hamilton, Leon Allen ("Goose") Goslin, and Joseph Michael ("Ducky") Medwick were good enough for the Hall of Fame selection committee, they are good enough for us. That took care of the outfield. (George Case, Doc Cramer, and Mike Tiernan were all stellar performers, though.)

Braun and Torborg were easy picks, too, for no other Jersey-borns seem to claim any distinction in the designated hitting or post-1900

TABLE 6
The All–New Jersey–Born Team

Position	First Team	Second Team	Pre-1900 Team
Right-handed starting pitcher	Don Newcombe	Andy Messersmith	
Left-handed starting pitcher	Al Downing	Johnny Vander Meer	
Right-handed relief pitcher	Joe Black		
Left-handed relief pitcher	Ron Perranoski		
Catcher	John Romano	Frankie Hayes	
First base	John Briggs	Joe Cunningham	Kid Gleason
Second base	Danny O'Connell	Dots Miller	Hardy Richardson
Shortstop	Red Shannon	Eddie Kasko	Billy Shindle
Third base	Wid Conroy	Joe Stripp	
Left field	Goose Goslin	Doc Cramer	Blondie Purcell
Center field	Billy Hamilton	George Case	Mike Tiernan
Right field	Joe Medwick	Charlie Jamieson	
Designated hitter	Steve Braun		
Manager	Jeff Torborg		Patrick Powers

managing categories. Likewise Joe Black and Ron Perranoski, as rightie and leftie relief pitchers.

The starting pitcher choices were not much more difficult. For example, Don Newcombe and Andy Messersmith both led their leagues in one positive stat or another fourteen times during their careers. No other right-handed starters native to Jersey came anywhere close. But Newcombe did it in two fewer years and won nineteen more games than Messersmith while losing nine fewer. Newk's total pitching index (TPI), according to *Total Baseball*, came out substantially higher than Messersmith's.

In the left-handed starter category, Al Downing finished handily ahead of the legendary Johnny Vander Meer. Though Vander Meer was the only man ever to fashion two consecutive no-hitters, he actually won fewer games than he lost over a thirteen-year career in the majors. Downing, on the other hand, won 123 while losing 107 and led his league once each in fewest hits allowed per game, total strikeouts, strikeouts per game, lowest opponent batting average, and shutouts.

Now the picks get tougher, starting with the catcher's position.

If you wander down to River Road, below Castle Point in Hoboken on any sunny summer afternoon, you may happen on a committee of sixtyish gentlemen in bathing suits, fresh from a dip in the Hudson. These gentlemen have no trouble at all naming the best catcher ever to emerge from Jersey: John ("Honey") Romano, the pride of Hoboken. In the end, we agreed with these biased experts. But Romano's numbers were not that much better than those of our runner-up, Frankie Hayes, who finished his fourteen-year career in the majors a decade before Romano started his ten-year stint in 1958. Romano and Hayes both came out ahead of several Garden State backstops whose names may be more familiar to some baseball fans: Charlie Berry, Rick Cerone (number ten among catchers in lifetime fielding average), Jeff Torborg, and Steve Nicosia.

"And what about Moe Berg?" someone is sure to ask, recalling Moe's exploits at Newark's Barringer High and Princeton University. The fact is, Berg does not qualify, for he was born in New York City. But for his exploits alone he deserves a mention here.

In truth there probably never was anyone quite like Berg. Authors Louis Kaufman, Barbara Fitzgerald, and Tom Sewell concisely sum him up in the title of their book *Moe Berg: Athlete, Scholar, Spy.* Son of Russian Jewish immigrants, Berg was gifted not only with athletic talent but also with an acuteness of mind and ear that made him a world-class linguist. Getting to Princeton on an academic scholarship, Moe took four years of French, three of Italian, two and a half each of Latin and Spanish, one each

Jeff Torborg, Plainfield-born, Westfield-raised, and Mountainside resident, as Rutgers University Star about 1960 and as manager of Chicago White Sox, 1990. (Sports Media Relations, Rutgers University and the Chicago White Sox)

of Greek and German, and a course in Sanskrit. Always something of a mystery man and loner, and feeling out of place among the prep school alumni who dominated Princeton in 1919–1923, he used baseball as his only diversion from studies, excelling equally at ball and books. In his senior year, he batted .386 to lead a Tiger team that compiled nineteen straight victories.

After graduating from Princeton, Berg signed with the Brooklyn Dodgers and had a decent but far from spectacular first season in the majors. A part of his mind surely was on Paris and the Sorbonne, to which he traveled at season's end to study linguistics with the great Professor Rousselot. With that out of his system, he returned to baseball in 1924 and resumed building what would be a fifteen-year career in the big leagues, mostly with Chicago, Washington, and Boston of the American League.

But linguistics remained a lifelong love, and his awesome language skills made Berg an instant hit with the locals during postseason tours of Japan in the mid-1930s with Babe Ruth, Lou Gehrig, Jimmie Foxx, and others. Berg began studying Japanese just a few months before the 1932 tour and reportedly was proficient by the time his boat docked at Yokohama. This same easy fluency undoubtedly served Berg well a few years later in a second career, that of spy for the Allies during World War II in Europe.

Had Moe Berg been born in New Jersey, would he have beaten out Romano or Hayes on our all-star team? Probably not, for his major league career, though longer than theirs, did not quite measure up either offensively or defensively. But throw in scholarship and clandestine exploits, and Berg would be a shoo-in!

Moving down to first base on the all–New Jersey team, John Briggs gets the nod over the better-hitting Joe Cunningham thanks to much slicker glove work. Before taking fielding into account, *Total Baseball* gives Cunningham a total average of .857 compared to Briggs's .782. But when play in the field is added, Briggs gets a total player rating of 6.1, more than double Cunningham's 3.0. Among the better-known also-rans at first were Mike Jorgenson (number 9 among first basemen in lifetime fielding average) and Dennis Walling.

At second Danny O'Connell, who played briefly in New York before the Giants decamped for San Francisco, was a fairly obvious choice for first team. He gave away little in batting to the other contenders and sparkled in the field. But the pre-1900 choice, Hardy Richardson, batted nearly forty points higher on lifetime average, knocked in five hundred more runs, and earned a total player rating of 25.9 versus O'Connell's 2.0.

Dots Miller and Eddie Miksis, who each received a solitary vote for the

Hall of Fame, and Larry Milbourne were among the other Jersey boys in contention for the keystone slot.

Major league shortstops are in short supply among New Jersey natives. Miksis, Miller, Milbourne, and some others played the position, but not primarily. Among those who did, only one wound up with a positive total player rating—Red Shannon. Though Shannon's major league career was relatively short and undistinguished, the shortstop spot goes to him, with Eddie Kasko (good hitting, no fielding) in the runner-up slot.

Finally, at the hot corner, Wid Conroy takes top honors, with Joe Stripp the bridesmaid. Conroy, who played just after the turn of the century, displayed a nice balance of hitting for average, hitting for power, and fielding. One voter thought him good enough for the Hall of Fame. Stripp performed in the 1930s, mostly for Brooklyn, got no Hall of Fame votes, and also had well-balanced numbers, though not quite as good as Conroy's.

In brief, here are the records of the first team (players) and a few of the more stellar runners-up:

Don Newcombe, right-handed starting pitcher, ten years in majors
Born: Madison (grew up in Elizabeth)
Principal team: Brooklyn/Los Angeles Dodgers, 1949–1958
Record: Won 149, lost 90
Led league: wins (1 year), win percentage (2), strikeouts (1), strikeouts per game (1) fewest walks per game (2)

Al Downing, left-handed starting pitcher, seventeen years in majors
Born: Trenton
Principal teams: New York Yankees, 1961–1969; Los Angeles Dodgers, 1971–1977
Record: Won 123, lost 107
Led league: fewest hits per game (1), strikeouts (1), strikeouts per game (1), shutouts (1)

Joe Black, right-handed relief pitcher, six years in majors
Born: Plainfield
Principal team: Brooklyn Dodgers, 1952–1955
Record: Won 30, lost 12, saved 25
Led league: no leads—but in a hard-to-beat rookie performance, helped Dodgers to pennant with fifteen wins, fifteen saves against only four losses.

Ron Perranoski, left-handed relief pitcher, thirteen years in majors
Born: Paterson
Principal team: Los Angeles Dodgers, 1961–1967, 1972
Record: Won 79, lost 74, saved 179
Led league: win percentage (1), games (3), saves (2)

Johnny Vander Meer, southpaw starting pitcher, thirteen years in
   majors
Born: Prospect Park
Principal team: Cincinnati Reds, 1937–1949
Record: Won 119, lost 121
Led league: fewest hits per game (2), strikeouts (3), strikeouts per
   game (3), consecutive no-hitters versus Boston (June 11, 1938)
   and Brooklyn (June 15, 1938)

John Romano, catcher, ten years in majors
Born: Hoboken
Principal teams: Chicago White Sox, 1958–1959, 1965–1966; Cleve-
   land Indians, 1960–1964
Record: Lifetime batting .255, 706 hits, 129 home runs, 417 runs bat-
   ted in
Led league: no leads

John Briggs, first baseman, twelve years in majors
Born: Paterson
Principal teams: Philadelphia Phillies, 1964–1971; Milwaukee
   Brewers, 1971–1975
Record: Lifetime batting .253, 1041 hits, 139 home runs, 507 runs bat-
   ted in
Led league: no leads

Danny O'Connell, second baseman, ten years in majors
Born: Paterson
Principal team: Milwaukee Braves, 1954–1957
Record: Lifetime batting .260, 1049 hits, 39 home runs, 320 runs bat-
   ted in
Led league: no leads

Hardy Richardson, second baseman, fourteen years in majors
Born: Clarksboro
Principal team: Buffalo (National League), 1879–1885

Record: Lifetime batting .299, 1688 hits, 68 home runs, 818 runs batted in

Led league: hits (1), home runs (1), runs batted in (1)

Red Shannon, shortstop, seven years in majors
Born: Jersey City
Principal team: Philadelphia Athletics, 1917–1921
Record: Lifetime batting .259, 277 hits, 0 home runs, 91 runs batted in
Led league: no leads

Wid Conroy, third baseman, eleven years in majors
Born: Camden
Principal team: New York Yankees, 1903–1908
Record: Lifetime batting .248, 1257 hits, 22 home runs, 452 runs batted in
Led league: no leads

Goose Goslin, left fielder, eighteen years in majors
Born: Salem
Principal team: Washington Senators, 1921–1930, 1933, 1938
Record: Lifetime batting, .316, 2735 hits, 248 home runs, 1609 runs batted in
Led league: triples (2), runs batted in (1), batting average (1), number 18 on all-time runs batted in list
Elected to Hall of Fame in 1968

Doc Cramer, left fielder, twenty years in majors
Born: Beach Haven
Principal teams: Philadelphia Athletics, 1929–1935; Boston Red Sox, 1936–1940; Detroit Tigers, 1942–1948
Record: Lifetime batting .296, 2705 hits, 37 home runs, 842 runs batted in
Led league: hits (1), number 8 on all-time putout list for outfielders

Billy Hamilton, center fielder, fourteen years in majors
Born: Newark
Principal teams: Philadelphia Phillies, 1890–1895; Boston Braves, 1896–1901
Record: Lifetime batting .344, 2158 hits, 40 home runs, 736 runs batted in

Doc Cramer, Beach Haven-born, unveils a sign renaming Manahawkin street in his honor. (Times Beacon Newspapers)

Led league: runs (4), hits (1), walks (5), batting average (2), number 1 in all-time runs per game, number 2 in all-time stolen bases
Elected to Hall of Fame in 1961

George Case, center fielder, eleven years in majors
Born: Trenton
Principal team: Washington Senators, 1937–1945, 1947
Record: Lifetime batting .282, 1415 hits, 21 home runs, 377 runs batted in
Led league: runs (1), stolen bases (6), number 21 in all-time stolen base average

Mike Tiernan, center fielder, thirteen years in majors
Born: Trenton
Principal team: New York Giants, 1887–1899
Record: Lifetime batting .311, 1834 hits, 105 home runs, 851 runs batted in
Led league: runs (1), home runs (2), walks (1), slugging average (1)

Joe Medwick, right fielder, seventeen years in majors
Born: Carteret
Principal team: St. Louis Cardinals, 1932–1940, 1947–1948
Record: Lifetime batting .324, 2471 hits, 205 home runs, 1383 runs batted in
Led league: runs (1), hits (2), doubles (3), triples (1), home runs (1), runs batted in (3), batting average (1), slugging average (1)
Elected to Hall of Fame in 1968

Steve Braun, designated hitter, fifteen years in majors
Born: Trenton
Principal teams: Minnesota Twins, 1971–1976; Saint Louis Cardinals, 1981–1985
Record: Lifetime batting .271, 989 hits, 52 home runs, 388 runs batted in
Led league: no leads

IF THE ALL-TIME team of Jersey-borns is great in the outfield and near great on the mound, a team made up of those who played some of their professional career in New Jersey is spectacular nearly everywhere. There will be some quarrel with the selections in Table 7. Maybe even some burst blood vessels. Where, someone will shout in outrage, is Willie Wells? He played in Newark, did he not?

Ducky Medwick (Bettman Archives)

TABLE 7
The All-Time "Played in Jersey" Team

Position	First Team	Second Team
First base	Monte Irvin* Newark Eagles	Mule Suttles Newark Eagles
Second base	John Henry Lloyd* Atlantic City Bacharachs	Larry Doby Newark Eagles
Shortstop	Honus Wagner* Paterson Atlantics	Dick Lundy Atlantic City Bacharachs
Third base	Ray Dandridge* Newark Eagles	Oliver Marcelle Atlantic City Bacharachs
Left field	Goose Goslin* Trenton Giants	Chaney White Atlantic City Bacharachs
Center field	Willie Mays* Trenton Giants	George Case Trenton Giants
Right field	Edd Roush* Newark Peps	Bob Seeds Newark Bears
Catcher	Yogi Berra* Newark Bears	Biz Mackey Newark Eagles
Pitcher	Walter Johnson* Newark Bears	
	Don Newcombe Newark Eagles	
	Leon Day Newark Eagles	
	Ed Ruelbach Newark Peps	
	Vic Raschi Newark Bears	
Manager	Bill McKechnie* Newark Peps	Ed Barrow Paterson Atlantics, Newark Eagles

*Hall of Famer

He sure did—at shortstop for the Eagles from 1937 to 1945, with some time off for Latin American ball. He appeared in the first Negro League East-West All-Star game in 1933, when he played for the Chicago American Giants, and repeated in 1934, 1935, 1937, 1938, 1939, 1942, and 1945. Lacking a "cannon" for an arm, he nonetheless nailed the runners he should have, and then some. He ranged deep into the outfield for short fly balls, giving his outfielders the freedom to play deeper than they otherwise would have dared. Though not a home run threat, he averaged consistently above .300 at bat.

But ahead of Wells in the played-in-Jersey shortstop category stands Honus Wagner, Hall of Famer, generally acknowledged to be the greatest shortstop of all time. (In truth, we stretch a point with Wagner. In his one full season and one partial season with the Paterson Atlantics—1896 and 1897—he never did play shortstop. First base and third base were his posts. But if we give him one of those on our first team, then Irvin or Dandridge must move to shortstop—and Wells remains outside the white lines.) And there is also John Henry Lloyd, "the black Honus Wagner," whom we stationed at second base to get all Hall of Famers onto the first team. And Dick Lundy, thought by many to be the peer of Lloyd. What were we to do with Wells?

Another who gets slighted unavoidably is Joe Gordon, who starred at second for the Newark Bears before moving on to do the same for the New York Yankees. A member of the 1937 Bears "wonder team," Gordon hit .280 with twenty home runs in the not-so-friendly confines of Ruppert Stadium.

But there sits Hall of Famer Lloyd in the second base slot on the first team (he played the position often as age stole shortstop range from his arm and legs). Second-team honors go to Larry Doby, who outhit Gordon by a considerable margin during comparable American League careers. Gordon probably was the better fielder, though Doby was converted from second to the outfield by the Cleveland Indians, making comparison impossible.

Monte Irvin, primarily a shortstop and outfielder during his years with the Newark Eagles, emerges at first base on our played-in-Jersey all-stars for the same reason Lloyd winds up at second base. This not only blocks Mule Suttles from the first-team slot, which he might otherwise deserve, but it also eliminates from contention Babe Dahlgren—a .340 hitter for the 1937 Newark Bears and eventually the replacement for Lou Gehrig on the Yankees.

Cleveland Indians' owner Bill Veeck signs Paterson's Larry Doby as the first black player in the American League, 1947. (Cleveland Indians)

Most of the played-in-Jersey first team picks get ample notice elsewhere in this book (Lloyd, Dandridge, Irvin, and Day in the Negro League chapter; Roush, McKechnie, and Ruelbach in the Federal League chapter; Goslin and Newcombe earlier in this chapter; Wagner in Chapter 3 on the beginnings of professional baseball). The other four—Mays, Berra, Raschi, and Johnson—need little introduction, but a few words on their New Jersey playing days are in order.

Mays, Berra, and Raschi were on their way up when they passed through the Garden State. Johnson was on his way down.

Mays spent part of 1950 with the Trenton Giants before moving on to the Minneapolis Millers, where he leaped, slugged, sped, and hollered for the rest of the season prior to breaking in with the parent New York Giants in 1951. The Trenton team was unfortunately on its last legs in that city during Mays's stay. They finished fourth after the "Say, Hey Kid" departed, and left town for good in the off-season.

Willie wound up playing twenty-one seasons for the Giants—in New York and San Francisco—then returned briefly to New York for a season and a half with the Mets. He batted .302 lifetime and led the league in homers four times, steals three times, and batting average once. He finished sixth on the all-time games-played list, sixth in at-bats, fifth in runs, ninth in hits, third in home runs, third in total bases, seventh in runs batted in, tenth in slugging average, and first in outfield putouts. A case can be made that he was the greatest ever to roam a Jersey ball field.

Berra and Raschi were teammates on the 1946 Newark Bears before moving up to the Yankees late in the season. Berra, a longtime resident of New Jersey though a native of St. Louis, went on to spend eighteen seasons with the Yankees and came out of retirement in 1963 to play in four games with nine at-bats for the Mets. Though he never led the league in anything, except maybe malapropisms, some experts call him the best catcher of all time. His lifetime batting average was only .285, but the damage he did to the opposition in crucial situations (especially the Dodgers, it seems to at least one old Brooklyn fan) made that average worth thirty or forty points more. He still stands second in home runs for catchers and holds the catcher record for most chances handled without an error. He also continues to lead in World Series hits with seventy-one. When his playing days were done he went on to manage in the majors (seven seasons so far with the Yankees and Mets, including one divisional and one league championship). He was elected to the Hall of Fame on his second try in 1972.

TABLE 8
New Jersey Cities and the Major Leaguers They Have Produced

Location	Number of Major Leaguers	Location	Number of Major Leaguers
Newark	31	Burlington	4
Camden	25	Harrison	4
Jersey City	21	Ridgewood	4
Paterson	21	Atlantic City	3
Trenton	21	Beverly	3
Hoboken	10	Bloomfield	3
Passaic	10	East Orange	3
Bayonne	9	Englewood	3
Elizabeth	9	Perth Amboy	3
New Brunswick	6	Phillipsburg	3
Orange	6	Ridgefield	3
Plainfield	6	Somerville	3
Hackensack	5	South Amboy	3
Montclair	5	Vineland	3

Raschi joined Eddie Lopat and Allie Reynolds and was in turn joined by Whitey Ford on the incomparable Yankee pitching staff of 1946–1954. The big right-hander won 132 games while losing only 66, leading the American League in win-loss percentage (.724) in 1950 and strikeouts (164) in 1951. In 1975 he received thirty-seven Hall of Fame votes out of a total of about four hundred.

We stretch another point with Walter Johnson. His New Jersey career consisted of just a short stint as player-manager of the Newark Bears in 1928, the first year of Paul Block's enlightened and relatively munificent ownership. Before that, Johnson put in twenty-one seasons in the majors, every one of them with the Washington Senators. He won 417 games to 279 losses, led the league six times in wins, twice in percentage, five times in complete games, seven times in shutouts, four times in innings pitched, and eleven times in strikeouts. He made the Hall of Fame in its inaugural year, 1936, with 189 votes.

IN REVIEWING the list of major leaguers who were born in New Jersey, the temptation was strong to see which city produced the most. As we were compiling the figures, though, it occurred to us that the cities listed for the players were not necessarily the towns their parents were living in when they were born. Especially after the born-at-home era passed, the birthplaces listed in many cases were the closest towns with hospitals. For example, Jeff Torborg, who now lives in Mountainside, grew up in Westfield. But his birthplace is listed as Plainfield, the location of Muhlenberg Hospital.

With that caveat, we still think a compilation of birthplaces has sufficient meaning to include here. In Table 8 we list only those towns claiming three or more Jersey boys

A complete list of the Boys of Jersey can be found in Appendix A.

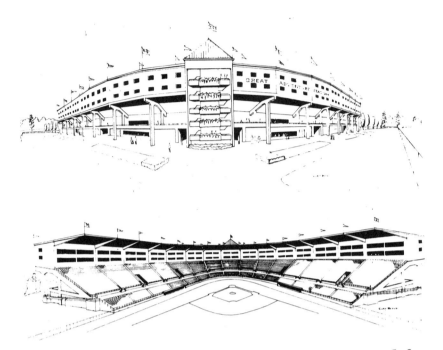

Rendering of a minor league stadium proposed for Great Adventure Amusement Park in Jackson Township. (Six Flags/Great Adventure)

AFTERWORD

In one of the school songs of Rutgers, New Jersey's state university, the institution is compared to the Raritan River, upon whose banks it lies, as "ever changing, yet eternally the same." That description is apt, as well, for the game of baseball. Its evolution, its new characters, events, and controversies—all make it a living part of our society. But its sameness, for nearly 150 years, gives it a bedrock quality that ties together generations and offers a dependable future.

What does the future hold for baseball in New Jersey? A minor league team may play at Great Adventure in this decade, another may appear in Trenton. As the major leagues expand, business, media, and political forces may well attract a franchise to a Garden State venue.

Hoboken's recently formed American Baseball Heritage, Inc. may follow through on its plans to honor Alexander Cartwright, build a museum, and push for a national celebration of the first match game played on its Elysian Fields, though we earnestly urge it to target October 21, 1995, rather than the June 19, 1996, date it has erroneously focused on.

With these developments and others occurring even now at every level of the sport, we expect baseball to remain "the Jersey game." The story goes on.

APPENDIX A
NEW JERSEY–BORN MAJOR LEAGUERS

Name	Birthplace	Born	Position	Batting average	Seasons	Principal Team (League)
Alyea, Brant	Passaic	1940	O	.247	6	Min (A)
Armstrong, George	Orange	1924	C	.167	1	Phi (A)
Atherton, Charlie	New Brunswick	1873	3	.248	1	Was (N)
Baldwin, Frank	High Bridge	1928	C	.100	1	Cin (N)
Bates, Ray	Paterson	1890	3	.233	2	Phi (A)
Batten, George	Haddonfield	1891	2	.000	1	NY (A)
Berra, Dale	Ridgewood	1956	S	.236	11	Pit (N)
Berry, Charlie	Phillipsburg	1872	C	.267	11	Bos (A)
Berry, Charlie	Elizabeth	1860	2	.224	1	KC (U)
Bierman, Charlie	Hoboken	1879	1	.000	1	FW (n)
Borgmann, Glenn	Paterson	1950	C	.229	9	Min (A)
Bradley, Scott	Glen Ridge	1960	C	.270	5	Sea (A)
Braun, Steve	Trenton	1948	O	.271	15	Min (A)
Briggs, John	Paterson	1944	O	.253	12	Phi (N)
Bruggy, Frank	Elizabeth	1891	C	.277	5	Phi (A)

(continued)

Appendix A (*Continued*)

Name	Birthplace	Born	Position	Batting average	Seasons	Principal Team (League)
Burns, Joe	Trenton	1900	C	.105	1	Chi (A)
Burt, Frank	Camden	1882	O	.111	1	Bal (a)
Buzas, Joe	Alpha	1919	S	.262	1	NY (A)
Byers, Randy	Bridgeton	1964	O	.269	2	SD (N)
Calderone, Sam	Beverly	1926	C	.291	3	NY (N)
Campbell, Mike	*	†	1	.146	1	Elz (n)
Carey, Tom	Hoboken	1849	2	.275	8	StL (A)
Carlstrom, Swede	Elizabeth	1896	S	.167	1	Bos (A)
Case, George	Trenton	1915	O	.282	11	Was (A)
Castiglia, Jim	Passaic	1918	C	.389	1	Phi (A)
Cerone, Rick	Newark	1954	C	.241	14	NY (A)
Charles, Chappy	Phillipsburg	1881	2	.219	3	StL (N)
Cicero, Joe	Atlantic City	1910	O	.222	3	Bos (A)
Clark, Allie	South Amboy	1923	O	.262	7	Cle (A)
Connors, Joe	Paterson	†	O	.091	1	Atl (U)
Conroy, Wid	Camden	1877	3	.248	11	NY (A)
Cramer, Doc	Beach Haven	1905	O	.296	20	Bos (A)
Crolius, Fred	Jersey City	1876	O	.244	2	Bos (N)
Cunningham, Joe	Paterson	1931	1	.291	12	StL (N)
Curry, Jim	Camden	1893	2	.229	3	Det (A)
Cusick, Jack	Weehawken	1928	S	.174	2	Chi (N)

Name	Hometown	Year	Pos	Avg	No.	Team
Daly, Bert	Bayonne	1881	2	.190	1	Phi (A)
Davis, Gerry	Trenton	1958	O	.301	2	SD (N)
Deane, Harry	Trenton	1846	O	.167	1	FW (n)
Dente, Sam	Harrison	1922	S	.252	9	Was (A)
Dineen, Kerry	Englewood	1952	O	.324	3	NY (A)
Dinges, Vance	Elizabeth	1915	O	.291	2	Phi (N)
Dunleavy, Jack	Harrison	1879	O	.241	3	StL (N)
Dwyer, Double Joe	Orange	1904	H	.273	1	Cin (N)
Eagan, Bill	Camden	1869	2	.236	3	StL (a)
Easton, John	Trenton	1933	H	.000	2	Phi (N)
Elsh, Roy	Penns Grove	1892	O	.262	3	Chi (A)
Fallon, George	Jersey City	1916	2	.216	4	StL (N)
Farrell, Jack	Newark	1857	2	.243	11	Pro (N)
Fisler, Wes	Camden	1841	1	.315	5	Ath (n)
Ford, Ted	Vineland	1947	O	.219	4	Cle (A)
French, Walt	Moorestown	1899	O	.303	6	Phi (A)
Gallagher, Dave	Trenton	1960	O	.285	2	Chi (A)
Geraghty, Ben	Jersey City	1912	S	.199	3	Bos (N)
Gigon, Norm	Teaneck	1938	2	.171	1	Chi (N)
Giordano, Tommy	Newark	1925	2	.175	1	Phi (A)
Gleason, Harry	Camden	1875	3	.218	5	StL (A)
Gleason, Kid	Camden	1866	2	.261	22	Phi (N)
Glynn, Bill	Sussex	1925	1	.249	4	Cle (A)
Goldy, Purnal	Camden	1937	O	.231	2	Det (A)
Goslin, Goose	Salem	1900	O	.316	18	Was (A)

(continued)

Appendix A (*Continued*)

Name	Birthplace	Born	Position	Batting average	Seasons	Principal Team (League)
Grasso, Mickey	Newark	1920	C	.226	7	Was (A)
Graulich, Lew	Camden	†	C	.308	1	Phi (N)
Green, Danny	Burlington	1876	O	.293	8	Chi (A)
Gunning, Hy	Maplewood	1888	1	.111	1	Bos (A)
Haas, Mule	Montclair	1903	O	.292	12	Phi (A)
Hamilton, Billy	Newark	1866	O	.344	14	Phi (N)
Hargreaves, Charlie	Trenton	1896	C	.270	8	Bro (N)
Hatfield, Gil	Hoboken	1855	3	.248	8	Was (a)
Hatfield, John	*	1847	2	.272	5	Mut (n)
Hayes, Frankie	Jamesburg	1914	C	.259	14	Phi (A)
Helfrich, Ty	Pleasantville	1890	2	.240	1	Bro (F)
Hermann, Al	Milltown	1899	2	.234	2	Bos (N)
Heubel, George	Paterson	1849	O	.275	2	Ath (n)
Hoffman, Izzy	Bridgeport	1875	O	.233	2	Bos (N)
Huber, Otto	Garfield	1914	2	.273	1	Bos (N)
Husta, Carl	Egg Harbor	1902	S	.136	1	Phi (A)
Jamieson, Charlie	Paterson	1893	O	.303	18	Cle (A)
Johnson, Bill	Montclair	1918	3	.271	9	NY (A)
Jorgenson, Mike	Passaic	1948	1	.243	17	Mon (N)
Karkovice, Ron	Union	1963	C	.168	3	Chi (A)
Kasko, Eddie	Linden	1932	S	.264	10	Cin (N)

Name	City	Year		Avg		Team
Kavanaugh, Marty	Harrison	1891	2	.249	5	Det (A)
Kearns, Teddy	Trenton	1900	1	.278	2	Chi (N)
Kelly, Jim	Bloomfield	1884	0	.297	3	Pit (F)
Kelly, John	Paterson	1859	C	.226	3	Bal (a)
Kelty, John	Jersey City	1867	0	.237	1	Pit (N)
Kenders, Al	Barrington	1937	C	.208	1	Phi (N)
Knothe, Fritz	Passaic	1903	3	.220	2	Bos (N)
Knothe, George	Bayonne	1898	2	.083	1	Phi (N)
Knox, John	Newark	1948	2	.274	4	Det (A)
Kopshaw, George	Passaic	1895	C	.200	1	StL (N)
Krenchicki, Wayne	Trenton	1954	3	.266	8	Cin (N)
Kryhoski, Dick	Leonia	1925	1	.265	7	StL (A)
Kubiak, Ted	New Brunswick	1942	2	.231	10	Oak (A)
Laga, Mike	Ridgewood	1960	1	.199	7	Det (A)
Lajeskie, Dick	Passaic	1926	2	.200	1	NY (N)
Lally, Dan	Jersey City	1867	0	.263	2	StL (N)
Lamere, Pete	Hoboken	1874	C	.182	2	Chi (N)
Larsen, Swede	Jersey City	1913	2	.000	1	Bos (N)
Lee, Billy	Bayonne	1892	0	.186	2	StL (A)
Leip, Ed	Trenton	1910	2	.274	4	Pit (N)
Lennox, Ed	Camden	1885	3	.274	6	Bro (N)
Lis, Joe	Somerville	1946	1	.233	8	Phi (N)
Lucas, Fred	Vineland	1903	0	.265	1	Phi (N)
McCormick, Mike	Jersey City	1883	3	.184	1	Bro (N)

(continued)

Appendix A (*Continued*)

Name	Birthplace	Born	Position	Batting average	Seasons	Principal Team (League)
McCrea, Frank	Jersey City	1896	C	.200	1	Cle (A)
McGuckin, Joe	Paterson	1862	O	.250	1	BB (a)
Maddox, Elliott	East Orange	1947	O	.261	11	NY (N)
Mahoney, Jim	Englewood	1934	S	.229	4	Was (A)
Maier, Bob	Dunellen	1915	3	.263	1	Det (A)
Malkmus, Bobby	Newark	1931	2	.215	6	Phi (N)
Martin, Jack	Plainfield	1887	S	.237	2	Phi (N)
Mathews, Bob	Camden	†	O	.333	1	Phi (a)
Medwick, Joe	Carteret	1911	O	.324	17	StL (N)
Mellor, Bill	Camden	1874	1	.361	1	Bal (A)
Merritt, George	Paterson	1880	O	.213	3	Pit (N)
Miksis, Eddie	Burlington	1926	2	.236	14	Chi (N)
Milbourne, Larry	Port Norris	1951	2	.254	11	Sea (A)
Miller, Dots	Kearny	1886	1	.263	12	Pit (N)
Mills, Everett	Newark	1845	1	.281	5	Har (N)
Mills, Ruppert	Newark	1892	1	.201	1	New (F)
Molinaro, Bob	Newark	1950	O	.264	8	Chi (A)
Monchak, Alex	Bayonne	1919	S	.143	1	Phi (N)
Moore, Ferdie	Camden	1896	1	.500	1	Phi (A)
Murphy, Frank	Hackensack	1880	O	.219	1	Bos (N)
Narleski, Bill	Perth Amboy	1899	S	.265	2	Bos (A)

Nash, Cotton	Jersey City	1942	1	.188	3	Min (A)
Nicosia, Steve	Paterson	1955	C	.267	8	Pit (N)
Nixon, Al	Atlantic City	1886	O	.277	9	Bos (N)
O'Brien, Eddie	South Amboy	1930	S	.236	5	Pit (N)
O'Brien, Johnny	South Amboy	1930	2	.250	6	Pit (N)
O'Connell, Danny	Paterson	1927	2	.260	10	Mil (N)
O'Malley, Tom	Orange	1960	3	.256	7	SF (N)
Orsino, John	Teaneck	1938	C	.249	7	Bal (A)
Orsulak, Joe	Parsippany	1962	O	.276	5	Pit (N)
Peterson, Hardy	Perth Amboy	1929	C	.273	4	Pit (N)
Pfeil, Bobby	Passaic	1943	3	.242	2	NY (N)
Pfister, George	Bound Brook	1918	C	.000	1	Bro (N)
Picciuto, Nick	Newark	1921	3	.135	1	Phi (N)
Pitko, Alex	Burlington	1914	O	.259	2	Phi (N)
Pittaro, Chris	Trenton	1961	3	.221	3	Det (A)
Puhl, John	Bayonne	1875	3	.182	2	NY (N)
Purcell, Blondie	Paterson	†	O	.267	12	Phi (a)
Radcliff, John	Camden	1846	S	.265	5	Bal (n)
Reilly, Charlie	Princeton	1855	3	.250	8	Phi (N)
Reiss, Al	Elizabeth	1909	S	.200	1	Phi (A)
Richardson, Hardy	Clarksboro	1855	2	.299	14	Buf (N)
Rochefort, Ben	Camden	1896	2	.176	1	Phi (A)
Rodin, Eric	Orange	1930	O	.000	1	NY (N)
Romano, John	Hoboken	1934	C	.255	10	Cle (A)

(continued)

239

Name	Birthplace	Born	Position	Batting average	Seasons	Principal Team (League)
Rothfuss, Jack	Newark	1872	1	.313	1	Pit (N)
Sabo, Alex	New Brunswick	1910	C	.375	2	Was (A)
Sanicki, Ed	Wallington	1923	O	.294	2	Phi (N)
Saunders, Rusty	Trenton	1906	O	.133	1	Phi (A)
Savage, Don	Bloomfield	1919	3	.256	2	NY (A)
Scala, Jerry	Bayonne	1926	O	.223	3	Chi (A)
Schroder, Bob	Ridgefield	1944	2	.217	4	SF (N)
Senerchia, Sonny	Newark	1931	3	.220	1	Phi (N)
Shannon, Joe	Jersey City	1897	O	.200	1	Bos (N)
Shannon, Red	Jersey City	1897	2	.259	7	Phi (A)
Shindle, Billy	Gloucester	1860	3	.269	13	Bro (N)
Smith, Ernie	Totowa	1899	S	.241	1	Chi (A)
Snyder, Charles	Camden	†	O	.273	1	Phi (A)
Snyder, Redleg	Camden	1854	O	.160	2	Cin (N)
Stanley, Joe	*	†	O	.238	1	Bal (U)
Stansbury, Jack	Phillipsburg	1885	3	.128	1	Bos (A)
Steelman, Farmer	Millville	1875	C	.218	4	Phi (A)
Stephenson, Dummy	Petersburg	1869	O	.270	1	Phi (N)
Stires, Gat	Hunterdon	1849	O	.271	1	Roc (n)
Stripp, Joe	Harrison	1903	3	.294	11	Bro (N)
Sullivan, John	Somerville	1941	C	.228	5	NY (N)

Sweasy, Charlie	Newark	1847	2	.190	5	Cin (N)
Tesch, Al	Jersey City	1891	2	.286	1	Bro (F)
Tiernan, Mike	Trenton	1867	O	.311	13	NY (N)
Torborg, Jeff	Plainfield	1941	C	.214	10	LA (N)
Wagner, Hal	East Riverton	1915	C	.248	12	Phi (A)
Walling, Dennis	Neptune	1954	3	.276	14	Hou (N)
Walsh, Walt	Newark	1897	R	—	1	Phi (N)
Ward, Hap	Leesburg	1885	O	.000	1	Det (A)
Williams, Earl	Newark	1948	C	.247	8	Atl (N)
Williams, Otto	Newark	1877	S	.203	4	Chi (N)
Wood, Jake	Elizabeth	1937	2	.250	7	Det (A)
Yates, Al	Jersey City	1945	O	.277	1	Mil (A)
Zak, Frankie	Passaic	1922	S	.269	3	Pit (N)
Zimmerman, Eddie	Oceanic	1883	3	.186	2	Bro (N)

PITCHERS

Name	Birthplace	Born	Record	ERA	Seasons	Principal Team
Acker, Tom	Paterson	1930	19–13	4.11	4	Cin (N)
Armstrong, Jack	Englewood	1965	4–7	5.82	1	Cin (N)
Bakely, Jersey	Blackwood	1864	77–125	3.67	6	Cle (a)
Bauer, Lou	Egg Harbor City	1898	0–0	—	1	Phi (A)

(continued)

Appendix A (Continued)

242

Name	Birthplace	Born	Record	ERA	Seasons	Principal Team (League)
Behney, Mel	Newark	1947	0–2	4.50	1	Cin (N)
Bicknell, Charlie	Plainfield	1928	0–1	6.83	2	Phi (N)
Bittiger, Jeff	Jersey City	1962	4–5	4.55	3	Chi (A)
Black, Joe	Plainfield	1924	30–12	3.91	6	Bro (N)
Bogle, Warren	Passaic	1946	0–0	4.30	1	Oak (A)
Borden, Joe	Jacobstown	1854	11–12	2.89	2	Bos (N)
Boris, Paul	Irvington	1955	1–2	3.96	1	Min (A)
Borowy, Hank	Bloomfield	1916	108–82	3.51	10	NY (A)
Boswell, Andy	New Gretna	1874	3–4	5.91	1	Was (N)
Bouton, Jim	Newark	1939	62–63	3.58	10	NY (A)
Brady, Jim	Jersey City	1936	0–0	30.00	1	Det (A)
Brady, King	Elmer	1881	3–2	3.06	5	Phi (N)
Brodowski, Dick	Bayonne	1921	9–11	4.75	6	Bos (A)
Brown, Boardwalk	Woodbury	1887	38–40	3.47	5	Phi (A)
Brown, John	Trenton	†	0–1	7.20	1	Bro (N)
Brown, Mike	Haddon Township	1959	12–20	5.76	6	Bos (A)
Buckingham, Ed	Metuchen	1874	0–0	6.00	1	Was (N)
Burchell, Fred	Perth Amboy	1879	13–15	2.93	4	Bos (A)
Campbell, Archie	Maplewood	1903	2–6	5.86	3	Cin (N)
Campbell, Hugh	Elizabeth	†	2–16	—	1	Elz (n)
Carroll, Ownie	Kearny	1902	64–90	4.43	9	Det (A)

Name	Birthplace	Year	Record	ERA		Team
Ciardi, Mark	New Brunswick	1961	1–1	9.56	1	Mil (A)
Citarella, Ralph	East Orange	1958	0–1	4.09	3	StL (N)
Clark, Mike	Camden	1922	3–0	5.31	2	StL (N)
Clemenson, Bill	New Brunswick	1919	1–1	5.57	3	Pit (N)
Cogan, Dick	Paterson	1871	2–3	5.00	3	Chi (N)
Connors, Joe	Paterson	†	0–2	5.57	1	KC (u)
Cuccurullo, Cookie	Asbury Park	1918	3–5	4.55	3	Pit (N)
Cullen, Jack	Newark	1939	4–4	3.08	3	NY (A)
DeMott, Ben	Green Village	1889	0–4	6.19	2	Cle (A)
Dewald, Charlie	Newark	1867	2–0	0.64	1	Cle (P)
Dillman, Bill	Trenton	1945	7–12	4.53	2	Bal (A)
Doran, John	*	1869	5–10	5.43	1	Lou (a)
Downing, Al	Trenton	1941	123–107	3.22	17	NY (A)
Dugan, Dan	Plainfield	1907	1–4	6.65	2	Chi (A)
Dustal, Bob	Sayreville	1935	0–1	9.00	1	Det (A)
Eastwick, Rawly	Camden	1950	28–27	3.30	8	Cin (N)
Errickson, Dick	Vineland	1914	36–47	3.85	5	Bos (N)
Estelle, Dick	Lakewood	1942	1–2	3.23	2	SF (N)
Estock, George	Stirling	1924	0–1	4.35	1	Bos (N)
Fagan, Everett	Pottersville	1918	2–7	5.49	2	Phi (A)
Fallenstein, Ed	Newark	1908	2–1	5.49	2	Phi (N)
Fanning, Jack	South Orange	1917	1–4	8.45	2	Phi (N)
Fanok, Harry	Whippany	1940	2–1	5.29	2	StL (N)
Farrell, John	Monmouth Beach	1962	19–11	4.03	2	Cle (A)

(continued)

243

Appendix A *(Continued)*

Name	Birthplace	Born	Record	ERA	Seasons	Principal Team
Ferguson, Alex	Montclair	1897	61–85	4.90	10	Bos (A)
Finneran, Happy	East Orange	1891	25–33	3.31	5	Bro (F)
Flitcraft, Hilly	Woodstown	1923	0–0	9.00	1	Phi (N)
Foxen, Bill	Tenafly	1884	16–20	2.57	4	Phi (N)
Fuchs, Charlie	Union City	1913	6–10	4.85	3	Phi (N)
Garoni, Willie	Fort Lee	1877	0–1	4.50	1	NY (N)
Gaston, Milt	Ridgefield Park	1896	97–164	4.55	11	StL (A)
Gebrian, Pete	Bayonne	1923	2–3	4.50	1	Chi (A)
Gorsica, Johnny	Bayonne	1915	31–39	4.18	7	Det (A)
Green, Fred	Titusville	1933	9–7	3.49	5	Pit (N)
Grevell, Bill	Williamstown	1898	0–0	14.25	1	Phi (A)
Halicki, Ed	Newark	1950	55–66	3.62	7	SF (N)
Hands, Bill	Hackensack	1940	111–110	3.35	11	Chi (N)
Hannan, Jim	Jersey City	1940	41–48	3.88	10	Was (A)
Hanson, Erik	Kinnelon	1965	2–3	3.21	1	Sea (A)
Harkins, John	New Brunswick	1859	51–83	4.09	5	Bro (a)
Harper, Harry	Hackensack	1895	57–76	2.86	10	Was (A)
Heimach, Fred	Camden	1901	62–69	4.46	13	Phi (A)
Henderson, Ed	Newark	1884	1–1	4.15	1	Pit (F)
Hesterfer, Larry	Newark	1878	0–1	7.50	1	NY (N)
Hiller, Frank	Newark	1920	30–31	4.42	7	Chi (N)
Holmes, Chick	Beverly	1896	0–0	13.50	1	Phi (A)

Name	Town	†	Record	ERA		Team
Hopper, Lefty	Ridgewood	†	0–2	4.91	1	Bro (N)
Howell, Harry	*	1876	131–146	2.74	13	StL (A)
Hunter, Willard	Newark	1934	4–9	5.68	2	NY (N)
Husted, Bill	Gloucester	1867	5–10	4.88	1	Phi (P)
Imlay, Doc	Allentown	1889	0–0	7.07	1	Phi (N)
Jackson, Mike	Paterson	1946	2–3	5.76	4	Phi (N)
Jakucki, Sig	Camden	1909	25–22	3.79	3	StL (A)
Jones, Ken	Dover	1904	0–1	5.32	2	Bos (N)
Keegan, Ed	Camden	1939	0–3	9.00	3	KC (A)
Kellett, Al	Red Bank	1901	0–1	8.10	2	Phi (A)
Keriozakos	West Orange	1931	2–5	5.59	3	Was (A)
Kiely, Leo	Hoboken	1929	26–27	3.37	7	Bos (A)
Klimkowski, Ron	Jersey City	1944	8–12	2.92	4	NY (A)
Kucks, Johnny	Hoboken	1933	54–56	4.10	6	NY (A)
Kunkel, Bill	Hoboken	1936	6–6	4.28	3	KC (A)
Lapihuska, Andy	Delmont	1922	0–2	7.04	2	Phi (N)
Laxton, Bill	Camden	1948	3–10	4.70	5	SD (N)
Lazorko, Jack	Hoboken	1956	5–8	4.20	5	Cal (A)
Leiter, Al	Toms River	1965	6–6	4.61	2	NY (A)
Lemongello, Mark	Jersey City	1955	22–38	4.06	4	Hou (N)
Lombardo, Lou	Carlstadt	1928	0–0	7.20	1	NY (N)
Lowe, George	Ridgefield Park	1898	0–0	0.00	1	Cin (N)
Mackinson, John	Orange	1923	0–1	7.36	2	StL (N)
McLaughlin, Warren	North Plainfield	1876	3–3	4.75	3	Phi (N)

(continued)

Appendix A (*Continued*)

Name	Birthplace	Born	Record	ERA	Seasons	Principal Team
McRae, Norm	Elizabeth	1947	0–0	3.18	2	Det (A)
Makosky, Frank	Boonton	1910	5–2	4.97	1	NY (A)
Meads, Dave	Montclair	1964	8–4	4.45	2	Hou (N)
Merena, Spike	Paterson	1909	1–2	2.88	1	Bos (A)
Messersmith, Andy	Toms River	1945	130–99	2.86	12	Cal (A)
Meyer, Brian	Camden	1963	0–0	1.50	1	Hou (N)
Milacki, Bob	Trenton	1964	2–0	0.72	1	Bal (A)
Mirabella, Paul	Belleville	1954	15–27	4.39	11	Sea (A)
Montefusco, John	Long Branch	1950	90–83	3.55	13	SF (N)
Morris, E.	Trenton	†	0–0	9.00	1	Bal (U)
Nagy, Steve	Franklin	1919	3–8	6.45	2	Was (A)
Narleski, Ray	Camden	1928	43–33	3.61	6	Cle (A)
Neubauer, Hal	Hoboken	1902	1–0	12.60	1	Bos (A)
Newcombe, Don	Madison	1926	149–90	3.56	10	Bro (N)
Nolan, Edward "The Only"	Paterson	1857	23–52	2.98	5	Ind (N)
Ohl, Joe	Jobstown	1888	0–0	2.00	1	Was (A)
Otis, Harry	West New York	1886	2–2	1.38	1	Cle (A)
Pacillo, Pat	Jersey City	1963	4–3	5.82	2	Cin (N)
Perranoski, Ron	Paterson	1936	79–74	2.79	13	LA (N)
Pfister, Dan	Plainfield	1936	6–19	4.90	4	KC (A)
Pierson, William	Atlantic City	1899	0–1	3.27	3	Phi (A)
Pitula, Stan	Hackensack	1931	2–2	3.10	1	Cle (A)

Pounds, Bill	Paterson	1878	0–0	6.00	1	Bro (N)
Prall, Willie	Hackensack	1950	0–2	8.40	1	Chi (N)
Puleo, Charlie	Glen Ridge	1955	28–38	4.24	7	Atl (N)
Rambo, Pete	Thoroughfare	1906	0–0	13.50	1	Phi (N)
Ratzer, Steve	Paterson	1953	1–1	7.29	2	Mon (N)
Robinson, Jack	Orange	1921	0–0	2.25	1	Bos (A)
Salmon, Roger	Newark	1891	1–0	9.00	1	Phi (A)
Santorini, Al	Irvington	1948	17–38	4.28	6	SD (N)
Schacht, Sid	Bogota	1918	0–2	13.91	2	StL (A)
Schaffernoth, Joe	Trenton	1937	3–8	4.58	3	Chi (N)
Schultz, Barney	Beverly	1926	20–20	3.64	7	StL (N)
Schultze, John	Burlington	†	0–1	6.60	1	Phi (N)
Sebra, Bob	Ridgewood	1961	12–24	4.52	4	Mon (N)
Seward, Frank	Pennsauken	1921	3–3	5.17	2	NY (N)
Sima, Al	Mahwah	1921	11–21	4.62	4	Was (N)
Sivess, Pete	South River	1913	7–11	5.38	3	Phi (N)
Smith, Eddie	Columbus	1913	73–113	3.82	1	Chi (A)
Snook, Frank	Somerville	1939	0–2	3.67	1	SD (N)
Snyder, Brian	Flemington	1958	1–2	6.43	1	Sea (A)
Stecher, Charlie	Bordentown	†	0–10	10.32	1	Phi (a)
Steineder, Ray	Salem	1895	3–2	4.86	2	Pit (N)
Stember, Jeff	Elizabeth	1958	0–0	3.00	1	SF (N)
Strelecki, Ed	Newark	1905	1–3	5.82	3	StL (A)
Stroud, Sailor	Ironia	1885	20–20	2.94	3	NY (N)

(continued)

Appendix A (*Continued*)

Name	Birthplace	Born	Record	ERA	Seasons	Principal Team
Stryker, Dutch	Atlantic Highlands	1895	3–8	6.60	2	Bos (N)
Sykes, Bob	Neptune	1954	23–26	4.65	5	StL (N)
Terlecki, Bob	Trenton	1945	0–0	4.85	1	Phi (N)
Thormahlen, Hank	Jersey City	1896	29–30	3.33	6	NY (A)
Valentinetti, Vito	West New York	1928	13–14	4.71	5	Chi (N)
Van Atta, Russ	Augusta	1906	33–41	5.59	7	StL (A)
Vander Meer, Johnny	Prospect Park	1914	119–121	3.44	13	Cin (N)
Viau, Lee	Wayne	1868	83–77	3.32	5	Cin (a)
Vickery, Tom	Milford	1867	41–42	3.75	4	Phi (N)
Walsh, Junior	Newark	1919	4–10	5.91	5	Pit (N)
Wenz, Fred	Bound Brook	1941	3–0	4.71	2	Phi (N)
Williams, Ace	Montclair	1917	0–0	16.00	2	Bos (N)
Wolf, Ernie	Newark	1889	0–0	6.00	1	Cle (A)
Wolfe, Bill	Jersey City	†	0–1	5.00	1	Phi (N)

*City of birth unknown; all players so marked played in the 1800s.
†Date of birth unknown; all players so marked played in the 1800s.

Position
Abbreviations

1 First base
2 Second base
3 Third base
C Catcher
H Pinch hitter
O Outfield
R Pinch Runner
S Shortstop

Principal Team Abbreviations

Ath Philadelphia Athletics
Atl Atlanta
BB Baltimore/Brooklyn
Bal Baltimore
Bos Boston
Bro Brooklyn
Buf Buffalo
Cal California
Chi Chicago
Cin Cincinnati
Cle Cleveland
Det Detroit
Elz Elizabeth Resolutes
FW Fort Wayne Kekiongas
Har Hartford
Hou Houston
Ind Indianapolis
KC Kansas City
LA Los Angeles
Lou Louisville
Mil Milwaukee
Min Minnesota
Mon Montreal
Mut New York Mutuals
New Newark
NY New York
Oak Oakland
Phi Philadelphia
Pit Pittsburgh
Pro Providence
Roc Rockford (Ill.) Forest City
StL St. Louis
SD San Diego
SF San Francisco
Sea Seattle
Was Washington, D.C.

League Abbreviations

a American Association
A American League
F Federal League
n National Association
N National League
P Players League
U Union Association

249

APPENDIX B
NEW JERSEY
BASEBALL MILESTONES

ca. 1832–1833	Olympic Club of Philadelphia plays first match game of base ball (town ball), Camden
1837	Olympic Club drafts first written constitution for a baseball club
1845	First modern baseball club—the New York Knickerbockers—locates in Hoboken
	October 6. First recorded game (intrasquad) of modern baseball, New York Knickerbockers, in Hoboken
	October 21. First recorded match game of modern baseball, New York versus Brooklyn, in Hoboken
	October 22. First newspaper report of a modern baseball game appears in the *New York Herald*
1855	First New Jersey team organized in Newark
1857	New Jersey team—Liberty of New Brunswick—represented at first general baseball convention
1858	New York game introduced to Princeton University by L. W. Mudge, H. S. Butler, and Henry L. Sampson, Brooklyn ball playing freshmen
1860s	All-black team in New Brunswick
1863	October 22. First intercollegiate baseball game in New Jersey, Seton Hall versus Fordham, at South Orange
1865	May 5. First intrastate college game, Princeton versus Rutgers

August 3. First game for "Championship of the United States," in Hoboken

September 28. First scandal in baseball: universally recognized thrown game, in Hoboken

1866   First college curve ball pitcher, E. Davis, Princeton class of 1870

1872   E. B. Wood of Jersey City elected first president of National Association of Amateur Base Ball Players

1873   Elizabeth Resolutes join first professional league in baseball

1879   Princeton University becomes charter member of College Baseball Association

1880   New York Giants' antecedent, Orange (New Jersey) Metropolitans, formed by John B. Day

1883   July. Brooklyn Dodgers' antecedent, Superbas, staffed with defunct Camden Merritt

1884   Trenton wins first championship of Eastern League

1886   Jersey City Little Giants win Eastern League pennant

1898   September 18. First Brooklyn Dodgers–New York Giants Sunday game, in Weehawken

1901   Creation of baseball trust, in Red Bank

1906   First motion picture with baseball plot, *How the Office Boy Saw the Ball Game*, by Thomas Edison, in West Orange

1915   April 16. First home game of New Jersey's only major league team, the Newark Peps, in Harrison

October. Last game featuring a New Jersey major league team

1921   First radio broadcast of a World Series, on wjz, of Newark

1928   October 3. First World Series no-hitter pitched by "Red" Grier, of Atlantic City Bacharachs, in Baltimore versus Chicago

1929	October. Second World Series no-hitter pitched by Luther Farrell, Atlantic City Bacharachs versus Chicago
1932	Newark Bears win International League pennant
1937	Newark Bears, International League champs, win Little World Series, defeating Columbus Cardinals of American Association
1938	Newark Bears win International League pennant, lose Little World Series to Kansas City Blues
1939	May 17. First telecast of a baseball game, Princeton versus Columbia
	Linden Athletic Club wins championship of Major Division of American Amateur Baseball Congress
1946	April 18. Jackie Robinson breaks baseball's color line, Jersey City
	September 29. Newark Eagles win Negro World Series
1947	July. New Jerseyan Larry Doby breaks American League color line
	September. Trenton Giants win Interstate League pennant
1948	Trenton Post no. 93 wins championship of American Legion Baseball
1949	Hammonton wins first Little League World Series
1956	Trenton wins Babe Ruth League Championship
1957	Last major league game in New Jersey, Dodgers versus Giants, in Jersey City
1961	September 1. Jersey City Jerseys, last minor league team in New Jersey, end final season
1972	Maria Pepe appears in Little League game in Hoboken; court challenge eventually opens Little League to girls nationwide

BIBLIOGRAPHY

BOOKS

Adelman, Melvin L. *A Sporting Time: New York City and the Rise of Modern Athletics, 1820–70.* Urbana: University of Illinois Press, 1986.

Allen, Lee. *The American League Story.* New York: Hill and Wang, 1961.

———. *The Cincinnati Reds.* New York: G. P. Putnam's Sons, 1948.

———. *The Giants and the Dodgers: The Fabulous Story of Baseball's Fiercest Feud.* New York: G. P. Putnam's Sons, 1964.

———. *The National League Story.* New York: Hill and Wang, 1961.

Bartlett, Roland W. *The Fans Vote! 100 Baseball Superstars.* Palm Springs: ETC Publications, 1983.

The Baseball Encyclopedia. New York: Macmillan, 1969, 1982.

Brooks, Van Wyck. *The World of Washington Irving.* Kingsport, Tenn.: Kingsport Press, 1944.

Chadwick, Henry. *The Sports and Pastimes of American Boys.* New York, 1884.

Church, Seymour. *Baseball: The History, Statistics and Romance of the American National Game from Its Inception to the Present Time.* San Francisco, 1902.

Danzig, Allison, and Joe Reichler. *The History of Baseball, Its Great Players, Teams and Managers.* Englewood Cliffs: Prentice-Hall, 1959.

Deutch, Jordan A., Richard M. Cohen, Roland T. Johnson, and David S. Neft. *The Scrapbook History of Baseball.* Indianapolis: Bobbs-Merrill, 1975.

Dunshee, Kenneth Holcomb. *As You Pass By.* New York: Hastings House, n.d.

Graham, Frank. *The Brooklyn Dodgers: An Informal History.* New York: G. P. Putnam's Sons, 1945.

Gruber, Frank. *Zane Grey: A Biography.* New York: G. P. Putnam's Sons, 1945.

Henderson, Robert W. *Ball, Bat and Bishop: The Origin of Ball Games.* New York: Rockport Press, 1947.

History of the North Hudson County Railway from Its Earliest Days to the Present Time. West Hoboken: Reporter Printing Company, 1893.

Holway, John B. *Blackball Stars.* Westport, Conn.: Meckler Books, 1988.

James, Bill. *The Bill James Historical Baseball Abstract.* New York: Villard Books, 1988.

Kaufman, Louis, Barbara Fitzgerald, and Tome Sewell. *Moe Berg: Athlete, Scholar, Spy.* Boston: Little, Brown, 1974.

Kirsch, George B. *The Creation of American Team Sports: Baseball and Cricket, 1838–72.* Urbana: University of Illinois Press, 1989.

Krout, John Allen. *The Pageant of America: Annals of American Sport.* New Haven: Yale University Press, 1929.

Larkin, Jack. *The Reshaping of Everyday Life, 1790–1840.* New York: Harper & Row, 1988.

Leitner, Irving A. *Baseball: Diamond in the Rough.* New York: Criterion Books, 1972.

Lieb, Fredrick. *Baseball as I Have Known It.* New York: Coward, McCann, 1977.

Linthurst, Randolph. *Journal of Leo Smith: Story of a Nineteenth Century Short-stop.* Chicago: Adams Press, 1976.

————. *Newark Bears.* Trenton: White Eagle Printing, 1978.

————. *The Trenton Giants.* Trenton: White Eagle Printing, 1982.

Lowrey, Philip J. *Green Cathedrals.* Cooperstown: Society for American Baseball Research, 1986.

Lurey, H. Rodney. *The Story of Milltown.* South Brunswick: A. S. Barnes, 1971.

Manchester, Herbert. *Four Centuries of Sport in America, 1490–1890.* New York: Benjamin Blom, 1931.

Mayer, Grace M. *Once upon a City.* New York: Macmillan, 1958.

Mayer, Ronald A. *The 1937 Newark Bears: A Baseball Legend.* Union City: William H. Wise, 1980.

Menke, Frank G. *The Encyclopedia of Sports.* 6th ed. Garden City, N.Y.: Doubleday, 1977.

Noverr, Douglas A., and Lawrence E. Ziewacz. *The Games They Played: Sports in American History, 1865–1980.* Chicago: Nelson-Hall, 1983.

Okuhn, Joanne, and Cynthia Roberts. *Garden State Memories: New Jersey Day by Day.* Lyndhurst, N.J.: Wheal-Grace/Emil R. Salvini, 1986.

Orem, Preston D. *Baseball (1845–1881): From the Newspaper Accounts.* Altadena, Calif.: Orem, 1961.

Pavlovich, Louis F., ed. *Collegiate Baseball (Since 1957).* Tucson: Pavlovich, 1983.

Peterson, Harold. *The Man Who Invented Baseball.* New York: Charles Scribner's Sons, 1973.

Peterson, Robert W. *Only the Ball Was White.* Englewood Cliffs: Prentice-Hall, 1970.

Peverelly, Charles A. *The Book of American Pastimes, Containing a History of the Principal Base Ball, Cricket, Rowing, and Yachting Clubs of the United States.* New York: Peverelly, 1866.

Presbrey, Frank, and James Hugh Moffatt. *Athletics at Princeton: A History.* New York: Frank Presbrey, 1901.

Ritter, Lawrence S. *The Glory of Their Times.* New York: Collier Books, 1966.

Rogosin, Donn. *Invisible Men.* New York: Atheneum, 1983.

Schlossberg, Dan. *The Baseball Catalogue.* Middle Village, N.Y.: Jonathan David, 1980.

Seymour, Harold. *Baseball: The Early Years.* New York: Oxford University Press, 1960.

———— *Baseball: The Golden Age.* New York: Oxford University Press, 1971.

Siegel, Alan A. *Out of Our Past: A History of Irvington, New Jersey.* Irvington: Irvington Centennial Commission, 1974.

Sipes, William B. *The Pennsylvania Railroad: Its Origin, Construction, Condition and Connections.* Philadelphia: Passenger Department of the Pennsylvania Rail Road, 1875.

Spalding, A. G. *Base Ball: America's National Game.* New York: American Sports, 1911.

Sterling, Adalaine W. *The Book of Englewood.* Englewood: Irvington Centennial Committee, 1922.

Sutherland, Daniel E. *The Expansion of Everyday Life, 1860–1867.* New York: Harper & Row, 1989.

Thorn, John, Pete Palmer, and David Reuther. *Total Baseball.* New York: Warner Books, 1989.

Tocqueville, Alexis de. *Journey to America.* Edited by J. P. Mayer. New Haven: Yale University Press, 1962.

Turnbull, Archibold Douglas. *John Stevens: An American Record.* New York: American Society of Mechanical Engineers, 1928.

Twombley, Wells. *200 Years of Sport in America: A Pageant of a Nation at Play.* New York: McGraw-Hill, 1976.

Voight, David Quentin. *American Baseball: From Gentleman's Sport to the Commissioner System.* Norman: University of Oklahoma Press, 1966.

Wainwright, Nicholas B., ed. *A Philadelphia Perspective: The Diary of Sidney George Fisher Covering the Years 1834–1871.* Philadelphia: Historical Society of Pennsylvania, 1967.

Walker, Edwin Robert et al. *A History of Trenton, 1679–1929: Two Hundred and Fifty Years of a Notable Town with Links in Four Centuries.* Vol. 2. Princeton: Princeton University Press, 1929.

White, Sol. *Sol White's Official Baseball Guide.* Philadelphia: H. Walter Schlicter, 1907.

Winfield, Charles H. *History of the County of Hudson New Jersey, from Its Earliest Settlement to the Present Time.* New York: Kennard & Hay, 1874.

Young, Jenny J. *The Ceramic Art: A Compendium of the History and Manufacturing of Pottery and Porcelain.* New York: Harper & Brothers, 1878.

MAGAZINE ARTICLES

Adelman, Melvin L. "The First Baseball Game, the First Newspaper References to Baseball, and the New York Club: A Note on the Early History of Baseball." *Journal of Sport History* 7 (Winter 1980): 132–135.

Allen, Oliver E. "The First Family of Inventors." *American Heritage of Invention and Technology* (Fall 1987).

"Amateurism." *Outing Magazine* (July 1898).

Henderson, Robert W. "Baseball and Rounders." *Bulletin of the New York Public Library* (April 1939): 303–314.

OTHER MAGAZINE SOURCES

Baseball Magazine

Baseball Research Journal

NEWSPAPER SOURCES

New Jersey

Atlantic City Press

Jersey City Daily Courier and Advertiser

Jersey Journal

New Brunswick Home News

New Brunswick Times

Newark Daily Advertiser

Newark Evening Journal

Newark Evening News

Newark Star Ledger

Paterson Evening News

Trenton Times

New York

Brooklyn Daily Eagle

New York Clipper

New York Daily Times

New York Herald

New York Times

Porter's Spirit of the Times

Spirit of the Times

Wilkes' Spirit of the Times

Pennsylvania

Philadelphia Inquirer

INDEX

Absecon, N. J., 199
Ace bandage, 201
aces [runs], 10–11
Acme Colored Giants [team], 138
Actives [team]: based in Hoboken, N. J.,
    34–35, 168; of Reading, Pa., 66, 73
Adams, Dan, 18–19, 192
Adidas USA, 201
Adriatics [team], 168
Alerts [team], *see* Seton Hall Alerts
Alexander, Grover Cleveland, 144
Alger [player for Harvard University],
    178
Allaire, N. J., 54, 199
Allentown (Pa.) Cardinals, 95, 97
Allison, Art, 47, 177
Allison, Doug, 42, 44–45, 47, 177
All-Star Game of Major League Base-
    ball, 204
Alpine [team], 169
Alston, Walter, 93
Amateur Athletic Union, Junior Olym-
    pics of, 188
Amateur Sports Act of 1978, 188–189
American Amateur Baseball Congress,
    188
American Association, 60, 65, 71, 73,
    91, 114, 127, 136
American Baseball Coaches Associa-
    tion, 185, 188
American Baseball Heritage, Inc., 231
American Bridge Company [team], 171
American College Baseball Associa-
    tion, 178–179
American Giants, 141–144, 146, 225
American League, 54, 56, 60, 66, 85, 91,
    225, 228; and competition with
    Federal League, 109, 111–112, 114,
    127–128; first black player for, 135,
    151, 226; MVP award, 151
American Legion Baseball, 188

American Negro League, 141, 144–145
American Sports Publishing, 122
Americus [team], 169
Amherst College, 30, 138, 175, 178
Amity [team], 26–27
Anson, Cap, 45, 137
Arlington, Lizzie, 196
Armstrong, Jack, 199, 204
Asbury Park, N. J.: as spring training
    site, 56; team, 68, 80
Astrodome, 202
Atlantic Association, 69, 77
Atlantic City, N. J., 140–141, 142, 147,
    159; as hometown, 228; as spring
    training site, 56; minor league teams
    of, 68, 75, 80. *See also* Bacharach
    Giants; Johnson Stars
Atlantic City Press, 145
Atlantic Collegiate Baseball League,
    185
Atlantic Highlands, N. J., 209
Atlantic League, 68–69, 77, 80, 207
Atlantics: of Brooklyn, N.Y., 29–34,
    37–38, 44–47, 49, 175, 177, 179; of
    Jamaica, N.Y., 26; of Trenton, N. J.,
    169–170. *See also* Paterson Atlantics
Auston, Henry, 47
Avila, Bobby, 151

Babe Ruth Baseball, 188, 193, 201
Babylon (N.Y.) Athletics, 137
Bacharach, Harry and Burt, 140
Bacharach Giants, 140–147, 224
Bachman, John, 9
Bailey [player for Irvington, N. J.,
    team], 44
Ball, Phil, 111, 128
Baltimore: early amateur team of, 30;
    early professional team of, 71; Elite
    Giants, 146, 153; Marylands, 44, 47;
    Orioles, 80, 82–83, 85, 91, 100, 112–

261